# i want to be like you

# i want to be like you

## Life With Asperger's Syndrome

Travis E. Breeding

Tate Publishing & *Enterprises*

Published by Tate Publishing & Enterprises, LLC
127 E. Trade Center Terrace | Mustang, Oklahoma 73064 USA
1.888.361.9473 | www.tatepublishing.com

Tate Publishing is committed to excellence in the publishing industry. The company reflects the philosophy established by the founders, based on Psalm 68:11,
*"The Lord gave the word and great was the company of those who published it."*


*Cover design by Rebekah Garibay*
*Interior design by Joel Uber*

Published in the United States of America

ISBN: 978-1-61663-918-1
1. Biography & Autobiography, Personal Memoirs
2. Psychology, Psychopathology, Autism Spectrum Disorders
10.11.01

# Dedication

I Want to be Like You is dedicated to any adult or child who has autism spectrum disorders. It is with great hope that by sharing my story more neurotypical people will begin to understand some of the challenges that people with ASD face on a daily basis. We have a long way to go in the goal of educating the entire neurotypical community in the world; however, we have come such a long way and should be proud of all of the hard work done by professionals around the world as well as those of us on the spectrum.

# Table of Contents

# Foreword

In a book like no other, Travis brings the reader through his developmental trajectory as a man with Asperger's syndrome. While the literature is replete with research describing the difficulties people on the autism spectrum have with understanding others and themselves, this book demonstrates that with the work and dedication Travis has shown in gaining self-knowledge, the contrary is very possible.

Travis struggles mightily to understand a confusing world of social interaction and academics in school. Like a great majority of those of us on the autism spectrum, Breeding was mercilessly bullied and misunderstood by his teachers. Flying in the face of a popular myth regarding a desire to isolate in people on the autism spectrum, Travis demonstrates a strong desire to make connections with others. The question continuously asked by Travis and by so many of us on the autism spectrum is how to develop these relationships. And Travis provides a lot of insight to the processes that many of us on the autism spectrum struggle with.

For example, the reader will learn of the incredible lengths Travis, desperate to develop those connections, went to, such as bribing people with money and material goods to attempting to work out an appropriate friend-to-acquaintance ratio for obtaining a modicum of social interaction that made sense to him. Fortunately, due to his hard work, Travis has grown to treasure the benefits of true, experientially based friendship.

Similarly to the efforts Travis has made in social interaction, the reader will learn how he works through challenges in the areas of communication, sensory issues, and motor control as they presented difficulties in academics as well as developing understanding relationships with teachers, therapists, and other students. As much as I Want to be Like You is about a person's life with autism, this is also a story of Travis coming of age as he continues to deepen his understanding of how autism affects him and others he interacts with.

Travis tells us about his experiences with autism in a no-holds-barred fashion, just like it is with his victories, challenges, and triumphs. Travis has presented the autism community a gift that will help further the knowledge of what it is like to have autism but more importantly what it is to be a human being.

—Stephen M. Shore, Ed.D<br>
Assistant Professor of Special Education at Adelphi University<br>
Internationally known autism consultant and<br>
speaker on issues pertaining to autism<br>
Board of Directors of the Autism Society and other<br>
organizations related to autism

# Introduction

*I Want to be Like You* is a book that I decided to write to give other adults with autism spectrum disorders an inside look at what it can be like to grow up and live with AS. But more importantly, I wanted to write this book for parents of kids who are on the spectrum, to give them some insight as to what they and their child might experience when their children grow up and become young adults.

This book is written by an adult who is living with Asperger's syndrome and has experienced everything that comes along with having AS for many, many years. It is my goal that one day we will have a lot more resources available for adults and that we will continue to get better at diagnosing autism spectrum disorders in early childhood. It is crucial that the diagnosis comes very early in life so that one can spend lots of time learning the basic communication skills necessary for survival.

As we all know, autism spectrum disorders are not something that is taken lightly. Everyone who has an autism spectrum disorder experiences it to their own degree and level. In this book, you will see firsthand how Asperger's syndrome has affected me and my life. I was one of those who had a late diagnosis. I got diagnosed in the fall of 2007. I was twenty-two years old at the time, and getting the diagnosis was somewhat of a relief; but at the same time, it was somewhat frustrating. While it's great to know that you're not just some crazy psycho roaming around the world and there's actually something pretty severe in nature wrong with you, it can also be overwhelming to realize that there's really not much that can be done as far as a cure or making it go away. You will now realize that you have a lot of work ahead of you.

In this book, you will see real-life examples. I think that the bad things really stand out, and I tend to focus on them quite a lot; therefore, it's made it easy to remember nearly every detail and to pass it along to you today. While I must admit there have been some good things that have happened in life, unfortunately, none of those have ever had anything to do with social relationships.

Just recently, I've had the pleasure of meeting a couple of women who have experience in the autism world. I've met Kara Skaggs (who runs an Asperger's support group here in town) as well as Sue Christman (who works for an agency that provides assistance to people with disabilities). I would highly recommend that if you are an AS individual, you get hooked up with a support group and also make connections with as many people as you can so that you can get the best available help that's out there. I've found that there are people that care; you just have to do the research and find them. As a person with AS, it's very important that you have at least one or two people who fully understand what autism is and what you're going through on your side. I cannot stress how important it is for you to find one or two people who get you and understand you, who are willing to listen to you and provide assistance in any way in which they are capable of doing.

Unfortunately for me, I didn't know of the support that was out there when I was first diagnosed with Asperger's syndrome. I got diagnosed in October of 2007 and spent about a year or so just saying, "Okay. What now? What do I do? I don't fit in, and I don't know how to." I continued trying to attend school and obtain employment, and it just wasn't working out. Finally, in late March or early

April of 2009, I got lucky and something turned up. I was able to find out about the Asperger's support group that was meeting at a local hospital in town, and I became very interested in finding out more about it. I called Kara, and I learned that the next meeting was only a few days away. I knew I had to attend if I was going to have any chance at succeeding in life.

On Monday, April 12, 2009, I was able to convince myself to go to the meeting. I will admit that it was extremely difficult to go to the meeting. I kind of figured that I'd probably end up just sitting there and listening to everyone else talk since it was my first time there. Somehow, that's not exactly what happened. They had actually had the meeting set up that evening so that siblings of people with an AS diagnosis were speaking and answering questions on what it was like to be a sibling to someone on the spectrum. It was very insightful to me. As the night went on, to my surprise, I was able to contribute to the conversation and had some parents of AS kids asking me questions and wanting to learn about me. I feel that I really put myself out there and provided a lot of valuable information to those parents that night; however, there is still so much more to get out there to them.

Through the meeting on April 12, 2009, I was also able to make the connection with Sue, who can help people on the spectrum obtain benefits and provide all kinds of valuable resources and information. To my surprise, there are several resources available to all of us on the spectrum; and I highly recommend that if you have AS, you should take advantage of all of the available resources. If you do not know of any resources available in your area, please Google it and find out.

Today, as I write this, I am still very much in the process of figuring out the resources that are available and learning about Asperger's syndrome. It's kind of like Asperger's in itself has become some sort of a special interest for me. Maybe there's nothing wrong with that at all because in all actuality I'm learning about myself and I am my special interest. We cannot learn to interact with others until we have learned how to interact with ourselves and be happy with whom we are.

What you are about to read in this book are the events that have happened in my life that have gotten me where I am today. These events are and will always be a part of my life and have made me who I am today. I hope that I can continue to grow and become better aware of communicating with NTs. There is so much to learn. At the same time, I hope that I can help you, the reader (parent of someone on the spectrum or if you yourself are on the spectrum), become more educated on what it might be like for an adult to live his or her life with an autism spectrum disorder. Please note that I am telling my story, and a lot of the events that have happened to me seem pretty bad. I tell you this not to discourage you but to provide an education and to encourage you to seek help and prevent as much of this as possible from happening to you, your son/daughter, or anyone else you may know who's on the spectrum.

# Coloring Outside the Lines

I had never really had a friend before preschool, as I grew up with two cousins very close in age who lived nearby. What I remember most about preschool was swimming and trying to learn to play with the others. For some reason, this wasn't very natural for me. I couldn't relate to the other kids like most of them related to each other. I struggled with knowing what my role was in the game being played and also in knowing when I was supposed to say or do something. It seemed to come with ease for the other children. I did manage to make an acquaintance with another kid by the name of Eric. I can't remember a whole lot of the preschool years, but I think it's safe to say that Eric and I probably played together some at that level.

Some of the activities we were doing in preschool involved learning how to color, and others included anything from cutting things out to gluing them to paper. All of these activities are something that should be fairly easy for any child to learn how to do. However, for me, it was different for some reason. I could never stay in the lines, and it always hurt my hand and fingers when I had to color for an extended period of time. Cutting wasn't much easier for me, as I struggled in just understanding how to hold the scissors. To me, coloring, cutting, and gluing seemed so uninteresting and pointless.

What I enjoyed most about preschool was being around a group of people. It was good to be hanging out with other kids. Other than the two cousins who were near my age growing up, I'd never had a lot of social interaction with children my age before. One of my favorite activities during preschool was swimming time. I loved the water and how it made me feel. I've always enjoyed swimming. My grandfather had a pool, and as a kid I would spend most of my summers there either with my cousins or by myself.

After the preschool years came time to go to kindergarten. At five years old, I was ready to go off to school for the next thirteen years of my life. I had mixed emotions about this. In the fall of 1990, I went to kindergarten round-up at Andrews Elementary School. My parents were there with me, and I remember that the teacher had all kinds of activities for the children to do. She also talked a little about school. It did seem quite overwhelming to me. I would now be expected to go to school every day as opposed to just a couple days a week. I would have to meet new and more students to interact with. It would also become increasingly more difficult as I was going to be expected to participate in activities such as coloring time or nap time.

As a kid, I had many difficulties with fine motor skills. For example, I would often just randomly have a tick and shake my head and have no control over it. I also had problems with other fine motor skills, such as balancing or standing on one foot, throwing, and catching. Hand-eye coordination was a huge problem for me. Even little things such as holding a pencil or crayon properly were a huge issue. So after the kindergarten round-up, my parents and the teacher conferred and decided that it was best for me to wait to start kindergarten a year later. To this day, I am not sure how I feel about that. I mean, I'm sure there were many pros to having that extra year to try to develop my skill set, but at the same time, it made me a year older than most of the other kids.

Then the experience began. In late August of 1991, I started kindergarten. Luckily for me, I would have a really great teacher.

Mrs. Price was very understanding and caring. I had to use the bathroom a lot, probably more so than most kids. Luckily, we had a restroom in our classroom. This was back at the time when we had half-day kindergarten, so school didn't become too overwhelming for me or last too long.

From what I can recall of kindergarten, playing and making friends seemed to come easily for me. I got kind of close with a couple of kids. Luckily, the kid I had mentioned before, Eric, was also in my kindergarten class.

The first time I got invited to another kid's birthday party was in the spring of the school year in kindergarten. I was invited to go to Chuck E. Cheese. I went with about three or four other boys and played some of the games and had some pizza. I can't really remember how well the social interaction was for me during that event, as it was so early in life, but I do remember coming home and feeling kind of left out or different. In fact, there were a number of times during kindergarten where I started to and did feel different. However, I didn't think anything of it.

Now that kindergarten was officially over, I was ready to move on to the first grade. At least I thought so. First grade very well could have been where I first really felt different and out of place.

# Distractions and Difficulties

Going from kindergarten into first grade was quite a significant change for me. Now, instead of only being at school for a half day, I had to be there for the better of six or seven hours, the entire day. I wasn't sure what to think about this change. There was a lot more structure to the day. Not only was I learning more classroom written rules, but there were a few more social unwritten rules to observe. This was where I first noticed that the change of routine thing became difficult for me.

During my first-grade year, I was somehow able to develop an even better friendship with Eric. Eric and I were always out on the playground together, playing some kind of game involving running around, hiding, or chasing each other. There were a few other kids that played with us. While most of the kids were often running around, starting some kind of trouble with one another, I seemed to be rather quiet and kept to myself as much as I could. Even within the group that I was playing those games with, I often seemed to wander about by myself and not really fit in with the rest of the group.

I was spending much of my time alone because I didn't seem to be able to fit in or hang out with the other kids. Even in the classroom, I felt like the other kids seemed to know something I didn't about socializing, and this really threw me for a loop. Of course, I had no idea that there was any meaning behind socializing, nor do I think I even knew what the word socializing meant in itself, but I could tell there was just something different about the other kids or something different about me.

First grade was the first time in my life when I experienced someone being mean to me or teasing me. Recently, I found a definition in the dictionary about what a bully is. A bully is "a blustering, quarrelsome, overbearing person who habitually badgers and intimidates smaller or weaker people." One of the bullies that I most remember is a boy by the name of Stephan. Stephan was a rougher kid who didn't seem to know how to follow the rules set forth in the classroom. No matter what the teacher would ask Stephan to do, he always seemed to end up doing something completely opposite and disrupting the class. There was another bully by the name of Shawn. He was a really big kid who, if he wanted to, could pretty much scare any kid. Between these two students, I was often made fun of, if not a little bit abused. To this day, I'm not sure if it's something that they meant to do or if they were just being themselves and not realizing that they were bothering or hurting someone else. A lot of times it's just assumed that everyone knows social rules and norms. It's just something we expect people to know and follow. Sometimes neurotypicals can be programmed to have a negative reaction to someone who is not following the social norms the way that they think they should be.

I am someone who likes and needs for things to be pretty quiet. I don't like a lot of loud noises or distractions, especially when I'm trying to learn. If there is too much else going on in the room, I'm not able to focus on learning the material that is being presented to me.

So with a lot of kids not realizing or understanding the need to be quiet when the teacher or someone else of importance was talking or leading a group discussion, I was never really able to focus in and learn what was being taught. It seemed like a lot of kids just didn't really notice or care that there was a teacher up in front of the classroom, trying to do her job and teach the students relevant information that they needed to learn. I was always very puzzled that when the teacher asked us to be quiet, I would always still hear kids whispering to each other if not talking aloud to one another in the classroom. I could never understand this. To me, be quiet means exactly that: be quiet.

I was very fortunate to have my cousin in the same first-grade class as I was in. This was something that really helped me cope with everything that was going on. My cousin and I had always gotten along and spent a lot of time together in childhood. We had always gotten along pretty well with no problems. Unfortunately, there was a day in first grade that was severely tragic to the development of my self-esteem. It wouldn't really bother our relationship in the long term since we were both so young, but in the short term I was devastated.

I had always had trouble with bedwetting and controlling bowel movements. Sometimes I would have problems at school. I always hated to ask the teacher if I could get up and leave the classroom, as I felt like I was bothering her in some way.

One day in the first grade, toward the end of the day, I had this horrible experience. We had a substitute that day. I never enjoyed having a substitute teacher, as it most likely meant that the flow of my day or routine was going to be interrupted somehow. It's nearly impossible for a substitute to keep a regular teacher's schedule intact exactly down to the moment. Unfortunately, we might have missed a restroom break or two during the day, and I ended up having an accident, a bowel movement, in the classroom.

I was trying to make it through to the end of the day, but my cousin ended up coming over to me and smelling something. Now, my cousin was aware of the fact that I would often have these accidents, and he probably suspected that I had an accident. Not only did he smell it, but he got down on his knees and proceeded to put his nose down near my butt and sniff. Then he proceeded to get the entire class's attention and point out to them that I'd had an accident, and it was all downhill from there. Other kids then got down on the floor and started sniffing, and I started crying. Everyone in the class knew that I had an accident, and they were really getting a good laugh out of it with each other. Once again, I was singled out and completely embarrassed in front of all my peers.

Later that night, I went home and felt so low and was completely distressed about the situation. I was extremely upset but wasn't sure with whom to be upset. I thought that this was just happening to me because I was a bad kid and other kids hated me. I was stupid, fat, ugly, and worthless. I didn't belong at the school or didn't deserve to be liked or have friends. There wasn't much of a rift between my cousin and me, as we were young enough that I think he apologized and we just let it go. Little did I know that that was just the beginning of a long series of events.

Somehow I managed to make it through that horrific accident in first grade and pass. In second grade, I got a great teacher. Mrs. Finley was a great woman.

I learned a lot of things in second grade. We started to learn a little bit more advanced math. We might have gotten into some multiplying and dividing toward the end of the year. Math has always been one of my strong points. I loved doing math. It was relaxing and something I was very good at. It was fun because it was turned into a competition with a few of the other students in the class who also excelled in math to see who could get done first and be most accurate. In elementary school I was really good at everything, and no subjects gave me trouble.

Peer relationships in the second grade seemed to be about like they were in the first grade for me. Once again, Eric was that person that I really grew to like. He was the type of kid who was what I call the "leader of the pack." He seemed to always be the kid that the other students would want to follow around and sort of worship in a way. I often wondered to myself why the other kids liked him more than they did me. Eric always had some creative game to play, and often I didn't really understand why we were playing the game we were, but I just knew that I was playing with someone and making it through school.

As far as the bullying, there were still the same kids that were causing problems in the first grade, always talking and being a distraction in class and really interfering with my, and I'm sure other students', ability to learn. Bullying comes in all forms, some of it severe and some of it less severe. Another student talking aloud during class and distracting other students from learning what they should be learning is also a form of bullying. I seemed to behave more like the girls in the class. I didn't understand the behavior of my male counterparts. I was more soft and delicate and not wanting to bother anyone or become a distraction. It often seemed to me that boys were just looking to cause trouble or to become the center of attention. I never understood this.

Another huge thing that was a problem for me involved my sensory motor skills. Toward the end of second grade, I started to try to write in cursive. Unfortunately for me, this was a huge struggle at first. I already knew that I had trouble with penmanship, but I didn't know why at the time. Luckily for me, Mrs. Finley was a very patient person, and she was always very encouraging. She took the time to practice with me and help me learn how to hold the pencil and write the letters. I traced letters for hours upon hours. This got a little boring to me, and again, I really struggled to see the point to us learning how to write letters in a different way. I could not make any sense of it.

Third grade was an important year for me. I got lucky and ended up with a really great teacher. Mrs. Sees was one of my all-time favorite teachers, and I was fortunate enough to have her twice in elementary school, as she ended up moving up to sixth grade.

Schoolwork seemed to come pretty easy to me in that year. That was also the year that things started to heat up at school socially. This was probably the first time I can recall going to afterschool events with other kids. It was one thing for me to be able to talk to other students during the day; but as I was about to find out, it was something totally new and different, something extremely challenging for me, to go to afterschool events and try to socialize with other kids outside of the school day. It becomes more difficult to socialize in extracurricular activities because of the lack of supervision. In elementary school, during the school day there is always a teacher or a teacher's aide there giving instructions for what you are supposed to be doing or how you are supposed to act. Afterschool events are much less supervised and freer to let the students decide what socializing should be going on. This is where all of these nonverbal cues come into play. Not understanding how to go with the flow and read other people's body language, I struggled to fit in. I would say things out of order and not be in the flow of conversation, and sometimes I would talk about my special interest too much. At this point my special interest was definitely basketball. I watched every basketball game there was on television with my dad. I've always been really good with statistics and sports and can tell people who won the championships in all professional sports back to 1980.

There was also no teacher on hand to make sure that other students weren't being bullies and pushing kids around or making them do things they didn't want to do. This is a key point in life for all students, as it's one of the first times in which you are set loose on your own to make things happen socially and interact with each other. As I'm writing this today I have to wonder how these other students did this so fluently with little trouble and no effort. It would seem that they came preprogrammed with some special skill set that I didn't come with.

As a kid growing up, it was always a goal of mine to become a professional basketball player. Well, in third grade, I had a cousin who was in the sixth grade and was playing on the elementary basketball team. One of the girls in my class, Sarah Hanson, had an older sister who was on the girls' basketball team. Her name was Kortney. She was the same age as my cousin. I started going to all of the basketball games, as basketball was always my favorite sport. I would often try to sit with Sarah. To this day, I don't know if Sarah and I are actually friends. To me, she was always a good friend and extremely nice, but we've never really hung out outside of the school day since about fourth grade.

As I was watching the basketball games, I began to notice something very strange about myself. I was enjoying watching our girls' basketball team a lot more than the boys' team. This could be due to a few reasons, one of which was the girls' team could have surely beat our boys' team hands down, which meant they were winning a lot more games and were more fun to watch.

I really became interested in the two stars of that team. The stars of the team were Kortney, Sarah's sister, and then a girl by the name of Alexia Shields. Alexia was like Michael Jordan to me. That girl would throw up shots that only MJ would dream of taking and somehow manage to get the roll and have the shot find the bottom of the net.

Basketball—in particular girls' basketball and the individual players, who were really talented and the stars of the team—became a fascination to me. I wanted to know everything about them. I wanted to memorize their stats from every game. One of the things that I've noticed is that I like to talk about things a lot and have often seemed to overtalk about things I'm interested in until it gets to the point of driving the other person crazy. This happened with Sarah, as I would always want to talk to her during the school day about the previous day's basketball game or the upcoming basketball game. I am almost sure she hated me for always bugging her about her sister or the games.

I also started to become very interested in the high school team. The high school, Huntington North, had a very good basketball team that was extremely talented that year. In fact, that was the year in which they went to state and won their second state title over Lake Central.

As far as the rest of third grade, it seemed to be pretty normal. I really started to notice that groups seemed to be developing. It seemed like people were forming more friendships with other students and congregating in groups more so than they seemed to in the previous two or three years of school. I wondered why so-and-so was hanging out with such-and-such a group. I was never really included in those groups. I would have liked to have been, but for some reason, which I could not figure out (and I spent a lot of time just trying to figure out exactly what it was), they just didn't really want to include or interact with me. I managed to pass the third grade with flying colors. Cursive writing was still very much a struggle for me and something that I had to work at extremely hard.

# The Last Kid Picked

Fourth grade was probably one of my most favorite years in elementary school. I had the opportunity of having a really cool teacher who was fresh out of college. I was amazed that this teacher was only twenty-three years old at the time. I thought, Wow. He's not that much older than I am. As always, it was difficult for me to adjust to the new teacher and the new school year. Each teacher has his or her own routine, and each classroom has its own environment. For me, I'd spend about three to four months at the beginning of each school year learning the new teacher's teaching style and the classroom's environment. Each year I'd have to go back and do the same thing. It was frustrating because it took me a long time to adjust to the new school year and really get into the flow of things. There would be a lot of new beginnings that year. Just like in the past, most of these kids were better equipped to handle the challenges of the change.

On the first or second day of school, there was a rather humorous situation. Our teacher, Mr. Graf, had taken us outside to read a story, and we were gathered around a tree. Somehow, his pants ripped. The new year seemed to start off okay, and I was just getting back into the flow of things from having the summer off.

There were a few changes in the fourth grade. One of the major ones for me was the fact that we were now required to start having gym clothes so we could change when we went to gym and then change again at the end of gym class. This was a good thing because at about that age we all start to sweat and smell after gym. However, it seemed really awkward for me. I'm not sure why. Maybe it was because I struggled with tying shoes due to my poor motor skills. Either way, I somehow managed to survive changing in the locker rooms.

Another huge change for me was that we were now in the upstairs part of the building. For the first four years of my school career, we were downstairs. Now I was upstairs for the remaining three years of elementary school. I was never very fond of stairs, and this would come back to haunt me within that following year or so. I was scared to walk up the stairs due to not knowing if I would be able to stand up or stay on my feet. Then I would see these kids that were taking two steps at a time and everyone thought it was cool, so I would think that I needed to take them two at a time so I could fit in.

The year went pretty well for me as far as school. I generally got all A's. It was an adjustment for me to have a male teacher for the first time, however. I was worried at first that he would not be able to be as nice or understanding as the female teachers I'd had and/or not as willing to help. But it turned out that he was very understanding. He would encourage me to do a lot of things and push me to excel.

Throughout my school career, teachers were trying to teach me how to be more clean and organized as far as school stuff. For example, I often had the habit of just throwing the textbooks and my notebooks back in my desk. I could see the logic in trying to put them in there neatly because I was just going to pull them back out again later on. It just didn't make sense to me, and I wouldn't have known how to organize them. So somehow I'd always manage to have the messiest desk of any student in the classroom.

One day, I was encouraged by Mr. Graf to organize and clean my desk. So as I tried to clean, I was thinking that I would come up with a really good system for keeping things neat. I wrote down all of my books and where they were going to be at in my desk. I taped this list to my desk. This told me which book was on which side of my desk and also which book was on top of what book so I could just reach in and quickly grab the book I needed without any worries or consuming too much time. When the teachers were ready to start a lesson in a new subject, I would often be searching for my book, and they'd end up waiting on me to find my book before they would start the lesson. This was kind of embarrassing to me because this meant that every other student was sitting there staring at me and laughing at me while I was searching for my book.

In my system, I did what was logical to me, which was probably completely illogical to the other NTs in the room. I abbreviated the first three letters of the subject that the book was about. So English was Eng, Math was Mat, Science was Sci, and so on. We had an assignment book that students were supposed to use to keep them more organized and to make sure they wrote all of their homework down so they didn't miss or forget about an assignment. Well, the first three letters of that book were Ass. So I wrote that down, and I didn't think anything of it. Later on, another student saw that and pointed it out to the teacher and caused a huge scene. I couldn't figure out why this other student was pointing something on my desk out to a teacher. I hadn't done anything wrong. Mr. Graf had to explain to me why we should change that and make it more appropriate. I would have never even thought of that, but maybe it was because I never used foul language. To this day, those little things like that still really don't make sense or register in my brain.

Socializing in fourth grade was a unique experience to say the least. I noticed that some things were changing about the way kids were playing on the playground. No longer were the girls playing babies or something to that nature. No longer were the boys running around, chasing each other, playing cowboys and Indians. In fact, the boys weren't chasing the boys anymore. They started to chase the girls.

It seemed like these boys did a one-eighty. Throughout my first few years of school, it was like the playground was segregated. The boys would do their own thing, and the girls did their own thing. Somewhere along the lines, something happened, and boys and girls became fascinated with each other. Not to an extreme. This was still the point where girls were saying boys had cooties or something. I could never understand that comment. I went around asking parents and grandparents what cooties were after hearing that at school the first couple of times.

Eric was still the leader of the pack in my group. It seemed like everywhere he went, we went. Some kids started to play sports at recess. Since I had always loved basketball, I would try to play along with the other boys who were playing. I was pretty good, but for some reason, no one wanted me on their team. Kids do a thing where they have team captains and the team captains pick the teams. I was always the last kid picked, which to me meant I was worthless and only picked by someone because they were forced to pick me. Some kids would swing on the swing set and talk. Talking started to become more of a thing in making friends at this level. It was less play, more talk.

Earlier, I spoke about how in third grade I had an obsession with girls who played sports, mainly girls that played basketball. The Huntington North Lady Vikes won the Indiana state basketball championship in 1995. I watched those state finals games on television. The 1995-96 season promised to be a great season, with the possibility of repeating. The girls were remarkable. My parents took me to almost every game. They quickly became nationally ranked, as they were already the number-one team in Indiana.

There were several good players on that basketball team; however, my favorite was a girl by the name of Lisa Winter. Lisa was a beautiful girl, and she was extremely talented with a basketball. I became fascinated by Lisa, and I tried to sit close to the team bench in every game, just hoping that she'd say hi to me. Lisa would later go on to be named Miss Basketball for the state of Indiana in 1996.

The team cruised to an undefeated regular season, and I was super excited about the tournament. Back then, when it was actually still "Hoosier Hysteria," the tournament was a breeze for us at Huntington North. We would play small schools in the sectional and blow them out. We would rarely see a worthy opponent until the championship game of the region or semi-state. We ended up running into a very worthy and determined opponent in the semi-state championship game that year. Kokamo High School would upset the Lady Vikes. I was so sad because we had tickets to the state finals the Saturday after at Market Square Arena in Indianapolis. Nevertheless, I was totally into Lisa and just wanted to meet her.

At that time, it wasn't really an "Oh my gosh, she's hot" thing for me. She was more of a role model. She was something that brightened my day and gave me something to look forward to whenever I could go see a basketball game at the high school.

Fifth grade would prove to be a significant year for me. I had a great teacher and still excelled academically, but something happened in October. Eric, the only kid whom I was kind of friends with, told us while sitting on a swing set that his dad had gotten a job in Cedar Rapids, Iowa, and the family was moving away. I was stunned. I couldn't believe this was happening. This kind of set me back in some ways. We spent the next month enjoying all of the time we had left together, and then we had to say our good-byes and part ways. I really struggled with this. Luckily, my teacher was aware of the situation and quickly acted to ensure that I made another friend I could count on. Mrs. Ross was understanding and a good teacher. For some reason, her teaching style was easiest for me to handle.

Somehow I ended up being friends with Austin Davenport. Austin was completely different than Eric, more adventurous. We did different types of things like play basketball and more athletic stuff. We seemed to get along pretty well and would start to do some things outside of school. We would attend high school basketball games and hang out at each other's houses.

Fifth grade was very exciting to me, as we had a new basketball coach and this was the first year that I could play elementary basketball. I didn't start that year, but I played in quite a few games and took a few shots. The sixth graders were pretty decent that year, and we had a good time. We played and went all the way to the semifinals of the county tournament, in which Central Elementary beat us by a final score of 34-31. I really enjoyed the year of basketball and was looking forward to the next year with Mr. Ginder as a coach. He seemed to have a good understanding of basketball and how to teach it.

I survived the rest of fifth grade, managing to get good grades and get by socially. Fifth grade was also the year that a major change at home was about to take place. I grew up as an only child, but I had always wanted a brother or sister, someone to play with more often. Well, one day when I was in fifth grade, my mom told me she was pregnant. Quite a shock to me. I was going to finally have a sibling. I was very excited. I wasn't sure how to handle the change, though.

As I touched on earlier, it was about this time that something strange was happening in social relationships. Boys were starting to become fond of girls. I watched them interact with each other with little or no interest in girls at the time, meaning I didn't think about it or wonder about it as much as the other boys did. My cousin, Dusty, whom I mentioned earlier in this book, was one of these boys that was crazy about girls. There was one girl in particular he seemed to take a liking to. Her name was Shellie VanGorden. Shellie was and still is a very attractive girl. Dusty would talk and talk to these girls for a long time, especially Shellie. I would always wander up to his house at night after school, and he'd be talking on the phone forever before he would come out. At that point in time, I had no interest in girls, nor did I have an interest in chatting it up with a girl—or anyone for that matter—on the phone. Talking wasn't my forte. I just never knew what to say.

# Just Passing Through

Getting into the beginning of the sixth-grade year was an exciting opportunity for me. I was glad to be excelling through school and was glad to have the friendship with Austin to replace what was lost when Eric and his family moved away. No friendship can be replaced, but having another friend or someone to talk to can help lessen the pain of losing a friend to a move.

I had Mrs. Sees again for my sixth-grade year. There was something a little different about sixth grade. In sixth grade, we had two teachers. We had a teacher who would teach us for one period of the day that was not our regular classroom teacher. I couldn't understand this change. Why would I need two teachers? Nonetheless, that's how it happened. For me, this was very difficult. I had trouble adapting to the fact that each of these teachers seemed to have a completely different teaching style. I was used to Mrs. Sees's teaching style, but when I went over to learn about science, I was not equipped to handle the style of Mr. Winter. Also, having the contrast of a female and a male teacher at the same time was a difficult concept for me. Teaching styles are just so different, and their ability to be understanding and caring sometimes isn't quite the same. Some male teachers I've had have been wonderful in explaining things. However, a lot of them would just give an assignment and then expect you to be able to start and complete it without needing any help.

I did survive the year academically. However, I managed to receive my first C. This was the first time that school was a little bit of a challenge to me. My handwriting was improving a little. (It was still nowhere close to being neat.) I was grasping the concept of writing in cursive finally.

In fifth and sixth grade, I had the opportunity to participate on our cross country teams. I'm not sure exactly why I decided to join that team, but I somehow managed to take something away from it. I was a terribly slow runner and completely uncoordinated. Every race we had, I would finish near the back of the pack. I was always the last runner from our school to finish any race. After being last over and over again, it kind of put me down, and I just didn't think I was any good. I mean, yeah, I finished the race, but the other kids were already off, celebrating finishing and running off without me.

Basketball was and has always been my favorite sport. I played a little in fifth grade but didn't see a whole lot of game action. Sixth grade promised to be an exciting year for me, as I was one of the tallest and biggest kids to be on the team. We had a new coach take over, as Mr. Ginder would depart after teaching just one year at Andrews Elementary. Mr. Winter would be the new coach, and he definitely had a unique coaching style.

I was so excited about basketball. The only thing I hated about basketball was that we had to do a lot of running that didn't even have anything to do with basketball. I could never understand why it was necessary to run up and down the stairs so many times and waste about an hour of practice just running. Our team only won one game that year, as we struggled to understand our roles on the team.

I made it through basketball season that year, but it was very frustrating. I had originally won the starting center position. After two games, the coach pulled me aside to let me know that I wouldn't be starting anymore because I wasn't fast enough. I was really discouraged, and I wanted to quit. Everyone would always make fun of me when we ran because I ran weird and extremely slow. I managed to finish out the year.

In sixth grade, we were offered a chance to join the band. I was always more interested in athletics than anything else and had never been interested in joining the band. However, my cousin, Dusty, was pretty pumped to join the band and play the drums. He talked me into joining as well. Little did I know at the time just how important this decision would be for me.

I didn't really have any interest in playing percussion, so I was looking at other sections in the band to try out. I was really fond of the trumpet, so I tried to play the trumpet, but it was extremely difficult. It turns out that my mouth was just too big for the trumpet. So the next instrument that was handed to me was a trombone. Well, this was an interesting instrument to me because, unlike any other instrument, the notes could be played by moving a slide. I thought, Wow. This is something unique, and I can handle this. I played it and quickly fell in love with it.

We would have many opportunities to present concerts that first year. Mr. Campbell was the band teacher. We learned how to play together and make music. I would quickly become fascinated in the trombone and the noises that you could make with it. I started taking it home and practicing literally every day. I decided that I wanted to become a master at the instrument. I fell in love with band because it was comfortable. It was something that I also became very good at. Unlike with any other activity I'd ever participated in, this one didn't require me to say too much or participate in too many conversations, as I would always have an instrument up to my mouth. I loved escaping into the feeling of the music, as in a way it was escaping into imagination or getting inside of my make-believe world.

Often, people with Asperger's syndrome will become obsessed with their special interest. Sometimes, we tend to carry on and on about it for too long. In sixth grade, there was a time when our girls' team got beat. Our girls' teams were really good, so this didn't happen very often. But one of the girls on the team, Sarah Hanson, whom I mentioned before, got injured in one of those games.

The next day following the game, I ended up talking about the game that took place the night before with Sarah. She got upset and said that she didn't want to talk about it anymore. She then proceeded to tell several other kids that I was bugging her by going on and on about the game. I felt bad that I had hurt her in some way, but I didn't understand what I was doing wrong or what could be so hurtful about talking about a game from the night before.

In June of 1998, I was done with elementary school. I was ready to move on to the next chapter of my life. This next area of life would be one that was challenging for me. It was full of many changes, changes that I had a difficult time adapting to.

Junior high is a crucial time period for everyone. NTs and Aspies alike have to go through so many changes and adapt to so many different things. Puberty kicks in, and changes start happening to our bodies; without proper knowledge and understanding, this can be really depressing for individuals.

At the time, I didn't have a diagnosis and didn't have any idea about just what autism was. If I would have had a diagnosis at the time, then there could have been some proper steps taken to make sure I was successful in middle and high school.

There are several advantages to having the diagnosis in the elementary years. One of the major ones is that the individual will grow up knowing they have Asperger's syndrome and be very aware of where they have difficulties, whether they be at school, play group, home, or anywhere where people might be around.

If someone is aware of having Asperger's or any form of autism at that young of an age, they might be able to receive the right kind of help in school. I would recommend that if you have a child who's been diagnosed, you report this to the school. Also report this to the child's individual teacher, as he or she will be better able to assist your child.

There are several good things about reporting this to the school. Once the school is aware that the child has a disability, there are a number of things they can do to provide assistance. They might already have special education teachers on staff, and if they don't, they will begin the search to find someone to help your child. Some schools even go as far as to hire someone who is educated in autism and can provide adequate assistance to make sure the student is successful in his or her academic endeavors.

It wasn't until about 1996 when we first began to acquire an understanding of the CNS (central nervous system) and its effect on sensory development. Therefore, in my case, it wasn't easy to recognize the signs of Asperger's syndrome, as we just weren't aware of what we know now. Let me briefly discuss what should be some red flags that should send off a signal in a parent's head to say, "Hey, I think we have a problem. Let's go talk to someone about it."

> When I started school, I was held back a year due to a lack of motor skills and trouble with simple tasks, such as writing or coloring. Today, this would tell me that I had problems with sensory development as well as controlling motor skills. Knowing what I know now, I could educationally tell myself that there is possibly a dysfunction in the CNS.
>
> I had problems with controlling ticks. I had a tick in my head so that I would just randomly shake my head for no reason. This was most likely due to Tourette's syndrome.
>
> As we now know today, Tourette's can be a side effect of having Asperger's syndrome or autism.
>
> There will be a lack of ability to socialize with peer groups in early elementary years.
>
> I was socially unaware of my surroundings and how to make and maintain friendships. With Eric, I got lucky, as being such a young age, friendships kind of happen on their own and don't really need any facilitating to be successful. As we get older, it becomes more necessary to put some time and effort into the friendship and then also use some social skills to keep the friendship going.

> There might be accidents with bed-wetting and bowel movements and social problems.
>
> I would often have problems with bed-wetting and bowel movements. I recently read a study that said people with Asperger's syndrome could possibly have trouble with bed-wetting as well as bowel movements. This was a huge aha-moment for me. Now I can finally make my mother understand that I wasn't doing it on purpose.
>
> The development of a special interest leads to losing track of the real world and creating a make-believe world.
>
> I now know that it's common for people with autism or Asperger's syndrome to develop a special interest or two. In doing this, they will become experts in their special interest area, and they might lose interest in other areas. Some might lose interest in socializing in general.
>
> Autistic individuals will often create their own make-believe world to escape the pain of the real world. I have done this time after time, hoping that my make-believe world would somehow become my real world. I've tried to change who I was in real life because I had imagined that I was someone else in the make-believe world. This can be and usually is extremely dangerous and harmful when it becomes too intense.

These are five very important indicators that tell me I might have had a problem or that something just wasn't right. I sometimes wish that the knowledge that's available today could have been available to professionals and teachers back in the early 1990s when I was in school so that my Asperger's could have been detected and I could have worked hard to become as normal of an NT as possible. However, this isn't the case anymore, as I know it's much too late for me to fix myself and become a perfect NT; I wouldn't want to be a normal NT individual now either, as I wouldn't really be who I am. This is who I'm supposed to be, and I'm currently in the process of continuing to accept my diagnosis and not only live with it but use it to make the world a better place for everyone.

# Failing Socializing

Seventh grade was a learning experience for me. It was like nothing I had ever experienced before. I was going to a new school that was a lot bigger than my elementary school. I would have to meet new teachers. I would also have to meet new students, as kids from other elementary schools would be going to the same middle school as I did.

All of this was a lot to handle. On the first day of school, I was terrified. Seventh grade presented many challenges for me, and it was also the first year that I can remember having some difficulty with academics. I had done poorly in penmanship before, but I'd never struggled in any other subject.

At Riverview Middle School, each grade was split up into two teams. They called them the red and gold teams. I was on the gold team in seventh grade. Each team had four teachers that would teach the main academic subjects of math, science, social studies, and English. Then we would have about two to three other teachers who taught band/choir, physical education, or keyboarding. There was also a teacher to teach industrial technology, or something to that effect.

I could never see the point in us having to take industrial technology; in fact, I hated it. It was because I was not very skilled at building or making things. With the sensory problems, I have always found it difficult to build things with my hands. Other people seem to be able to put things together with no problem, but for me, it's a real struggle, and it often gets frustrating.

The other kids would just sit and point while laughing at me. Then often whoever was teaching the class would get frustrated, and to me, it seemed like they thought I wasn't trying. However, I was trying really hard. Often, I felt like people just hated me. I couldn't see why they couldn't understand me.

Each team would have four academic subjects each day. We would be on a rotation with the same people. So at least the students in the class were always the same and knew each other. Seventh grade was the year when I really felt out of place and like something was wrong with me. However, I didn't speak to anyone about feeling this way until years later.

It was during each of these core subjects that I would try so hard to make friends and get to know people. For some reason, other kids would generally always be talking with each other in our free time. A lot of students would be laughing and enjoying one another's company. Whether it be socializing or gossiping, they all seemed to be engaged in conversation. I wanted to be involved in their conversations so badly, but I was scared to try. When I did muster up the courage to attempt to join in a conversation, it went terribly. Other students would barely acknowledge that I was there. I would try to relate to what they were talking about but ended up saying something completely different or off topic. I would sometimes get a one word response, other times a girl would ask me to be quiet, but most of the time a guy would tell me to shut up. With each rejection I became more depressed and wanted to shut down. There was nowhere to get help either because I didn't understand that there was a real problem. I just didn't feel I was as cool as they were or good enough for them. It was always a horrifying experience to me and very damaging to my self-esteem.

I got my first locker in seventh grade. I was such a mess because I was afraid I wasn't going to be able to remember the combination or get it opened. However, that was not the case at all, as I can still remember the combination to this day: 19-25-21. However, I would end up not enjoying the locker scene so much due to some other circumstances.

My locker ended up becoming an unorganized filing cabinet. I would have papers everywhere, as well as books. I am surprised that I was able to find the correct book at the time I needed it.

Another problem that I had with the lockers is that other kids would want to socialize near them before school, in between passing periods, and then again after school. It seemed like these kids were doing nothing but talking to one another all day long. How did they know what to say to one another? I would often think that someone had handed these kids and even adults a book that told them what to talk about. I was missing that book.

The problem in this was not only the fact that I quickly became frustrated when I saw what was going on. I could see them socializing with one another and talking about stuff. The stuff I am referring to is what NTs would refer to as small talk. This seemed to be something that other kids did with little or no effort at all. On top of this, several people would congregate around my locker to socialize with other students who had lockers near me but were so much more popular than I was and ever would become. So with everyone often crowding around my locker, I couldn't get to it when I needed to sometimes.

There were several occasions in which I went to get something from my locker or return something to my locker and there would be anywhere from five to ten people standing in front of my locker, just chitchatting. There were often times when I would need to get a book out of the locker to take to a class. I would stand around, waiting for the students to go away, but it seemed like they never did. Eventually, I would give up and just go on to class without the materials that I needed because I didn't want to bother them by trying to get something from my locker. There were also plenty of afternoons in which I wouldn't want to go to my locker after school, not because I didn't want to—in fact, I needed to—but because there were once again people standing around my locker and blocking it from me. I felt as if my own locker was off limits to me and that other kids were using it. Often, I would go home without a jacket or coat because of this.

I constantly wanted to be the first student to arrive at school in the morning. I panicked if the bus was running late or didn't get us to school on time. I wanted to be the first student in the building so I could just go to my locker and get what I needed. Sometimes I would try to carry around extra stuff for two or three class periods because I knew that I would have no chance of getting to my locker during the day. I didn't do this because I wanted to but because I felt like I had to. Even if on a rare occasion I did get to my locker, I didn't want to take the time because I wanted to be the first person in the classroom to pick a seat. If I picked my seat, then if another student had to sit beside me it was because they chose to or were the last one in the room. I always would feel bad if I was late and tried to sit next to someone. I would feel like I was hurting them because they didn't like me and that I didn't belong in the class with the other students.

I noticed in seventh grade how other kids would not only socialize with more success than I did at school, but their friendships started to go outside of school as well. Huntington was just opening a new movie theater called the Huntington Seven. Now, this was unique to Huntington because before this the theater was downtown and only had one screen.

Kids now had somewhere to hang out and socialize outside of school. Kids would be at the movies every Friday night with their friends. These friendships seemed to come in numbers now like I'd never seen before, meaning it seemed to me as if there were certain kinds of kids hanging out with each other in groups. During the school day and then again outside of school, people would congregate in groups. This was extremely uncomfortable for me, as I was never a part of a group and left to wander around by myself. These groups of kids would be at the movies on a Friday night with their friends, not their parents. I know this because when I was at the movies with my parents, I would see them all there, congregating outside of the theater with one another and having amazing social interactions. I became frustrated and tried to avoid going to the movies as much as possible. My parents didn't pay a whole lot of attention as to why I wasn't hanging out with other students outside of school. There could have been a couple reasons for this, one being that I had a couple of cousins my age who lived close by and I was with them sometimes. The other is that my parents just aren't very outgoing themselves and don't meet a lot of new people. Maybe they just thought it was normal to keep to myself and not have friends.

This was the year in which I really started to become bothered by the fact that I felt different and that other kids seemed "cooler" and more popular to me. Unfortunately for me, I didn't think too much of it at the time other than to myself. I became really down on myself at times and thought I was stupid. I didn't understand why I had such a hard time.

For me, one of the most horrifying experiences of middle school was riding the bus to and from school. I can't believe how rude kids can be and just how much trouble they can cause. I would get picked up early in the morning by my bus driver and then have to change buses at the elementary school in Andrews in order to get on another bus that was going to Riverview Middle School. The first bus was okay in the morning, as there weren't too many kids on it. I wished that bus would have taken us to Riverview.

My bus to Riverview was like a horror film. People would wad up spitballs and throw them all over the place. It was such a disaster. The bus driver couldn't even really focus on driving. It was so loud on there that it was overwhelming for me. I just wanted a calm and peaceful ride to and from school, but wow, was that ever hard to get. Overall I would say that the bus rides were very dangerous to me because the bus driver had absolutely no control at all. People would throw stuff and hit me. Sometimes people would be verbally abusive or mean to me. They would tease or bully me, tell me where I could or couldn't sit. It was like a nightmare for me. I was scared. But again, I didn't say anything to anyone—not even my parents—as I was starting to suspect that the way I was getting treated was the way that I was supposed to be treated.

Like always, I was very into basketball, and I decided to try out for the seventh-grade team. I attended the first night of tryouts and felt completely unwelcome and out of place. The other kids wouldn't even acknowledge that I was there. I felt so lonely and lost. We would scrimmage, and I'd be put in and didn't even get the ball. They would pass to other people ten to twenty times, and I didn't get the ball. I might as well have been out there playing basketball by myself because the other kids didn't want me to play with them or be on the team. I was just running around on the court with people laughing at me. They knew that I was different; even if they didn't come right out and say it, I knew that they knew it. This was also about the same time that the jazz band tryouts were taking place, and I knew I'd have to decide between doing one or the other anyway. I felt more comfortable in the band room than I did on the basketball court.

As I have discussed earlier, my dream as a very little kid was to become a professional basketball player. It was during my seventh-grade year when I attended basketball tryouts that I began to realize my dream was going to be just that. I didn't have the motor skills or the speed to keep up with the other kids, and I wasn't going to cut it at basketball. I was really discouraged for a few weeks.

Along with the transition to a new school came a new band director. Mr. Michael Flanagin was the band instructor at Riverview Middle School. The middle schools in Huntington had a summer band program, so my summer between the sixth and seventh grade came to an end a couple of weeks early. Both middle schools had the summer band program at Riverview because

Crestview Middle School was transitioning into their new building and it was not quite ready for them.

This was a unique experience for me. In sixth grade, we only had around ten to thirteen people in the band. Now, with all of the elementary schools going to the middle school, we would have a band of around fifty instrumentalists. I ended up really enjoying the summer band program that year. I had such a great time, and the best part was that I had fun without having to socialize with anyone or trying to make friends. I didn't have to say anything to communicate. I could communicate through my music or with my instrument, which I was naturally good at. Of course, there were still socializing activities involved with band, and I would feel awkward and left out in participating in them. However, most of the time was spent playing music, and I was able to be a huge part of that and felt like I belonged when we were playing. I loved music and loved making it. Since Crestview was at our school that year, we did a combined song called "La Bamba" at the end of the summer program. When the school year started, we had to play for Mr. Flanagin as an audition process. Unlike sixth grade, this time around, we were placed in our sections by talent level.

I won the position of section leader for the trombones. I was thrilled with this, and this gave me something to feel good about, as things that made me feel good came far and few between. Being a part of the band at Riverview was a really great experience for me. Without it, I would have become more depressed and secluded.

I loved to play the trombone and was very passionate about it. I can recall several songs that we did. One of them is one of my favorite songs to this day. It is actually done by the Canadian Brass, but even as a seventh-grade band, we were able to perform "Pachelbel's Canon." I fell in love with the tune even though it wasn't difficult at all. If you know anything about the song, you know that the low brass do not have a very exciting or challenging part.

We would do other songs like "Castlewood Fantasy." We did a piece for contest named "Pueblo." In eighth grade, we were starting to get really good. Again, I would be the trombone section leader. We did a lot of songs that year. One was called "Castlerock." We did a piece called "Cumberland Cross" that was a new piece out for band. A lot of the pieces we were performing were high school level pieces.

It was during band that I found an attraction to girls who were really good musicians and near the front of their section in rank. I'm not sure what my fascination was, but it had to do with a beautiful girl being good at something I was also good at—maybe a common interest. At the time this attraction to girls was almost the same as the other boys had. We still had the chase-them-around-the-playground mentality. For most neurotypical boys, that mentality about girls changes as they get through middle school and into their mid-teenage years. However, for someone on the spectrum, that may never change; and he may end up chasing girls his entire life out of the fascination of fixation he has with them.

The opportunity came for me to join the Riverview Jazz Ensemble, which was open to both seventh and eighth graders. I debated if I should audition or not. At the time, I was still very unsure of myself socially and musically. I knew that I enjoyed playing trombone, though. It was a way to escape all of the horrible things that were happening at school and have some good feelings for a change. So I took the chance and auditioned, and I'm glad I did.

We played a lot of cool stuff in jazz band. I also enjoyed it because this was a completely different type of music, more upbeat. At that point of time, being so young, I wasn't too thrilled by the classical music we played in concert band; but I loved what we were playing in jazz band. We performed pieces called "Louie, Louie," "Rock This Town," "Leader of the Pack," "The James Bond Theme Song," "Crazy Little Thing Called Love," "Satin Doll," "Make Me Smile," and "25 or 6 to 4," along with many other great tunes.

My ability to memorize things has always been one of my strengths. I can tell you the birthday of every single person I know. I had the ability to memorize every piece of music that I've ever performed on the trombone. It was strange because I never even had to look at the sheet music by the time we were performing. Throughout middle school and especially high school, I wouldn't even use music for the concerts. I would have it with me but didn't really look at it or need it. This was an amazing attribute to me being a good musician, especially in high school marching band and show choir backup band.

Being as into music as I was and having few or no friends at all, I quickly became fascinated by the trombone. I had a really good role model as a teacher; Mr. Flanagin cared a lot about his students and was very passionate about music. Without the skills to socialize with others, I quickly became fascinated with the trombone in itself and would bring it home every night. My parents seemed to enjoy the music, but I don't think they enjoyed me practicing quite so much at home. We lived in a small house, and it could get pretty loud in there. I would practice about two to four hours a night, which for a seventh grader is a really long time.

In middle school, we had practice logs that we had to fill out on a weekly basis and then return to school for Mr. Flanagin to check. I was the student who practiced the most hours several times. As much as I really wanted to be like the other kids, for some reason, I knew I was not. This was really depressing, but the trombone made it a little easier. Communicating through the trombone and through music was much easier and much more fulfilling for me than trying to socialize with my peers and build friendships, and it was a lot less painful.

# Escape into Fantasyland

In between my seventh- and eighth-grade years, I found out something that would be of importance to me. This is something that often happens to an individual who has Asperger's syndrome or autism. I would use this as a coping mechanism for years to come as well.

What I am going to talk about is something that Tony Attwood refers to as "escape into imagination" in his book, The Complete Guide to Asperger's Syndrome. Escape into imagination is not just your typical child or adult imagining something. This is much more intense for someone who's on the spectrum. Not only is it more intense, but it can also become meaningful to the person.

Just like the special interest having the capability of becoming the individual's best friend, escaping into imagination, or a make-believe world, as I like to call it, can also become the individual's best friend. Now this is something that is all right until it becomes the only means of survival for the individual. If this becomes their life, we've got a problem.

For me, this has been an issue many times. But at this particular time, I would escape into the imagination of movies and television shows. During that summer, my family had subscribed to receive HBO from Dish Network. While having HBO, I started watching more and more television. I would start watching the movies. I started to become interested in television more and more on a daily basis. While I was still playing my trombone quite a bit, I was spending the rest of my day watching movies on HBO.

I would search through the guide to try to find a movie. For some reason, what I was looking for was a movie where a really beautiful woman would be kidnapped. I was drawn to these movies. I loved the idea of being the superhero who comes in and saves the beautiful princess. I came across a wonderful movie on HBO one day. This movie would end up airing many times on HBO that summer, and I watched it over and over again. The movie description looked very interesting to me when I read it, so I decided to tape the movie as well. Soon after, I started taping every movie so I could have a library of movies. This was something that I did because I wanted to have someone to connect with whenever I wanted. Again, this would be a way of making friends for me.

The particular movie was Head Above Water. Cameron Diaz is the main star of this movie, and her character is Natalie. Cameron was great in this movie, and I quickly fell in love and became obsessed with her. She's absolutely beautiful.

I loved Cameron because she was so funny and attractive. I was really drawn to Natalie's arms in the movie. This is probably one of the strange special interests I had. It didn't take long until Natalie became my best friend. This is probably hard for NTs to understand, but when you don't have friends in real life, it becomes easy to become creative. This was great for me because this was something that provided meaning for me. Natalie was my best friend, and I would imagine every time I watched the movie that I was her hero and saving her.

There is a great scene in the movie where the guy puts Natalie in a bucket of cement or something and then proceeds to dump her into the ocean or a big lake. I wished that I was there to save the day. I would have dived into the water and pulled her to safety. Natalie was amazing to me, and I was extremely fascinated by her. I wished that I could meet her in real life.

After that, I would watch any Cameron Diaz movie that came out. I have most of them on video. Something about her just makes me happy. She would talk. I could talk to her, sort of. But I didn't have to worry at all what she thought about me. I could have a conversation and pretend what she was saying. I could tell her she was pretty, and she would say thank you. She was just nice and appreciative. It was helpful for me to be able to express myself to someone, even if it wasn't a real person; but in a sense it was a real person. To this day, she's one of my favorite actresses. I have a few others, but I still want to meet her someday. It would be like meeting my best friend in the entire world.

I also became more fascinated with television shows such as Saved by the Bell and Full House. Again, I formed a special relationship with the characters, with Zack Morris becoming the only guy that I really ever became friends with on television.

The summer of 1999 was pretty laid back for me, as I didn't do much of anything at all outside of my fake world. I went swimming on a couple occasions, but mostly the only people I saw were my parents and sister and some extended family. After finding a new best friend and having a best friend for the first time in about a year and a half, I was excited to start school, as I thought maybe it would be easier for me now that I had Natalie. If I was going to have a bad day, I'd be able to go home and have Natalie get me through it.

There were two things that got me through eighth grade: Natalie and band. Once again, I was excited for the summer band program. The seventh-grade band I was in was pretty talented, and it promised to be a pretty talented eighth-grade band as well. Once again, I was named section leader of the trombone section. I was extremely excited and practiced every day. There would be a time in eighth grade when a student by the name of Jeremy would challenge me for my position. I had been challenged before but had always won with ease. This time, though, Jeremy had won the challenge and played a little better than I had. That was a huge wake-up call to me. That would have been one of those signs that I was getting too involved with my make-believe world at home. I spent more time watching movies and imagining things than I did doing homework or playing the trombone. I had to put a movie in or escape into my imagination to pretend that I had some friends. Sometimes I would watch movies while practicing, just as something in the background. My grades also started to drop, and school became more challenging for me.

I was escaping into imagination a little too much at home that summer and even during most of my eighth-grade year. I had eased up on the practicing and focused more upon the make-believe world that I had created. I was devastated after losing the challenge because being first chair and section leader was something I was very proud of and extremely excited about. I moped around for a few days after that, but I immediately started taking my trombone home again and practicing as much as four to five hours a night. I was determined to get my position back, and as soon as I was presented the opportunity to do so, I would jump on it. I ended up winning my position back and never lost it again after that.

Eighth-grade band had another exciting year, as we would perform many outstanding pieces. Because we had such a great trombone section, we were able to perform a piece called "Lassus Trombones." This was the most amazing thing to me, as it involved playing extremely loud and fast, which is something I was very good at. We took the piece to contest and did fairly well.

Band was kind of a fantasy land for me in a way too. I mean, it was real. We were playing real notes and making music, but it was done through pushing air through instruments and banging drum heads. The only way anyone could talk was if they were a percussionist, and they often did. That is why it was kind of a make-believe world for me, because I was communicating through music and not by trying to hold a conversation with someone. It was relaxing, and I was free. Because I often had the music memorized and performing came pretty easily to me, I was able to play my part and still be in a dream in my head. I would dream often of being a conductor of an orchestra or performing for a professional orchestra.

Jazz band would once again prove to be a positive experience in the eighth grade. We would play many interesting pieces, and for the first time, we would do a song that had a trombone solo in it. I remember the piece, “Over the Rainbow.” Everyone’s familiar with it. I played the solo and enjoyed it. I practiced that solo over and over again for a few weeks. I wanted it to be perfect. It wasn’t even difficult, but I wanted it to be finesse.

I was also introduced to jazz band at the high school level. They were so much more talented than our jazz band was, and I wanted to be just like them.

It was during my eighth-grade year that I was introduced to Indiana University in Bloomington, Indiana. My band director, Mr. Flanagin, was a huge IU fan. Of course, being an alum of the university, he had reason to be a fan. He was crazy about IU basketball and football. At that time, he had a very good reason to boast about his Hoosiers and the basketball team, as Bobby Knight was still in command.

As it just so happened, my father hated the Hoosiers. More importantly, he strongly disliked Bobby Knight. So, naturally, growing up and being taught to hate the Hoosiers, I wasn’t a huge fan myself when I met Mr. Flanagin. In fact, if it wasn’t for him, I probably never would have had any interest in them or going to the university as a student. Most of the extended family on my mom’s side loved Bobby Knight and the Hoosiers. It would often be a little heated when they were discussed at a family gathering. I felt like I couldn’t like the Hoosiers because my dad didn’t want me to, so I just never said much about them.

Mr. Flanagin was probably the first person to really discover my talent for music and trombone. He talked to me a lot about going on and playing further, possibly even majoring in some sort of music in college. He informed me that I would need to purchase an intermediate trombone to continue playing, though, as I was quickly outgrowing my beginning one. Getting a new trombone was the best thing I'd ever done, as it improved my playing even more.

Mr. Flanagin talked a lot about the IU School of Music to me. I became very interested in IU and a possible career in music. I began listening to more classical music compositions and practicing harder.

In eighth grade, I had the opportunity to participate in an IBA, or Indiana Bandmasters Association, honor band. It was a great experience for me, as they take you in for the weekend and you rehearse for a day with other students that you've never met before. The best part about being in an honor band was the fact that you have the best players from each school in the band. So your weakest link is actually the best player from some school. Therefore, the playing level of the ensemble increases significantly.

During both my seventh- and eighth-grade years, I had the opportunity to play trombone in the school's talent show. We always had a few people from the jazz ensemble get together and play one of our favorite pieces. This was a lot of fun for me. I was nervous about playing for the entire school, though. At that time, it was one thing for me to play in front of adults, but to perform music that wasn't necessarily considered to be popular by the student body was a little more embarrassing and challenging. I really enjoyed it, though, and I played great. Unfortunately, there was no gain in feeling comfortable with myself. It's not like being the star basketball player at this age. It's not cool to be an amazing trombonist or even a musician unless you play guitar or drums. Kids in our society just don't appreciate that kind of music at that age. Therefore, it didn't make me feel any better about myself just because I played trombone.

Mr. Richison was our eighth-grade history teacher, and he was a very stern man. I ended up really liking him, but I remember that for those first few days, I was just a little scared of him. I was put into a cluster with a group of students that included my cousin and a girl by the name of Amy. Amy was by far the hottest girl in the eighth grade, and I wanted to talk to her so badly. However, I could never do so.

This class in eighth grade was where I noticed that there was something severely wrong with me. As we sat in the cluster of four people, the other three always had a big social interaction and were connecting with each other, sharing laughs and enjoying one another's company. I could never get myself included in the conversation. I did try on a few occasions, and when I would jump in the conversation, I sometimes got a strange look and sometimes was ignored, like I wasn't even there. This was frustrating for me. Luckily, I had the make-believe world I had created and would often escape into imagination in class while they were having an amazing social conversation. They would start talking about something that had happened at lunch or someone popular, and the other three in the cluster would have an awesome conversation about it. I kept trying to figure out how to get in the conversation and say something, but every time I would try, I would get ignored or nothing would come out of my mouth. What did come out of my mouth was completely unrelated to the topic they were discussing.

I really started to feel like there was something wrong with me. Something didn't make sense. I hadn't figured it out yet, nor did I tell anyone I felt this way.

Eighth grade had come and gone. Middle school seemed to blow by extremely fast. Overall, middle school was fun but also pretty challenging, both socially and academically. Now that middle school was finished, I was moving on to high school. I'd spend four years of my life in high school, and it was a pretty interesting four years for me. I was going to be a very small fish in a very big sea, and I'd find myself at the bottom of the totem pole once again.

# Following Freshman

After leaving the eighth grade, it was time to move on to something much bigger than I'd ever experienced before. It was time to go on to high school. This would create numerous changes that I'd have to deal with. I would be the youngest student again, making it extremely easy for me to get picked on.

Another huge change was the size of the building I was in and the number of students who were attending. There were a little over two hundred students in grades nine through twelve at Huntington North High School. Huntington only had one high school, and that meant that every student within the HCCSC, or Huntington County Community School Cooperation, all attended the same high school.

High school would end up being full of many exciting and wonderful opportunities for me in the music world; however, once again, the social world would end up being near nonexistent for me. High school was a frustrating time. I was starting to comprehend that there was something wrong with me. The feelings would get much worse as time would go on, but I would guess that between my freshman and sophomore years, I was able to put some pieces together and begin to realize that other kids hated me.

High school provided a much more competitive atmosphere in the music world. I loved this, as I would join groups that competed against other schools. Music became more interesting to me than it ever was before. I decided to join marching band. I made this decision in the eighth grade. I loved marching band and really enjoyed being able to spend a lot of time on the football field, both rehearsing and performing. This was good for me. It would help me get through all of the stress of the daily routine of school itself. School in itself would become one of my least favorite things, as I struggled with the social relationships with peers, and this caused me to do poorly in academics.

High school was a time when I would become nervous about a lot of things and have some anxiety. In the early part of high school, I became very interested in what other people thought about me. I could tell that others didn't like me, and this bothered me. I was bothered by the fact that I wasn't like the other students. Basically I could tell that I wasn't cool and popular and didn't fit in like they did. They thought I was weird, creepy, psycho, retarded, stupid, fat, ugly, worthless, and pathetic. At least in my mind, I felt that was how they felt about me. I wanted to have friends like they all did and wanted to be included in the activities that they were doing. I was very cautious of being bullied or taken advantage of, but despite this I would still try my best to be included. The rejection hurt, and each time I was rejected I threw myself into the make-believe world and started playing trombone more often.

Band camp was quite an experience. Since music was much more competitive in high school, there was also a lot more rehearsal. The biggest change was the fact that summer band wasn't just four hours out of your day for two weeks but had been doubled to eight hours out of the day for two weeks. At first, it would seem like such a long day, but as time went on, I'd quickly become used to it and enjoy it.

Music was fascinating to me, but when they told me I'd be playing music while on the move, I was a little worried. I could quickly imagine all kinds of problems that would be presented because of the whole moving thing. One time my freshman year, I got plowed over by a huge sousaphone player and, more importantly, the sousaphone itself. Luckily, I survived this accident and continued throughout my freshman year. A lot of people say that freshmen in marching band don't normally play. They normally just focus on the marching since it's a new concept to them.

I would end up being one of the rare freshmen who could march and play a show. If you would have asked me after my first day of band camp in my freshman year if I thought I was going to be good at marching band or able to march and play, I would have probably just stared at you and started crying. After one day, I was petrified. However, as time went on, I would quickly learn how to march and become an even better musician.

For NT individuals, there are some advantages of having band camp before school starts. Now, most kids obviously dreaded giving up the last two weeks of their summer vacation, but for freshmen, this provided a way to meet people and connect with upperclassmen. I would eventually make friends—or what I thought were friends—with a few upperclassmen in the band, and they'd kind of take me under their wings.

It was wonderful to be connected with someone who knew something about high school and where everything was in there. I was wandering the halls and just being in awe of how big the place was. It was fascinating to me but at the same time a bit overwhelming.

The conclusion of band camp meant that the summer had come to an end and it was time for students to put their thinking caps back on and head back to school. It was late August of the year 2000. It was a hot summer day, and I was headed into a new building with new teachers and many new students whom I had never seen before. I was feeling completely overwhelmed about the new situation. I was feeling a little scared. I'd heard all of the rumors about how seniors liked to come around and put freshmen inside of a locker and lock them in or how they liked to stuff freshmen in the trash cans. I was totally aware of this and was extra careful for the first week or two of school. Whenever I was in the hallway, I tried to be on the lookout for the big kids who were going to pick me up and harm me. I am happy to report that I never ended up being stuck in a locker or a trash can.

There were so many people within the high school. I graduated in a class in which I was eventually able to know who almost everyone was.

Huntington North High School had what they called a block four program. The day was divided into four ninety-minute periods, with lunch added into the mix.

Academics became increasingly more challenging for me. During my freshman year, I was struggling more so than before. This was obviously due to the amount of change that was going on in my life. There were times when I'd try to focus on a homework assignment and just not be able to focus on it for more than five to ten minutes at a time. I didn't really think too much of this at the time. I just thought that this was how hard school was supposed to be.

This is another situation in which being aware of having Asperger's syndrome would have been significantly beneficial to me. Had my parents or myself known this, I could have reached out for academic support from the school system. I honestly believe that I would have been an all A's and B's student, if not an all A's student, had I been able to get help and receive the proper support.

High school marching band would be much more intense than I could ever imagine. In middle school, it was still about the students learning how to get around the instrument, as I like to call it. They spent more time rehearsing and preparing than they did performing. While we would still spend much more time rehearsing than we did performing, high school marching band provided anywhere from fifteen to twenty-five performances between the months of August and October.

It was during this group of performances in my freshman year that I would feel left out. I thought I was weird and different than the other students. I would observe the social interaction of other students in the group. I'd see them laughing, talking, and having all kinds of fun with each other, but I was never able to become involved in those kinds of interactions. I was unable to connect with the students the way that they connected with each other. I also felt that I was different because I was one of the students who wanted to be good. If the teacher/band director said to be quiet, I was ready to be quiet and start, while the other students wouldn't stop talking or laughing or playing. I would try so hard to connect with them, and while they'd talk to me for a brief moment or two, they would quickly move on to someone whom I guess was much more appealing or interesting to them.

This is what I will refer to as the 97/3 equation. Due to the circumstances, the person with an Asperger's or autistic diagnosis has to put 97 percent of the effort into forming the friendship while the NT individual is only willing to put about 3 percent into it. The NT individual will acknowledge a person on the spectrum if the person on the spectrum is trying desperately to get their attention and approval but will never give them much more than a moment or two of their time and become quickly uninterested. This is quite simply because they think that someone on the spectrum is different or weird. In our society, when we see something new or different than we are used to, we are taught to run from it.

One of the biggest reasons as to why the Aspie/neurotypical friendship is so difficult to develop is because each party involved has a different definition of what the friendship is. People with Asperger's want instant friendship and instant companionship. We want to be calling and texting 24/7 and have the best friend instantly. Neurotypicals have about twenty different steps to making a friend. It may take a new neurotypical person a year to go from step one to step twenty and become a friend. The person with Asperger's has no concept or understanding as to what steps two through nineteen are. They are not even really visible to us. Again, we are talking about unwritten rules that society has created. Because of this, the person with Asperger's syndrome is trying to go from step one to step twenty within a day or two of meeting someone. This comes off as creepy, and people can even think you're a jerk because you are trying to push them to this intense level of friendship before they are ready for it.

High school marching band consists of going to perform at parades, performing at the high school's football games, as well as traveling to and performing at marching band contests throughout the state. For me, one of the most traumatizing experiences was the bus rides to and from the performance event.

I wanted to be cool and fit in with the other kids so much. However, for me, that was just not something that would be possible. It's like there was something in me that was blocking me from being like the other kids. I was getting onto the buses and seeing all of the other kids sitting together and laughing and having a good time. I wanted to sit with someone so badly, but no one would want me to. Often, I'd sit in a seat by myself, but whenever this wasn't possible, I'd be forced to come out of my comfort zone and ask someone if I could sit with them. I felt so bad for asking them or bothering them with a stupid question. Sometimes I would hear no, and other times I'd hear a yes. With the yes answers, it was almost like they said yes but with a look of disgust on their faces.

For me, the bus rides to and from performances wouldn't be a social event at all. Due to the lack of friendships and the fact that there would really be no one on the bus who wanted to talk to me, I would quickly do some escaping into the imagination and imagine the marching show that was getting ready to take place. I visualized every step of the show from warm-ups until we would get off the field.

I was often disturbed at the other kids' behavior on the buses. To me, this would become a quiet time of preparing for the upcoming show. It seemed like for these other NT students, the bus rides to and from the competitions and parades would become a social hour or game. There would be so much yelling and screaming, even throwing spit balls at one another, that I would often feel as if I was at a zoo rather than sitting on a school bus with a bunch of high school kids.

Throughout my high school career, I was constantly teased for how I took things so seriously—especially in the music world. I was so intense with performing and practicing my instrument, and the other kids just couldn't comprehend why I would be so interested in practicing. To them, practicing was a drag and something that they didn't want to do. For me, practicing to this level would eventually pay off for me.

High school marching band would also be a time of physical abuse from the older students. I often got pushed around while standing in a group of people. There were instances when other boys would come up to me and do something that they called a T bag. This was extremely painful. I hated having this done to me, but in order to fit in and be friends with these people, I would try to cope with it and let them do it to me over and over again. The only way to have friends was to allow myself to be treated this way. Sometimes they'd say they were my friends, and other times they would just say I was stupid.

There were other times in my life when I was physically abused in some shape or form, but because I was so desperate for friendship, I kept staying around these people, trying to gain their approval. All I wanted was a good friend or two to like me and not treat me so bad. I've known people who said they're my friends but yet did all kinds of this stuff to me. People who have tried to take money from me or tell me because they were a senior and I was a freshman it was my place to pay for their meals, movie tickets, or various other things. I let this happen to me over and over again. I didn't dare tell anyone because I didn't want to get anyone in trouble.

There was a time when people thought it was cool to randomly poke me in the face. This would be something that they'd do to other students as well, but I ended up hating it and wishing that they'd stop. People with Asperger's or a form of autism often have a comfort zone. If they are forced to go out of this comfort zone, it makes them very uncomfortable. Well, for me, this would be breaching that comfort zone, and it would hurt.

I really believed that in order for me to be accepted and liked by others, this was something that had to happen; this was something that was normal and happened to every kid. I was unable to pull myself out of abusive relationships with people whom I thought were my friends because I valued having someone to hang out with so much that I couldn't pull away.

In December of 2000, a cold, wintery night just before Christmas would bring about the first dance of a freshman's high school career. This was an exciting opportunity for everyone. I was so excited to go to the dance. I would quickly think about tuxedos, flowers for the girl, where to take the girl for dinner, how to open every door for her, basically how to treat her like a queen. Unfortunately, I was getting ahead of myself and forgetting one very important piece of the equation: the girl herself. I was always afraid of asking girls out.

Suddenly, I was puzzled. I had taken care of the preplanning for everything, even made dinner reservations to a nice restaurant. But I didn't have the girl lined up. I wasn't exactly good at talking to girls. I knew who a lot of girls were and thought that a handful of girls were beautiful. I knew who they were, knew which I was interested in, but the problem was I didn't know how to talk to them. Unfortunately, in order to ask someone to go to a dance with you, you must be able to talk to them. I would have to be able to initiate conversation with them and be bold and brave enough to ask them to be my date. This would be something that would require me stepping out of my comfort zone and taking one of the biggest risks I'd ever taken in my life. The question I had next wasn't for her; it was for me. I would ask myself, Am I capable of doing this?

Unfortunately, I would end up answering my own questions—except I didn't answer the question with just one answer. Hundreds of answers popped into my head. After spending a few days thinking through this and trying to decide if I was capable of asking her to be my date to the dance, so many negative thoughts came to mind. I don't know what to say to her. She's too pretty for me. I'm not brave enough. She's too good for me. She doesn't like me. I'm not as cool as the other guys she knows. I'm too stupid for her. I'm worthless. Even, I'm too fat and ugly for her.

The fact that all of these thoughts would immediately start rolling through my head was enough to quickly scare me out of asking anyone to go to the dance that year. However, I was determined, and I even preordered some flowers on the Thursday before the dance, thinking I would come up with the courage to ask someone to be my date on that Friday, with the dance being on Saturday. I never did end up asking a girl, so I guess I just bought myself some flowers.

# On the Outside Looking In

After a freshman year full of success in music and failure in peer relationships, I retreated to my home for the summer and didn't really go out much until I received my first job at a steakhouse in Huntington, Indiana. I was sixteen when I first started working there. After spending the summer doing many of the same things that I had been doing, such as creating a make-believe world of friends and escaping into imagination whenever possible, I would go back to school to become a sophomore.

During my late freshman year of high school and into the beginning of my sophomore year, I started watching the morning news every morning when I woke up as I was getting around for school. It was during this time that Wane-TV News Channel 15 in Fort Wayne, Indiana, had an excellent and award-winning morning newscast.

Tara Brantley and Mark Mellinger were the anchors on the morning show. I've always thoroughly liked both Tara and Mark, as I think they really have a passion for reporting the news and are real down-to-earth people.

However, it was during this time around my sophomore year in 2001-2002 when News Channel 15 decided to bring on board another morning reporter to do some special reporting for the show.

This reporter went around the city, doing specialized reports during every morning show.

Her name was Nicole Manskey. She was so pretty and fresh out of college. When I would see her on the news, I would just practically fall in love at that instant. She did a number of reports throughout a one- to two-year stand. Her stay was short-lived because she was so talented and would eventually move on to bigger cities.

Nicole did anything from reporting from local restaurants to reporting on snowfall out live in the snow. One of her stories included a visit to the hospital, during which she had to get blood drawn for some kind of medical awareness week that was going on in Fort Wayne.

I became infatuated with Nicole, and she was someone whom I could look up to; she was also very pretty. I looked forward to the morning news show all of the time. When I couldn't watch it, I would make sure I taped it and watched it later.

Nicole left Wane-TV News Channel 15 in April of 2004. At that time, I was a little devastated that my favorite morning show person was leaving and I'd no longer get to have a best friend in Fort Wayne anymore. Yes, for me, even though it was just a friendship that had been developed on television, it still hurt when I no longer got to see her over and over again. With the news reporters, it almost seemed as if it was even more real than the friendships with movie stars and professional athletes that I'd created in my make-believe world.

It was more real because with Nicole, she was a local reporter in the same city in which I was going to school and living. I saw her on the news five days per week, and at that time, I'd actually dreamed of growing up and marrying her.

After Nicole left, I felt a little lost because there wasn't that person to wake up to and listen to every morning anymore. It was like losing a best friend. At the time, I had no idea where she went. I didn't think about trying to find out where she had accepted a position.

Nicole was a tremendous influence to me and someone who would pull me through every day by motivating me. It's so strange how someone whom you've never met in person can be such an influence and great friend, but again, it's the lack of capability in developing real friendships in real life that allows this to happen.

As summer came to an end, it was time to head back to school. It was another interesting marching season. It was the best marching season out of all four years of high school for me. We had the best scores of any year during that season.

I still didn't like the bus rides, and I didn't like all of the yelling and screaming that went on during the bus ride. I noticed that randomly loud noises like screaming or yelling were starting to bother me. Now, it seemed strange to me, since I was so used to being around music.

On a day in January, the HNHS choir director, Mr. John Wenning, called me into his office. I had auditioned to be in his show choir backup band just a few months prior to that but didn't make it due to the fact that there were many upperclassmen auditioning and I, at the time, was just a freshman. Mr. Wenning asked me if I wanted to be in the show choir band for competition season. I was stunned. The Varsity Singers were an amazing group of talented singers, dancers, instrumentalists, and stage crew. Hearing the show choir perform in middle school was exciting to me. It was that Broadway-type style that I loved so much. Of course, I accepted his offer and immediately began practicing with the backup band to prepare the show.

Joining show choir backup band was the best musical experience that I had in high school. This group was extremely talented and motivated. The Varsity Singers had a great leader who knew how to compete and win. He is one of those music directors who, in my words, just gets it.

While the performing aspect of show choir was extremely fun and entertaining for me, the social part of it would prove to be yet another nightmare for me. Once again, I was just a worthless tag-along. At times it felt as if the other kids didn't even know that I existed. When I was included, it led to being made fun of while playing a card game or being asked to get them something or do something for them. No one ever wanted to be my partner in the card games, and if they were, they would make fun of me during the entire game or make jokes about me. Yes, even my own teammate would make fun of me or say I was stupid sometimes. It was never about just being friends. For me, I was looking for friendship and so desperately wanted and needed to be friends with these kids. Often, when we'd sit in the bleachers at events, I would feel out of place. While I was having all of these feelings on the inside, I never addressed them with anyone, because in my mind they already thought I was weird and hated me, so if I told them this, then what would they think? They'd probably think that I was a creepy psycho. I knew I couldn't tell anyone, and I also thought that these were completely normal feelings that I was having.

One of the perks to being a part of such a talented group of musicians was the fact that we would often win grand champion at numerous show choir competitions in the state of Indiana as well as some in the surrounding Midwest states. The first time that the choir won the grand championship at a competition with me being a part of the group, people ran the stage, and I thought there was some kind of a rock concert going on. I was amazed at the level of celebration. This particular group was a much more dedicated group as far as work ethic than any other group that I'd ever been a part of. If I would have had the proper social skill set, I think I really would have enjoyed this group.

As all members of the choir would quickly gather on the stage to begin celebrating being named grand champions of a competition, people would start hugging each other. I like hugs, and to me, this would be an exciting thing. I constantly thought to myself, Awesome. They're hugging, and then I waited, and waited, and waited some more. It was very rare that I would get a hug. The girls would run around, hugging other guys like there was nothing to it, and then it seemed like when they got to me, they gave me the look of "Oh gross. You're creepy. Go away."

I was devastated. This would happen to me over and over again at every show choir competition we would go to. What is wrong with me? I thought. I couldn't understand why these girls would just avoid hugging me. They must hate me, or, I must be a completely fat, ugly, worthless piece of trash, I couldn't help having these horrible thoughts about myself. I thought that I was a good person, and I couldn't understand why it was so hard for me to make friends or why girls thought of me in such a negative way. I couldn't figure out what I had done wrong or what I did to them that would make them treat me this way. At times, I would often think that they hated me just for being born into the world. I didn't get it. Something was wrong with me, and I had no clue what it was or how to fix it.

It was always a competition to see who would be the section leader. I was always the section leader in every ensemble (except when there were upperclassmen playing in the ensemble). One wintery day in 2002, I was sitting in my high school band class. I was always a student who would spend hours upon hours in the practice room, playing trombone. The other kids would always make fun of me and tease me because I had no life and practiced all the time. To me, the frustrating part was that these kids would often be the same kids who would shun me and not even give me a chance to be their friend.

Well, on this day, the comment that one of the students made was more hurtful and emotionally damaging than any other comment anyone had ever said to me up until that point. I was sitting in my chair, waiting to play my trombone, when I heard the words, "You practice your trombone so much that you're going to end up marrying your trombone and you'll never have a girlfriend." Now, obviously, most kids in a normal mind-set with any sort of a good self-esteem about themselves would have just let a comment like that go in one ear and right out the other ear. But imagine if you were someone who'd been laughed at, made fun of, pushed around, taken advantage of, and rejected all of your life. You'd probably really analyze what the other kid said. I know that's what I did.

I was completely stunned that he'd said that. My jaw dropped to the floor. Immediately, I would start overanalyzing it and become obsessed just with his particular comment. Was I wrong for practicing trombone so much? Was that why no one liked me?

I would spend the rest of that year being really lost. I wasn't sure if I belonged there. I would continue to try to develop peer relationships, and it just wasn't happening for me. I quickly became more and more frustrated.

Working at the steakhouse would start to present many more problems as well. I thought that maybe being at work would give me a chance to really fit in and feel like I belonged somewhere. Unfortunately, that didn't quite happen. I would quickly be pegged as someone who could be taken advantage of by people. The frustrating and sad part is that people who have autism or Asperger's syndrome simply aren't socially aware enough to recognize when someone's taking advantage of them. We don't have the capability of recognizing this sometimes—although sometimes I would be able to recognize it-but because we really want that friendship to develop with someone, we tend to stay in bad situations.

As the spring of 2002 came along, I would continue to go to school and pray that I could fit in. I would pray that I would make friends and be able to have a normal life. I was able to recover somewhat from the comment the student made about my trombone practicing and resume playing trombone and practice. In fact, I probably practiced more than ever before. I would have the chance to join the Fort Wayne Youth Symphony and begin taking private lessons from the principal trombonist of the Fort Wayne Philharmonic.

I would travel to Fort Wayne after school on most nights after a music rehearsal to take a lesson from Mr. David Cook. David has an amazing teaching style that's not comparable to anyone else I know. It's a little different, and it really motivated me to practice to achieve my best. That year, I would begin taking solos to ISSMA competitions and receive superior ratings. I even went on to state. I had a new sense of motivation for music and was losing interest in the social world again. Once again, it seemed like I just wanted to create my little bubble and hide in it. It was so much easier to just create a make-believe social life than to try to fit in to the real world. It was also a lot less painful.

During my sophomore year, I was in a German class with an amazing girl. We will call her Jennifer. She was also a member of Varsity Singers. I got to know her by sitting next to her in class. Since we were both involved in the show choir, we spent quite a bit of time together between class and rehearsals. After kind of getting to know her, I was very interested in her. Not only was she pretty, but she was understanding and had an awesome personality. She made a great friend. In February of 2002, I decided that I liked her and I was going to be brave enough to ask her out. Unfortunately, due to my lack of social knowledge, I did not know how to go about doing this. At first she was completely cool with me, until I crossed that line of friendship into being interested in her as a possible girlfriend.

My approach was to get her a necklace and a few other things, which I would proceed to give her after school and before a Varsity Singers' rehearsal on Valentine's Day. Somehow she found out about my intentions and tried to avoid me. As it ended up, I was able to give her the necklace and other gifts, except for now I felt bad because I knew that she thought I was creepy.

However, to this day, I can still recall giving the gift to her by the lockers and having her say, "You're a sweetheart," and then giving me a hug. You might be wondering why this was such a big deal to me. Well, for a guy who'd never had much success around girls, just to get a girl to say hi and talk with me was an accomplishment; but getting my first hug from a girl was an amazing feat. It was something that I've always remembered, and I will cherish it for the rest of my life.

The experience with Valentine's Day and Jennifer was the only real positive social experience that I can take away from high school. There were many other attempts at social success, but most led to failure, ridicule, and rejection.

# A Dream Discovered

The summer in 2002 would be spent working at the steakhouse and practicing my trombone. I would participate in a local summer concert band. The remaining time was spent swimming at a pond my grandparents owned. Again, there was no real social interaction with peers other than the forced ones that would happen at work.

As I was beginning to get older and maturing quite a bit, I was starting to become more aware of the situation. I was starting to become in tune with the fact that I really struggled socially. I couldn't figure it out, but then, at this point in time, there was never really much desire to even attempt to figure it out.

My job would continue to cause me problems socially, as I'd continue to be taken advantage of by both girls and guys that worked there with me. I'm not sure what it was, but I just felt like I was a target. What was I doing that was so wrong that was causing me to be treated in this way?

The previous year, while working at the steakhouse, I was a cashier, and this was really hard for me—no, not the mathematical part of the job, but more so the social part. I just didn't know what to say to the people as they went through my line. I had a hard time looking them in the eye. I was very nervous because I didn't want to say the wrong thing at the wrong time. I basically was able to say hello and carry on a small conversation. I related better to the senior citizens and older customers that were coming in because they weren't as judgmental. I learned how to cook for the buffet, which was a blessing because I was able to spend most of my time in back cooking. I loved coming out front to help the person run the front as well, though, and enjoyed seeing and meeting people. It was just frustrating due to my having Asperger's syndrome. I began to dread going to work to do that job, so I was relieved when they called me in and told me that they were moving me to a different position. I was now going to work with the food bars. There would be less socializing with customers and more time spent doing things that I sort of knew how to do and was somewhat good at.

This job was a little easier and less stressful for me, but I still struggled with my coworkers. I just wanted to be like them. I'd notice how a lot of times people would be whispering to each other, and I often wondered if they were talking about me. This would not only happen at work but at school and pretty much any other social setting.

Even though I would get made fun of at work, there were still some people I worked with who were nice to me and made me feel like I was someone of worth. While I never would develop what I would say was a true, everlasting friendship with any of these individuals, it did provide a comfortable setting for me. It was mostly the older people that befriended me at work. Older people have always seemed to be nicer to me than my peer group. This comes from their maturity and understanding of life. I tried to get to know them, and they were welcome to talking to me. I'd never hang out with anyone outside of work, but at least I had some people at work that I could talk to and listen to. Some of the older women were even able to listen when I needed to talk about a girl I liked. They were very understanding and tried to help me learn how to talk to her. It never worked out. But it was at least an effort on someone's part to help me.

I found myself constantly hanging out at the steakhouse, sitting there eating or just talking to people. This would become a security blanket for me, as I didn't have a social life of my own. The only socializing that I was able to do was preplanned or in a place where it was just naturally designed to happen for me.

I quickly became attracted to a girl whom I worked with, and she really made me feel good, at least at work. It was just nice talking to her, as I felt like this girl at least had a heart and was willing to listen. I constantly followed her around at work trying to talk to her and get her to like me, and I started sending her flowers and other gifts at work. Unfortunately, my attempts to develop this friendship outside of work failed miserably and led to ridicule from her and others. I wasn't sure what I'd done wrong, and once again, I just assumed that she, along with everyone else, hated me. This was extremely difficult to deal with, and I'd just try to become more withdrawn from society, basically only interacting with other people when I was forced to.

I withdrew to the make-believe world whenever I wasn't working. I would spend my hours at home, watching movies that I'd recorded a few years back and imagining me having a much more successful social life.

It was during that summer and the 2002-2003 school year that I really became interested in pursuing a music education degree from Indiana University in Bloomington, Indiana. I began to explore the possibilities of auditioning for the IU School of Music and quickly started playing harder music. Mr. David Cook would prove to be a tremendous help for me in this area, as well as Mr. Scott Hippensteel, who was an IU alum.

I began to practice hours upon hours. I went to all-region bands to play with some of the greatest musicians from across the state. I continued to try to keep up on my studies at school and kept playing in all the school ensembles. Between trying to go to school, working, and participating in musical ensemble rehearsals, I was so busy that I managed to be able to forget about most of my problems for at least a year or two.

My junior year was the best year of my high school career. I didn't try too hard to develop friendships because I was so busy doing the things that I loved to do and working. I actually enjoyed my job at the steakhouse. I would have liked it a lot more if I would have been able to fit in and avoid being tortured by being taken advantage of and even, at times, being physically tortured and abused. I never saw a reason as to why most guys had to be so tough and macho.

During my junior year, I was able to make a trip down to Indiana University. I went down there on a Saturday and spent the night. This was a good experience for me, and I really enjoyed the university. It was a huge place, and there were so many people there that I'd never seen before. I crowded into a dorm room with a room full of people for the evening. IU had a bowling alley on campus, and we were all able to go bowling.

As I continued to get older, I noticed that girls became more and more attractive. I really wanted to get a girlfriend, but I didn't have any idea how to. Dances at school would come and go, and I didn't have a date. I thought there was something severely wrong with me. I couldn't understand why girls wouldn't give me the same chance that they were giving other guys. Luckily, that year, I was able to keep myself focused on the work at hand with school and with my musical talents.

My junior year of marching band would prove to be a pretty horrible season. For some reason, we had a horribly difficult show and probably the least talented marching band of all four years. I would get frustrated with that season, as, to me, it would just seem like other students didn't care how good we were and how we looked to the public. I was at a performing level where I just wanted to be the best of the best in the musical world. I needed to be able to be involved with a group of people who would be as highly motivated as I was to be as successful as possible.

I would get this opportunity when I played with the Fort Wayne Youth Symphony. Playing with the youth symphony was fun because it was mostly playing with very little talking. The students in the group were much more focused on making professional-level-sounding music than they were on having a good time. This was a great experience that I learned a lot from.

Over the summer between my junior and senior year, I would put even more time into practicing. I officially decided that I was going to audition for the IU School of Music. I practiced a lot and repeated various technical exercises until I had them down perfectly.

This is a transitioning point in the story of my life. You would think a normal transitioning point in someone's life would come after their senior year of high school, but for me, my transition would begin toward the end of my junior year and into my senior year. While my senior year would prove to be a fun year as far as extracurricular activities, it would become more and more miserable as far as socializing. I would become more and more depressed and lost. The next part of this book is going to take you directly inside my brain as I graduated high school and began my college career.

# A Chapter Closes

It was finally here: senior year. I was ready to move on with my life. I began the year with lots of excitement and high hopes of being successful both in the music world as well as in the social world. I would continue to try to develop peer relationships with other students and would again struggle in this area. Struggling with peer relationships is something that would be a struggle for me over and over again. It wouldn't be something that would just naturally go away.

Marching band started out with a high note, as I quickly learned the band directors had decided on a show called Kipawatissmo for my senior year. In this show, there were three movements, and two of them were arranged to start with trombone solos. The middle movement, or ballad, had a baritone solo in the middle. It was very lyrical and smooth, so it would be something that would be much more difficult to play on a trombone. I really enjoyed the music to the show; I just wish we could have had a more talented group to perform it at times. Not so much a more talented group but a more determined and dedicated group that would be more interested in performing the music to the best of their ability. Again, I was a musician who, even in high school, wanted to be a professional musician and perform at a professional level.

I began preparing for my Indiana University School of Music audition the previous summer. I started preparing one of my all-time favorite trombone solos, a piece called "Concertino for Trombone" by David Fairdinando. This is probably one of the more challenging trombone solos out there on the market. It's a very demanding piece technically but also a very demanding lyrical piece.

I would take that piece to that state ISSMA solo and ensemble competition in late January of 2004. I would receive a perfect score at the contest, both at district and at state. This was something that was very commendable, as most students don't receive perfect scores at the state level. I was proud of myself for achieving this feat, and it motivated me even more for my audition that would be coming up just two weekends later.

It was the middle to end of September, and I became really frustrated with the other kids in marching band because they didn't seem to take being there seriously. As I've stated before, the previous three years bothered me, but this year would bother me more so than the others.

Eventually, I got to a point to where I wanted to just drop out and get out of there because it felt like a huge waste of time. I could be spending my time on my personal practice or even studying rather than having to waste five minutes every time the directors would ask the students to be quiet before we could start playing or marching. I managed to stick it out and put up with all of the frustrations and finish out the season, and I'm glad I did because I love marching band.

We would eventually make it through that marching season with a gold rating at the ISSMA District Contest and then receive a silver rating at the ISSMA Regional Competition in October of 2003. I was disappointed with the final result, as it was always my dream to march on the RCA dome floor in Indianapolis.

This was a busy time of year for me, as I was balancing all of the solo and ensemble contests along with Varsity Singers show choir competitions and, of course, preparing for the biggest day of my life. I was preparing to audition for the Indiana University School of Music. This was my dream, and IU had one of the top two music schools in the nation. I was so excited about this and put a lot of time and effort into practicing and preparing for it.

Meanwhile, I was still balancing the work schedule back at the steakhouse. This was becoming more complicated, as there was starting to be some trouble with the general manager at work. He was one of my favorite people there. However, somehow he'd get himself into a messy situation and eventually get fired from the company. They brought in another manager who took his place. At first, I wasn't a fan of this manager and struggled with the transition.

Like most things in life, for someone dealing with Asperger's or autism, changing out of a routine can be a very difficult thing to do. Therefore, when this new manager came in and had new ideas and new procedures, I was a little confused as to how to react to them. The change seemed to go okay with only a few minor speed bumps, but it was a struggle. I think maybe the other employees adapted to change much easier than me. The new manager was a lot stricter and had a temper. He had to have everything done his way or you were going to get fired. You didn't dare burn his meatloaf or make his buffets look bad, or you were going to be written up and fired. Thankfully I had a pretty good handle on my job and managed to avoid too much conflict with him. But I had to stay on my toes because I didn't want to lose my job at the time.

Meanwhile, back at school, I was having a hard time with some higher-level math classes and didn't really seem to be able to focus too much on homework or trying. With everything else going on, homework was the last thing I had on my mind. I mean, there was preparing for the IU audition, marching band, Varsity Singers, jazz band, and, of course, work. I was also trying to play in the Fort Wayne Youth Symphony at the time as well as take private lessons from the principal trombonist of the Fort Wayne Philharmonic. Needless to say, I didn't really have much time for a social life; therefore, I think my senior year might have been a little easier on me as far as being depressed, as I wouldn't allow myself time to get down in the dumps over my lack of ability to develop friendships with the other kids.

In the final days leading up to the Indiana University School of Music audition, I would not only become very focused on the outcome and goal that I had in mind, but I'd also become very anxious about it. I had never had a problem with becoming anxious before playing in front of anyone in my life, but for some reason, this time it was different. Of course, this was the biggest performance I'd ever been a part of up to that point. I was playing a trombone solo in front of three well-respected trombonists who were on faculty at Indiana University.

Professors Peter Ellefson, Dee Stewart, and Carl Lenthe would all be listening to me and critiquing my playing. I was extremely nervous and excited all at the same time. Luckily for me, I did so much ensemble playing while in high school that I didn't have to worry about being in shape. My chops were golden. Of course, if one's going to be auditioning for the IU School of Music, they had better not have to worry about their chops not being ready for the performance.

In the final days, I was extremely busy, as it was getting close to the Varsity Singers' competition season. This was an intense time for the show choir, as during the final week of preparation for competition season we would often have rehearsals every night. It was our last chance to polish up the show before we took it out on the road to compete with other schools.

In the final week heading into the competition season, I had a scheduling conflict. I probably tended to get myself involved in too many ensembles, as I would often have conflicts and have to pick and choose which ones I should attend. This was obviously creating a huge organization problem that I didn't like dealing with. As those of you on the spectrum know, keeping things organized can be a difficult task for us. For some reason or another, we just aren't too good at balancing things.

So that February evening when I had a conflict was a night in which the Varsity Singers had an evening rehearsal scheduled from

6:00 p.m. to 9:00 p.m. Meanwhile, the Fort Wayne Youth Symphony also had an evening rehearsal scheduled from 5:15 p.m. to 7:45 p.m. With Fort Wayne being about forty-five minutes away from Huntington, where I lived, this would make for an interesting dilemma. Somehow I had to be in two places at one time. I ended up splitting the time. I would go to the Fort Wayne Youth Symphony rehearsal but leave at 6:15 p.m. Then I jumped on the freeway and drove about eighty or ninety miles per hour to get back to Huntington North High School to rehearse with the Varsity Singers. Without even having time to eat or relax in between, I would get out my instrument and be ready to play the show choir show.

That particular evening, we had a guest clinician who would often come in and work with the choir and backup band. They had run the show once without me being there, and as I was walking in, the clinician accused the band of not being loud enough. Well, I was someone that was often known for my ability to play really loud. Let's just say I have a good set of lungs on me and can push amazing amounts of air through the horn. Well, when I got there and we ran through the show a second time, all of a sudden he said that the band was too loud. This was usually a good thing to hear, although I'll admit there can be times when playing too loud is not necessarily appropriate.

For someone who didn't have very much success in anything other than music in his life, just getting any kind of a compliment at all would put a beaming smile on my face. Even if it was at something that I already knew I was good at, I would still like it when someone would take notice and compliment me for a job well done. This was something that was able to help get me through high school. Without this, I just wouldn't have had anything successful going on in my life. You might say that I used music as a tool for making myself not only feel better but as a sense of acceptance. I was accepted by others through my music and not for my socializing.

I ended up being scheduled to work on the night before my Indiana University School of Music audition. This wasn't such a good thing, as I would have to spend the night before the audition working and trying to interact with other employees and customers. This was generally a very stressful task for me, and it would demand all of the attention and effort that I had. With the audition being the next day, my attention was supposed to be more so on that, but because of having to work, I was kind of scatterbrained and roaming back and forth between thinking about work and the audition.

The night before I was supposed to audition at Indiana University, we had a horrible ice storm. The roads got pretty bad, and I being hesitant as to if I wanted to go or not. I couldn't make up my mind if we should try our luck with the roads. I was supposed to be in Bloomington by eight o'clock that morning, and in order to be there on time, that meant leaving between 4:00 and 5:00 a.m. I hesitated all night long at work, thinking that we shouldn't go because of the weather. I was more scared and afraid of auditioning than I was worried about the weather.

I had never had any problems playing my trombone in front of anyone, and I was just naturally in the zone whenever I played. But this particular time, due to the magnitude and meaning of the performance, I was a nervous wreck.

My parents were able to calm me down enough to get in the car and head down there for the audition. It was snowy and icy. The roads were a mess, and we had to drive really slow, which drove me even more crazy, as it gave me more time to think and overanalyze the days ahead.

When I got to Bloomington, I was amazed at the sight. There were so many people there on campus, and I immediately heard students warming up and practicing in the practice rooms. For those of you who have never been to Indiana University, I think it's one of the college campuses worldwide that is a must-visit. You must see this university in the fall and spring, as it is absolutely gorgeous.

The first day I was there, I spent the majority of the day filling out paperwork, talking to people who were affiliated with the school of music, and taking tests. Yes, I said tests. This was not your standard university testing either. This was IU, one of the best music schools in the world. These tests would determine what level of theory and piano you would be in, should you end up being one of the lucky ones to be chosen and accepted to the school of music.

I was very anxious as I was taking the theory test. I was generally very good with anything to do with music; however, at our high school, there wasn't really much of a theory program, as is the case at most high schools.

After seeing three other students from my high school audition for the IU School of Music in each of the previous three years before me and not getting in, I was extremely nervous and afraid that I wasn't going to get in either. However, deep down in my heart, I knew that I was good enough. There was something about me and my determination of becoming the best that would push me and pull me through.

The morning of the audition, I woke up early and left the hotel with my dad to head over to the School of Music building, where the auditions were taking place. Each instrument was stashed off in their own little private section of the building. I walked into this building and was amazed at not only the size of the building but also at the number of students who were in the building. Then, when I reached the trombone studio, I couldn't believe how many trombonists had made the trip to Indiana for the auditions. All of these kids—literally thousands of high school trombone players—would be competing for just a handful of spots in the incoming freshman class of 2004.

I was standing in the hallway after warming up, and just visualizing the performance, I began to get excited and become tense. This would be the most pressure I'd ever encountered while performing, and it was the performance with the least amount of people listening. I was listening and amazed at how well all of these other students played.

As the time got closer for me to go inside and play for these three outstanding musicians, my heart instantly began pounding more so than ever before. Here I was. After seven years of playing trombone and trying to become a master of it, I was auditioning to my dream school for a dream position.

When I walked in the room, these three individuals who would be judging me seemed to be your average trombone professors. I had kind of put them up on a pedestal, thinking that they would be different, but to my liking, they were just like me. This would help me calm down and perform, as I'd feel less pressure. I was able to capture the moment and become part of the music. I lost all thinking of what was going on in the real world and became the piece of music.

I finished the performance and then proceed to do some sight-reading for them. Sight-reading is something in which I have always excelled. I am able to quickly visualize the notes on the page and put them into my head and then convert them from my hand to my arm to tell me what position to go to on the trombone to play that particular note.

Looking back on this phenomena now, I can conclude that my ability to sight-read at nearly a perfect level was probably attributed to my having Asperger's syndrome. You see, Asperger's can affect a person in several negative ways, but it can also leave a positive impact on someone. It can give and often does provide someone with a gift and most often a very inspiring gift, one that can even provide inspiration for others.

After leaving Bloomington and heading back to Huntington, I felt good about my chances. I performed the solo the best I had ever performed it and was thrilled with the way in which it came off to the trombone faculty. The trombone faculty seemed fairly pleased with my playing and asked me some good questions, which I was able to answer maturely and properly.

When I got back home to Huntington and went to school, the rest of the year would fly by. I would be so extremely busy with show choir competitions, Fort Wayne Youth Symphony, teaching some trombone lessons of my own, working at the steakhouse, and still trying to find time to practice. Yes. Even if I got into IU, it wouldn't mean that my work was done or that practice time was over. In fact, my work would just be beginning. I would be expected and want to practice even more and at a more intense level. I was excited about the opportunity that I had and was hoping that I would be accepted and get the chance to make the most of it.

In 2004, the Huntington North Varsity Singers had what I thought to be the most successful season out of all four of my years. We seemed to have developed a great sense of style, and the band really blended well with the singers to create an amazing sense of blend and balance and a terrific-sounding ensemble. It was a very memorable musical experience. We would win every competition but one that year. At the end of the season, we would make the trip down to Indianapolis and compete in the North Central competition. This would be the toughest competition that we'd ever competed in. There was a group nicknamed Attache. This group was from Clinton, Mississippi. They were supposedly the top-ranked show choir in the country, with the Varsity Singers consistently being in the top five or ten choirs in the country. We were extremely excited about the chance to compete with this group and really wanted to beat them.

Show choir competitions consisted of a morning or early afternoon performance in which every choir would have the chance to perform and show what they had. Then there was an afternoon awards program, in which they awarded special caption awards, such as best instrumental ensemble and best stage crew. They also occasionally had a best performer award. Then, after announcing all of those caption awards, they would pick the top six scoring choirs to go on to the finals in the evening. Each of the six groups would perform again in the evening in an order that was determined by a random drawing.

At the North Central competition, I had the honor of going up to the stage to accept awards after the end of the morning/afternoon performances. I was excited for this because I would get to go up with two girls. It was a custom that the guys and girls would lock elbows, so I was able to have a girl on each side of me, which meant so much to me. It meant the world because after a few years of seeing other guys being able to relate to girls and get girls to hug them or just interact with them in positive ways, this was the first time that I'd ever done something important with girls. While it was staged, they locked arms with me and went up on stage to receive our awards. This wouldn't seem like a big deal to the ordinary person, but when you're a guy who's wondering why girls hate him or why they think you're dumb, fat, stupid, and ugly, this is a huge accomplishment and breakthrough.

At this particular competition, I wasn't really expecting us to win best band, and I knew that winning grand champions at the competition was going to be a challenge in itself. To my surprise, when the gentleman read, "And the best instrumental ensemble goes to the Huntington North Varsity Singers," I was stunned. I was so happy, as we had just beaten the top show choir backup band in the country. This band was so good that the band itself had a nickname. They called themselves the Sound Machine.

After winning best band and having a brief moment to celebrate, it would be time to get back to business.

At the end of the first round of competition, we found ourselves in an unfamiliar spot. We were in second place, a few points behind Attache. We didn't often have to come from behind to win a competition, but if we were going to pull off the unbelievable upset, we would have to come from behind. In order to pull this off, we would need to have our best show of the season, if not the best show of our lives. We were pretty calm and confident. In fact, the parents of the students in our group were more nervous than we were. They wanted the championship for themselves more so than we (the students) wanted it. This would put the students under a tremendous amount of stress.

We had come to the point in time in which the senior class from Huntington North High School was to perform at their last show choir competition. The seniors, I'm sure, had mixed emotions, and I was just excited to play.

We performed our hearts out that night only to find out that it just wasn't quite enough. Attache, from Clinton, Mississippi, was just too good. While we managed to sneak out of there with the best band award in the morning session, we would fall short as a whole group. This was the only competition we lost in 2004. After finishing in fourth place, there was a lot of disappointment from the kids but more so from the parents. We had kind of spoiled the parents of the group members in previous years and then earlier that year by winning so much that the parents had a harder time dealing with defeat than the students did.

When the awards were over and we retreated to the room to get ready to leave, I'll never forget something that happened. You see, everyone who had been involved with the group knew that winning best band was exciting and an accomplishment, but winning that and not coming in first place overall meant nothing. While we band members knew that we could be excited about our accomplishment, we understood that there were more important tasks to be accomplished at these competitions. Well, one of the newest band members who was just experiencing not winning grand champion at a competition for the first time came back to the room and was yelling and screaming and celebrating because we'd won best band earlier that day. He didn't know why everyone was so down and depressed. Well, he got some dirty looks, and that was one time when I didn't feel like I was the only one who was out of place.

The ending of show choir season would bring one of my favorite times of the year. Springtime was right around the corner. This also meant that my birthday was coming up very soon, as I have a March 27 birthday. Birthdays were always such a drag to me. I had great family, and the support that the family would give me would be incredible, but I was missing something. Most of the time, kids going through school often have birthday parties not only for their family but also a party for their friends. Often, you would invite friends over to eat some pizza and just have a good time. I would try to accomplish this feat, but often no one or at least very few would show up. I know that my mother tried extremely hard to put on parties and try to get other children to come play with me. For some reason, no one would want to come to my party. Again, I attributed this to the fact that I was fat, ugly, stupid, and worthless.

Other kids at school would often pass out party invitations, but they would pass me up, as they didn't like me or didn't enjoy hanging out with me. I wanted to be invited to someone's birthday party so bad, but it just wasn't going to happen for me. I didn't have a birthday party for students that year or any other year that I can recall. I usually just had a party with my immediate family members at home.

It was mid-April when I came home from school to find a letter in the mail from the Indiana University School of Music. I was excited, anxious, and nervous all in one. I was prepared to handle the outcome no matter what the letter said, as I had a few other choices in mind for a college, but Indiana University was at the top of my list. As I opened the letter, my hands began to shake. After reading the letter saying that I had been accepted as a trombone performance major to Indiana University, I let out a huge sigh of relief. This was what I had wanted. This was what all of those hours and hours of practice had led to.

I immediately started to spread the word to everyone in my family that day, and I couldn't wait to spread the word to my music teachers at school and everyone who had been a huge inspiration in the music world for me. I felt so blessed to have a chance to pursue my dream of becoming a professional musician. I was ready for the next chapter of my life to begin and excited about the musical opportunities that would be presented to me. I was, however, still concerned with my social struggle to find friends.

The end of May arrived, and it was officially the end of a very challenging journey for me, a journey that was filled with some ups and downs—mostly downs. While I had had some success in the music world, I'd really struggled with academics and especially social relationships. I was still dumbfounded as to why I had such a hard time making friends. It was beyond my comprehension as to why no one wanted to be a part of my life. Why didn't a girl like me? Why didn't guys think I was cool like they were and want to be my friend? I had so many questions that had not been answered socially that I was just hurt and confused. I couldn't wait to get out of Huntington and get to Bloomington, as I thought maybe it was just the area I was in. Maybe only the people that lived in Huntington hated me and I would meet some people at Bloomington who would accept me for who I was and like me. I was trying to stay positive, and I just thought that maybe someone down there would accept me.

Before getting a chance to leave Huntington, I'd have a couple more high school events and a summer of working at the steakhouse to get through. Normally, events such as prom and graduation were meant to be meaningful and something that a high school student should enjoy. Unfortunately for me, due to my unusual circumstances, these events would be miserable and stressful. Everything socially was so hard for me to understand, and I would spend time overanalyzing it and beating myself up over any mistakes I'd made or at least mistakes that I thought I was making. I knew that something was wrong. There was something a little off about me that other kids just didn't like.

In the weeks leading up to prom, I became really stressed out. There wasn't really much going on for me to worry about as far as grades or auditions, but I was extremely worried about finding a date for the prom. This was extremely important to me. In the previous years, I'd missed out on nearly all of the Christmas dances that we had at our school, and I really wanted to go to prom with someone. I had decided that if I didn't have a date, there was no way I was going to take a chance on showing up there without a date and getting made fun of by my peers. I even had a plan ready in case I didn't get a date.

I didn't want to just stay at home and not go to prom because I wanted my parents to at least think I was successful in getting a date. I wanted them to think I was successful in at least finding one friend in high school. To them, getting a date wasn't hard. They would often wonder why I didn't show any interest in girls in high school, and so did many other people. I was often asked by people if I was gay due to the fact that I never had dates or even hung around girls.

Being asked if I was gay was the most frustrating thing in the world. No, I wasn't gay, but due to my poor social skills, it was easy for people to assume that. In fact, I was completely the opposite. I loved girls. There were more than a handful of girls whom I thought were the most beautiful and amazing people I'd ever known in my life while in high school. It wasn't that I didn't want anything to do with them at all but more that I didn't know how to have anything to do with them, at least in the way in which they wanted. Any attempts to try to talk a girl into going on a date with me would lead to rejection and ridicule, which would completely ruin my self-esteem. In each attempt I'd make to get a girlfriend, my self-esteem would drop a level due to the girl's reaction to me. Their reaction was like "Um. Wow. You like me? You of all people? How could that be? You're the most fat and ugly guy that I've ever had ask me out. You're pathetic and should be ashamed of yourself for asking me out." Now, obviously, I don't think they ever quite said it in those words, but unfortunately, that is what they were implying to me whenever I tried to develop a relationship with them.

After spending a couple of weeks trying to salvage a last-minute attempt at a date, it was Monday of prom week, and I had pretty much thrown in the towel and given up on going to prom. I had my plans all arranged to drive around on that Saturday night so my parents would think I went to prom. I just didn't want them knowing what a loser I was. I was going about my business during the week like normal—practicing trombone, working at the steakhouse, and doing some end-of-the-year things at school. I had decided that there was no hope for me in getting a date for prom. In fact, I'd decided that I was just stupid and girls as well as guys hated me.

I would often be the odd man out in a group of people. This was the case at lunch during all of my middle school and high school years, and it was no different my senior year. However, on Monday or Tuesday of prom week, a girl whom I ate lunch with had her boyfriend break up with her. She had her heart set on going to prom with this guy, as they had been together for quite some time. She seemed heartbroken, so I thought I'd offer to take her to prom. At first she wasn't too thrilled about the idea, and I think she was holding out to see if she could find a hotter date. But eventually, on Wednesday of that week, she called me at home and asked me if I would go to prom with her. This was a miracle, and I was amazed because I didn't even really have to do the asking. I simply offered. I had a prom date, and I was going to try to make sure that she had the best night of her life. Unfortunately, it would prove to be a very difficult task.

This girl was an extremely beautiful young woman, and she even played the flute in band. I was bound and determined to make sure that she had a good time at prom. I quickly began planning as I went to the flower shop and ordered a corsage and a dozen roses for that Saturday. The next couple of days we spent talking about what we wanted to do for prom.

We had decided that we were just going to eat dinner at Applebee's—nothing too fancy, as it was such a last-minute thing. Up until that Wednesday evening, I hadn't even planned on going to prom. So we went to Applebee's, but we did this in our regular clothes. We decided that it might be best to do this instead of wearing our prom attire and taking the chance of spilling something on it. Dinner was pretty good. She was also a naturally quiet person, so there wasn't much conversation at all. But we enjoyed the meal and then proceeded to go on with the rest of our evening.

After a great dinner, we went to her place to change clothes. I was getting really excited. Once we were ready, we took some pictures at her house for her parents and then went off to my house to take some pictures. I was so happy to be doing this, as this meant my mom and dad would see me with a girl. Just maybe they wouldn't think that I was a loser for never being around girls in the past.

Once we left my place, we headed over to the steakhouse where I worked to take some pictures and to show off my beautiful date to the people I worked with. I had told them all that I had an amazingly gorgeous date for prom, but they didn't believe me. So when I showed up with her, they were in awe. Later on, they asked me how I pulled that off, and I ended up telling them how it just sort of fell into my lap and I got lucky.

Needless to say, this would be a night in which I felt good about myself. Not only was I trying to save the day and rescue a beautiful woman by taking her to prom, but I also, for the first time, was enjoying myself in a social situation with an extremely beautiful woman who had an outstanding personality.

After leaving the steakhouse, we went on to meet up with her best friend and her boyfriend. We hung out at their place for a while and took some more pictures. We took some group pictures as well as individual couple pictures. After picture time, it was finally time to head off to the prom at the school. I was nervous, as I had never really even danced before. I was afraid that I was going to step on her foot or something. But even with being anxious about all of that, I still wanted to have a great time, and I was just amazed to have such an awesome date.

As we walked into prom, I noticed how couples were holding hands waiting in line. I was confused as to if I should do this with her or not. I'm glad I didn't try to do this, as it probably would have ruined the entire evening before it even started.

As we got inside, I was amazed to see how our high school had been transformed into a magical place for a dance. We picked a table and started to chat a little bit with the other people in our group. We then proceeded to get some refreshments and hit the dance floor.

I had only been to one other dance before this in my entire life, and I can't remember dancing with anyone when I was there. So this would be my first real dance. I was nervous, but at the same time, I was excited. It wasn't really as hard to slow dance as I thought it was going to be. In fact, I quickly learned that if I imitated her, I could do pretty well at it.

To finally be on a date with an extremely beautiful girl, to me, was like being on top of the world. Being with her that night made me feel special. I can't really describe the feeling to you other than by saying that it could possibly be like you having your first child or you getting married. To me, it was the most amazing and wonderful thing that had ever happened.

While dancing with her, I had another special moment. You see, I'd never so much as held a girl's hand before. Well, while dancing, gentlemen are supposed to put their hands on the woman's waist. While this would more than likely mean nothing at all to someone who has done this time and time again, for me to be able to just put a hand on her waist was like a dream come true. I was in awe of how beautiful she was and how amazing it felt just to be in that moment. I think some guys would kind of take these little things for granted, but for me, even the tiniest thing is cherished, as I never know if I'll get to experience it again.

We spent some time dancing, and I was having the time of my life, but something just wasn't right. She didn't seem to be enjoying herself too much, and I understood why, but I felt bad that she wasn't having a good time. I wanted to try to fix it so that she could enjoy her senior prom. I was trying to engage her and get her to dance for a while, and she did dance, but she just wasn't really there in the moment. Of course, I knew why, but still, I felt horrible.

One of her great friends tried to convince me that it wasn't my fault at all that she was having a bad time but it was probably strictly due to the fact that her long-term boyfriend had broken up with her that same week. I still felt bad though, as I just wanted everything to be okay for her and for her to have the time of her life at her senior prom.

We ended up going our separate ways before the evening was over due to circumstances that were out of our control. I was so privileged and honored to have had a chance to take such an amazing woman to the senior prom, and I enjoyed every moment of it. While I do wish that I could have saved the day a little better than I did, I realize that this would have been nearly impossible due to the events that had occurred earlier on in that week.

Later on in the following week, I got a thank-you card from her for stepping in and taking her to prom. This made me feel good about myself, as I had done something nice for someone to make a difference in their life. I still have the card and the prom pictures stored away in my room as memories of the greatest day of my life. To this day, this is one of only two or three women that I'm actually in a picture with.

The time had finally come for us seniors to take a walk across that stage one last time. But before doing that, there was one thing I would get to do that I really loved about Huntington North. Every spring, the choir program at Huntington North hosted a spring concert. It was tradition that at that spring concert the show choir would reunite and give one final performance of their competition show from that year. This was pretty exciting, as there was no pressure as far as competing and we could just perform the show and have fun while doing it.

It was often a goal of the band at these spring shows to do something that would be a surprise for the singers, such as playing a tune a little bit faster than it was supposed to go and watching them try to keep up with the dance moves on stage. This was pretty entertaining to me, as I would get to see it all. I always had every show memorized, and I wouldn't even need to look at my music. I could have left the music to the show at home and still played it nearly perfect.

The spring show in 2004 was a huge success. We were finally done with show choir. I'd never again get the opportunity to play in a group quite like this. While there are a few colleges in the area that have show choirs that use backup bands like at the high school level, the majority of college show choirs either do not use backup bands or they use a condensed-sized band. This is okay, and show choir can still be entertaining, but I would argue that when you have live music and a backup band, the intensity level of the show increases and makes for a much more entertaining show.

If there was ever such a day that could be a huge transition point in someone's life, it was high school graduation day. This is the case for anyone and not necessarily just people who are on the autism spectrum. High school graduation day is a time to reflect upon the past while looking forward to the future.

For most kids, reflecting on the past meant not only looking back at their previous academic and athletic achievements as well as their extracurricular activities at school; it was also a chance to sit around and reflect upon the special memories of social relationships. It was a time to look back and reflect upon the friendships that had formed. It was also a time to look back and reflect upon any relationships you'd had with a significant other as well as special bonds that you had formed with teachers in school. It was a time to think back to elementary school and remember your favorite teacher in those early years. Thirteen years, a majority of your life to that point, was coming to an end, and it was time to celebrate the ending of an era but also celebrate a new beginning and the future that was ahead.

For me, however, it was mainly a time of reflecting upon the past successes in the music world. Since I didn't have very much success with building social relationships, I was more focused upon the successes in the music world. Out of all of the awards I had won in high school for playing solos at ISSMA contests and all of the soloist awards at jazz ensemble competitions, the most memorable award for me was being accepted into the Indiana University School of Music.

Of course, another more memorable event that did happen socially for me was attending the high school prom. This would really stick out in my mind as an event that would provide meaning to life, and it helped motivate me to move on at the social level and try to develop friendships even more. Without this one sort of positive success, I probably would have given up at that point and quit trying. It provided the inspiration that I needed to stay motivated.

There were so many people there for graduation, and I felt a little overwhelmed. As we marched in, I was very aware that it was the end of an era and a new beginning. We received corsages to wear during graduation, and I had a hard time putting it on. I was also having another problem. It seemed difficult for me to balance and keep my cap on. I'm almost positive this had a lot to do with sensory problems that can be associated with having Asperger's syndrome or autism. But at that time, I just felt like a helpless loser.

Luckily, my cousin was able to help me figure out how to handle this problem and fit in somewhat. I was extremely nervous about walking across the stage at graduation. For some reason, I wasn't very good and coordinated at shaking someone's hand. I would get nervous and tense, as I wasn't sure how you were supposed to know what hand the other person was going to put out and when exactly they were going to put it out. I wasn't sure when they were going to be ready to shake hands, and I wasn't even sure how hard they would want to squeeze my hand or have me squeeze theirs.

The summer started with my graduation party. I had invited a lot of peers from high school, and only about two to three actually showed up. This was discouraging to me. Usually, when kids graduate together in a class of 450 or greater like I did, a student would at least have a hundred or so kids at his or her party.

Toward the end of August, I started packing up some of my things to head to Bloomington. I was still working forty to fifty hours a week, so I didn't have a whole lot of spare time. I also had to keep practicing trombone and piano so I could become an even better musician and have an advantage when starting school in September. That whole summer people pointed out to me that I practiced too much and that I didn't have a life. They would tease me and make fun of me. I would try to blow it off, but it was starting to really bother me. I was glad to be getting away from Huntington and trying to start a new life socially down in Bloomington. I wanted to keep the music aspect of my life, but I knew I had to get rid of the horrible social life that I had experienced and try to reestablish a better social life in Bloomington.

It was August 18, and my career at the steakhouse came to an end. I would run hot bar for one last senior night with the girl that I'd usually run it with. We were both headed off to college, and this was both of our last nights working there. We had a good time, and the night went smoothly; I must admit that it was kind of hard to say good-bye to the place and a couple of the adults there. But I had to. It was time to move on with life. I thought, *Surely there are better things ahead.* There have to be some friends to be made down in Bloomington, and life can only get better from here.

After the end of the summer, I spent my last week in town preparing for transition. I began to make some phone calls and get acquainted with the trombone faculty down at Indiana University. I would set up a lesson with my trombone professor, Mr. Peter Ellefson. I was amazed when I first met him, as he was such a fine musician. He had played for a few years with the Seattle Symphony, and, well, he knows his way around the trombone.

I moved into my first apartment the week before classes started. My cousin helped me move in, as he had a huge truck. I couldn't believe the amount of people who were already in Bloomington a week before classes had even started. I was going to be living on my own in an off-campus apartment. I wanted to have roommates, but due to my bedwetting problem at the time, I was unable to.

I thought that getting into Bloomington a week or so early would really benefit me not only socially but musically. I was looking to start my social life over, and I thought I'd spend a week or two doing this before classes actually started. I also wanted to get accustomed to my new surroundings and the new buildings.

There were so many changes to become accustomed to. I wanted to find out where all of my classes were. I also wanted to spend some time preparing the orchestra audition pieces. I knew that this was going to be a challenge.

The time had finally come for me to be a college student. I thought this was going to be an exciting experience and be completely different than being in high school. I was very much looking forward to the change and figuring out how to make friends. I thought for sure that I'd be able to make some good friends in the music school. I thought that maybe through common interest I would be able to just have some friends kind of fall into my lap, so to speak.

After spending a week down at Bloomington, getting things organized in my new apartment and figuring out how to get around town and mainly around campus, I was all situated. I thought that I'd come home for the weekend to say a few good-byes to some family. At that time, I thought I was going to be saying good-bye to them for quite some time, as I had no intentions of coming home until Thanksgiving. Little did I know at the time just how fast my plan would change.

# A Dream Dashed

After getting all situated in my new apartment down in Bloomington just off of the campus of Indiana University and coming home to spend the last weekend in Huntington, it was time for me to head back down to Bloomington on Sunday, August 22, 2004. Classes were slated to begin on Monday. I remember being extremely excited but very anxious and nervous. Indiana University was a huge place, and certainly I had many outstanding opportunities to develop friendships with not only guys but girls as well.

I couldn't wait to get down there and start playing my trombone with all of these amazing other talented musicians. This was my dream. This was my dream being fulfilled and coming true. I couldn't have asked for anything better than this musically. Socially, I was still looking for improvements in relationships with peers, and I thought that IU was the place in which this was going to happen for me.

I got into Bloomington at around 7:00 p.m. I didn't have much to do after getting there except for relax and get used to my new place. I had a really great apartment thanks to my grandparents, and I had imagined staying there all summer long and taking some summer classes.

As I came into town and began to see the beautiful scenery and realize that this situation was actually real and I was not dreaming it up, I began to think about the next few years of my life. I imagined myself making many amazing friends and meeting a woman of my dreams, graduating with a bachelor's in trombone performance, landing a professional gig, getting married, and having children. I had my life all planned out. I went to bed that evening feeling the best I'd felt about myself in a really long time.

I was thinking positively and was motivated to get up in the morning and begin my day. I thought that this was going to be perfect and I was going to be okay. I had a difficult time falling asleep due to the fact that I was so anxious, excited, nervous, and a little scared all at once. I was in a new place, with new surroundings and new people, but I knew that this opportunity had to be better than being in Huntington, where peers were always mean to me and no one wanted to be my friend.

After spending the night in my brand-new apartment, it was time for me to get up. I had a music theory class at 8:00 a.m., and I would have about a half-hour to forty-five-minute commute just to get there. Due to that fact that I was unable to live on campus, I had to drive to the university's football stadium and catch a bus there that would take me to campus and drop me off near my first class.

After waking up at around six and taking a shower, I immediately started doing crunches. Crunches were the beginning of a routine for me that would really disrupt other important things in my life. I started doing these crunches when I was a junior in high school because I had a cousin who was really big into working out. He did crunches every night and would lift weights occasionally. He was really big on being in shape, and I also wanted to be in shape.

I started doing crunches because I thought that I needed to lose weight. I thought that girls probably didn't like me because I was fat and ugly and it was time for me to do something about it. When I started doing crunches, I was only doing about thirty of them a day. By the time I had started my freshman year at Indiana University, I was doing two hundred a day. This would take me about five to ten minutes, which wasn't really a big deal.

For some reason, I noticed that I wasn't able to make myself do the crunches at night. Originally, when I'd started out doing these crunches, I was doing them at night, before going to bed. As time went on, I started having to do them in the morning before I could even go anywhere. This wasn't so bad, though, as I was only doing two hundred of them and it would only take a few minutes.

The reason I had to start doing them in the morning was because I thought that I was fat and ugly. I thought if I worked out in the morning before I left my house and anyone could see me, I'd look a lot better and be much more attractive to girls. It got to the point that I just had to do them. I couldn't make myself not do them. It became an obsession of mine. (Often, people with Asperger's syndrome will also have obsessive compulsive disorder, OCD. In fact, often, people who end up being diagnosed with Asperger's syndrome are originally misdiagnosed with OCD.)

This wasn't such a horrible thing for me at the time, though, as again I wasn't doing anything that would take up a whole lot of my time in the morning—just two hundred crunches and then off to class. For some reason, it made me feel better about myself to do this.

For my first day of school, I really wanted to be early so I could be sure to catch the bus and also get to class on time. In fact, as I did in middle and high school, I would want to be one of the first ones to class. I wanted to be in my seat before the other students got in there because I didn't want to have to be faced with walking up to one of them and asking them if it would be okay if I sat next to them. I thought they would get mad at me for even asking if I could sit in the same room. While I was trying to be optimistic about developing friendships, I was also realistic, as I knew what I had experienced before, and I had some reservations about trying to meet new people for fear of the same things happening. I didn't want to experience that painful process any more than I already had.

There were so many students waiting around to catch the bus that I felt overwhelmed. I wanted to retreat to my apartment because I didn't know how to handle being around all of these people.

Due to the fact that normally freshmen live on campus their first year and would never be riding this bus until the sophomore or junior year, I was the young pup who had no idea what to do or what was going on. These other people on the bus were so cool, and I wanted to be like them more than I could explain. They just had a sense of calmness about them. Meanwhile, I was freaking out.

One of the things I didn't like about having to ride on the bus like that was the fact that I was a music major and played trombone. So I had to carry a somewhat good-sized instrument on the bus with all of those other kids. It was crazy. I got many strange looks, and it seemed like people didn't want me on the bus or just thought I was dumb and stupid. I'm sure they wondered why I was carrying a trombone on the bus. Most students probably had a locker on campus because they lived on campus or close to campus, but I didn't have a locker yet, nor did I know how to get one. In fact, I never inquired about getting a locker while at Indiana University. I was too scared to ask someone how to get one because I didn't know who to ask or how to ask them. I would just carry my instrument back and forth on the bus every day that I was there.

Another thing that bothered me about the bus was the fact that there were so many students that would ride it but not that many seats. There was nowhere for me to sit down on the bus. I was carrying my trombone and a book bag, and I had nowhere to sit. Now, I'm sure that many neurotypical individuals would be quite capable and comfortable in this situation and be just fine with standing there and holding on to the railing. But for me, due to the fact that I had horrible balance issues due to my lack of sensory motor skills, trying to stay on my feet while on the bus was a nightmare.

I would often bounce back and forth and run into other students who would get really upset at me and curse at me or tell me, "Get off of the bus, you moron," as if I hadn't had enough verbal or mental abuse in high school. Here we were again, dealing with many of the same things.

In my elementary years, I had a bus driver who would start driving as soon as I would get on the bus. He would take off before I was able to sit down, and I would lose my balance and on some occasions fall. I was afraid of riding his bus, and there was a time in which I didn't want to ride a school bus at all. For me, if I'm to be riding in something, it's best that I'm sitting down so I don't roll around. There's no guarantee that I'll be able to stand on my feet on something that's in motion unless I'm sitting.

During the entire bus ride, I would be holding on for dear life. I still had to hold on to my trombone and my book bag. This would create a tremendous challenge for me, and I'm sure that to other students it was rather amusing, as it probably looked like I was riding on an out-of-control roller coaster. But it was just a bus that was only moving twenty to thirty miles per hour at best. I still had issues, and it was something that was completely out of my control. I was helpless.

This is another one of those classic situations in which a behavior or action is simply out of the individual on the spectrum's control. There was really nothing I could do to help myself stand up on the bus. I had to work extremely hard just to avoid knocking other students over. I often felt bad for accidentally making contact with a student on the bus. I felt as if I needed to apologize to them for running into them, and I often did.

After finally making it through the bus ride, I quickly got off of the bus at my first opportunity. I didn't care if I had to walk farther to find my class. I just wanted to get off of there, out of fear of being laughed at or made fun of. I think I would have walked an extra twenty miles just to get out of riding the bus. Being on the bus was just miserable for me, and I couldn't stand it. I wanted to be free of the pain of being pointed at and laughed at. I felt bad because I wasn't as cool as these other students.

After getting off the bus on the first day of school, I was overwhelmed at how many people there were on Indiana University's campus. Indiana University usually has about sixty thousand students enrolled in classes during the fall and spring semesters. I was used to going to school with about two thousand kids, but being at a place where there were sixty thousand plus people all trying to navigate themselves around the campus was amazingly challenging.

There were so many buildings, and I had a difficult time finding my first class. Luckily there were other people heading into the music building that I was going to, and I was able to find my way into class. Being one of the last ones in there, I would be forced to ask someone if I could sit beside them. I was so scared that they were going to say no and I was going to be standing up during the entire class. I prayed that they would say yes and I could find a seat. After asking two or three kids if I could have a seat next to them, a girl finally said I could, and I sat down and unloaded my books and my trombone.

As I got into class, I was amazed at how big the classroom was. There were anywhere between four to five hundred students all in the same lecture hall. I'd never seen anything like this. It was so overwhelming and stressful for me. But I quickly became attracted to just how talented all of these music majors were. We could hum pitches and scales without receiving a key, and we were right on. This would have never happened in high school.

After theory class, I had some time to relax, and I quickly ran over to McDonald's. I got a quick bite to eat and a drink and planned to sit outside, as it was so nice that day. There was really nowhere to sit, so I ended up standing against a wall. As I was looking around and observing some people, I noticed that most of the students were congregating in groups, just like they had done at my middle and high schools. I was a little disappointed when I noticed this because I was kind of expecting and hoping for the situation to be a little bit different for me down at Indiana University.

I quickly went back into my high school mode of thinking that I was the most stupid and worthless person in the world and that all of these people wanted to be friends with everyone except for me. Was my life a mistake? What had I done to people to be shunned and treated like I was a thing and not a person?

I quickly went about the rest of my day on campus. I had a couple more classes, and then I was able to retreat for the walk to catch the bus. The bus was a little more crowded this time, as it was late afternoon and people who had scheduled late classes were now awake and heading to their classes while others were going home. Once again, I was forced to stand up with my book bag in one hand and trombone in the other while trying to hold on to the pole. This was extremely hard for me to do, and it was so packed that we were shoulder to shoulder. The trombone just got in the way. I thought to myself that maybe playing trombone wasn't such a great idea. Why didn't I play something smaller or, better yet, not play any instrument?

I can't remember ever being so excited and anxious to get off of a bus in my entire life. Once I was off the bus, I raced to my car. I wanted to get out of that parking lot as soon as possible. I was hoping that maybe the next day would be a little easier, as I would be getting used to the magnitude of the campus. When I got home that evening, I immediately started playing trombone. Auditions for orchestra and concert bands were that Tuesday and Wednesday. I really wanted to land a spot in IU's top orchestra. In order to do this, I'd need to have a flawless performance.

I practiced for about two or three hours and then decided I was ready. I put the horn away and went out to the swimming pool that was at my apartment complex. I thought maybe I could meet some people out there and become friends with them. Who knows? Maybe I would get lucky and meet a beautiful woman who would at least maybe smile at me or say hi to me. I stayed at the pool for an hour or so without one person coming over and saying hi to me. Of course, due to my social history, I wasn't about to just go over and say hi to anyone at all, especially a gorgeous woman. I would be way too scared to do something like that.

I went back in and began to read some of my music theory homework. This was something that I'd never seen before. Again, we had some basic music theory in high school, but the kind of music theory that you see in high school is nothing at all like the kind you'll get in college, especially a college that has such a prestigious reputation as Indiana University's School of Music did.

After spending a couple hours studying, I fixed a late meal and watched some television. I was worn out. I then went off to bed and found myself unable to sleep as I began to replay the day's events in my head. I just couldn't get over the whole bus scene or how big the campus was. It was astonishing to me that so many people could be in one place at one time.

That night seemed really short. After getting to sleep, I slept pretty well, but 6:00 a.m. came very early. The sun was shining, and I was ready for another day. I was bound and determined to make this day better than the first one.

I started my morning off with my traditional glass of chocolate milk. Since my childhood, I have had a tradition of always starting off my day with a glass of chocolate milk. If I was ever unable to start my day with this traditional glass of chocolate milk due to traveling, my day would be horrible. It was one of those things that I just had to have in order to begin my day. Of course, we know that there are many things in life that someone who has autism or Asperger's syndrome do that are just like this. We tend to come up with a routine, and we want to stick with it. Changing it can cause distress.

After my morning glass of milk I proceeded to do my crunches. Once again, I completed two hundred of them.

It was about 7:05 a.m., and it was time for me to get in the car with my book bag and instrument and head over to the football field. The night before, I had come up with a solution for my problem: I was going to walk to campus instead of riding the bus. However, it turned out that from somewhere within me, I would pull out the courage to actually attempt to get on the bus again.

Once again, there were several hundred students gathered around, waiting for the bus. My hopes of being the first one to get on the bus were immediately shattered when I pulled in and there were that many people in line.

I was really tense and nervous as the bus pulled up. I had to wait a couple rounds, though, as I was far enough back in line that the first two buses weren't able to fit me on. This was bad because I had more time to think about the bus ride to the school. I was simply overwhelmed. I visualizing the whole bus ride as if it were a music performance. I imagined walking onto the bus without my instrument and acting cool like the other kids. I imagined that I could walk without having to hold on to something while the bus was moving. I imagined that somewhere on that bus ride there would be some other students who wanted to find out about me and would say hello or at least smile at me. I was feeling calmer, as I was kind of in a dreaming state.

When the bus pulled up I was forced to snap out of my dreaming state. It was such a good dream that I nearly forgot I had a trombone and almost walked off and left it.

I thought maybe the bus ride wouldn't be so bad. Unfortunately, when I walked up to get on the bus, I tripped and made a fool of myself. Everyone was staring, and, of course, they were laughing. I'd just provided them with some awesome entertainment, so now they had something to talk about on the bus ride to campus. I was frustrated as I got on the bus and ended up trying to lock myself into a corner, where I would be able to hold myself up and not move.

My book bag and trombone grazed a couple of people, and I got a few dirty looks. I didn't say anything at all, as I never did, and I looked straight at the ground. I wanted to get off the bus so badly, but I couldn't for just a few more minutes. During that Tuesday morning bus ride, I decided I was going to leave my trombone in my car every morning so I wouldn't have to carry it around all day. I thought this would make the bus ride easier and more comfortable for not only me but everyone involved.

This would, of course, mean that I'd have to ride the bus an extra time so I could go back to my car and pick up my trombone and then come back to campus with it. While I hated the bus, I thought the trade-off would be worth it.

I got off the bus and had to search for some new classes. Most colleges in the United States go off of a Monday, Wednesday, Friday/Tuesday, Thursday class schedule, meaning that you had the same classes on Monday and Wednesday, as well as Friday, along with having a Tuesday and Thursday class. I liked this, as it gave more time to prepare homework.

Going into my first college ear-training class was quite an experience. There were so many people there. Luckily for me, I was pretty musically inclined and was able to keep up with the brightest individuals. We would be asked to do things that I'd never done before. One of those things included singing in front of people. As soon as I found that out, I was a little nervous about it, but I knew that I was a talented musician and could most likely handle something of this nature.

What I didn't like was the fact that the professor would just randomly call on people. I just dreaded to be called on for an answer, and this was always the case throughout middle and high school. What if I didn't know the answer? What if I didn't know how to say the answer? I was always so worried about all of these little things, little things that the average neurotypical student wouldn't even think twice about.

I was glad that if it was going to happen in any of my classes, it would be a music theory or ear-training class. I knew what was going on in these classes, and I understood everything. It was those darn education classes, such as geology, that I would struggle with at times.

I managed to survive the first ear-training class, and it wasn't nearly as bad as I thought it would be. While there were no opportunities within that initial class period for me to make friends, I was successful with the musical aspect of it. I was glad to be doing something in which I knew what I was doing. Everything seemed so much easier when I knew how to do it.

After the end of my morning classes, I immediately tried to catch the bus so that I could go back to my car and pick up my trombone. I had parked my car in the parking lot where the bus had picked us up but left my trombone there in the trunk. I didn't want to carry it the first time around. So I then rode the bus back to my car later that afternoon to pick it up and then went back for my afternoon classes to where I'd need the trombone. I wanted to get back to the music building as quickly as possible so I could practice before the auditions that evening. The bus ride to and from the football stadium was a little more peaceful this time, as most people were eating lunch.

I quickly grabbed my trombone and waited to catch the next available bus. I made it back to campus with no problems and headed for the practice rooms. I spent about two or three hours that afternoon preparing for the auditions, and I was happy with how well I was playing. There were so many talented trombonists at Indiana University that just placing in the bottom of one of their ensembles would be a tremendous honor.

Orchestra auditions were done by a process that we call blind auditions. This means that when you go into the room to play for the professors or whomever it is that will be judging you, they are turned around and not facing you. This was good for me because I had enough on my mind without having three amazing musicians staring over the top of me.

There were probably around forty or fifty of us auditioning to play in the top groups. Everyone would get placed in some sort of group, but only the top ten or so would be placed in the university's most prestigious ensembles. I tried to listen closely to the individuals performing before me so I could get a good handle on what kind of competition I was going to have. I was simply amazed by how well everyone played. I felt like I was in trombone heaven.

There really wasn't a lot of socializing going on at an event like this, as they were much like me in the sense that before a big performance, they kind of get themselves in the zone. They really focus in at what's going on or getting ready to happen.

As the person who was scheduled to go before me entered the room for his performance, my heart began pounding. Here I was. It was August 24, 2004, and I was getting ready for the second biggest musical audition I'd ever had in my life.

As the kid before me finished up, I was ready to go. I was in the zone, and I entered the room and quickly became aware of my surroundings. I loved the atmosphere and enjoyed performing. I played the audition pieces to the best of my ability, and they couldn't have gone much better at all. After I finished playing, I how relieved I was to be done with the whole audition process in general. I mean, I loved to play trombone and usually didn't mind auditioning for groups. It was just a lot more fun to be able to play for pleasure. It was just more fun to be able to relax and enjoy myself while performing music.

The alarm clock rang, and I was awake and ready for my third day of school. I'd decided that I was going to leave a little earlier so I could walk from the football stadium to campus so that I could avoid having to deal with the crowds on the buses. So I woke up at 5:00 a.m. and had my traditional glass of milk and then proceeded to shower and get ready to go. I finished up my crunches, loaded up the car, and was on the road by 6:30.

As I pulled into the parking lot at the stadium, I quickly realized no one was there. I could just leave my car and start walking. I didn't realize how long the walk was. I planned on leaving early enough that I could arrive on campus by 7:30 so I could get situated and be the first one in the classroom that day. However, to my surprise, it took about an hour just to walk to the campus from the football stadium.

I got to school and got organized and was in my first class of the day about five minutes early. Luckily, I was able to find my own seat and wouldn't be forced to make someone sit by me. If they were going to sit by me, it was going to be their choice or because they were late and the last one there. I pulled out my books and glanced over some things before the professor got there.

Most of that day was stress-free; however, I was starting to notice how all of the other kids were mingling in groups. They were sharing laughs with each other and taking pictures. I'm sure some of them were just getting reacquainted with one another after a long summer. Again, I found myself wishing that I could be just like some of these guys. I started to look for guys whom I thought were cool and that girls were attracted to. I thought if somehow I could learn to mimic these particular guys and their behaviors, I would be as cool as they were and be able to make friends while getting a girlfriend.

This would also be the day we would find out the results of our playing auditions from the day before. I was nervous about this but thought that I had at least done well enough to place in an ensemble. As I walked up to the sheet, I closed my eyes and imagined I was on the list. As I opened to look, I saw my name listed to the IU concert band. I was going to be playing in one of the best ensembles in the country. I was thrilled with this and quickly ran out to call my mom and tell her.

Most people wouldn't understand the magnitude of an accomplishment like this, but for someone who didn't have any success in life outside of the music world, this was huge. Since music was like one of my best friends, it was like accomplishing something with my best friend. I was now going to be able to play some amazing music and become a better musician.

The rest of that day was spent touring the campus. I thought I might be able to accidentally meet someone by taking a walk around campus and becoming more familiar and comfortable with my new surroundings. I was able to go to the library as well as the student union, where students would often congregate; but once again, when they were congregating, they were usually in groups of friends and didn't have room for someone else like me. I wanted to have my own group to congregate with so badly. I just didn't have any understanding of how to form peer relationships. I was stumped, and I would continue to try, but things wouldn't get much better.

That afternoon, I practiced for a few hours and started to work on some solos for lessons. I signed up for a Thursday morning lesson time, which meant that I had to prepare for it on Wednesday nights. In all actuality, I should have prepared for it over the weekend, and I think I would have if I would have stuck around for a while.

That evening, I got on the bus and headed back to the football stadium. It was a lot less crowded later in the evening, and I was often able to find a place to sit, which made me much more comfortable. I arrived back at my car and loaded it up and took off. When I got home I saw a bunch of people by the pool, and I so wanted to try to meet some of them. So I grabbed a magazine and took a walk down to the pool. I sat and read for a little bit, thinking that maybe someone would walk up to me and ask me what I was reading. No one ever did walk up to me, so after an hour or so, I jumped in the pool for a few brief moments and then proceeded back to my apartment to fix dinner and watch some television.

This routine would become quite common for me over the next couple of days, as again, for me, it was easiest to get into a routine of things and follow the schedule. I had a hard time adapting to change. It was stressful and, at times, caused discomfort. That evening, I went to bed early.

As I woke up the next morning, I found myself a little depressed. The excitement of my first week and my musical accomplishments was beginning to wear off, and I was starting to come to grips with the reality of not having any friends to spend time with. The fact that the weekend was coming up helped draw my attention to that. What was I going to do for an entire weekend without any friends or family around?

The next day was much like the first three. This time, I forced myself to try the bus once again. Since I was leaving my trombone in my car and wouldn't have to drag it along on the bus for the morning commute, I thought it would be a little easier. I was able to get a good grip when holding on to the pole with having an extra free hand. I felt a little more sturdy and safe.

That day at school, I focused on schoolwork. I didn't really try to roam about the campus to make any new friends or anything that had to do with socializing. I was emotionally drained from trying so hard earlier in the week to find people to talk to or people who would talk to me. I just didn't have any more socializing capacity left in my brain for that week, so I studied for a while.

It was on that Thursday morning at 10:00 a.m. that I would have my first official trombone lesson. I had come down earlier that summer to do a lesson with Professor Ellefson before classes had begun. However, this would be the first time I'd actually have a lesson with him while school was in session. We immediately began to work on some solos.

Professor Ellefson had a unique warm-up system. He has written his own warm-up style that he uses daily, and he wants all of his students to use it to warm up as well. For professional level musicians, warming up can be something that takes anywhere from a half hour to an hour. It's not like high school, when players just blow a couple notes and are ready to go. It's much more complex. If you're warming up for a huge orchestra gig, you'd better expect to spend around an hour warming up.

His lessons were a little more laid back than the lessons I had taken in high school. It was a completely different teaching style than I'd had before. He was calmer but yet very serious about what we were doing. He liked to have fun but he wanted to make sure that we were getting the work done that needed to be accomplished.

After finishing my lesson for that day, I was done, as our ensembles didn't start rehearsing until the following Monday. I went to catch the bus back to the football stadium. I had decided I was going to spend that afternoon roaming about the city of Bloomington. I stopped for some lunch at Steak & Shake and had a milkshake. I then went to the mall to do some looking around. I was trying to find some people that maybe I could talk to. Of course, there were people all over the city and campus whom I could talk to, but I didn't know how to. This was driving me nuts, and none of them would ever just come up to me and start a conversation. This was killing me on the inside.

I really began searching for happiness and answers in the social arena. No longer was I okay with putting it off like it didn't bother me. No longer was escaping into imagination and creating a make-believe world good enough for me. Cameron Diaz still made for a great imaginary best friend, and I still watched all of her movies. I would still sit and watch the movie Head Above Water.

It was at this point that I began to do some searching. I was trying to find a group of people who would accept me. The only problem was there weren't exactly any groups that were out looking to do a random act of kindness and accept some loser into their group. This would be hard work, but I was bound and determined to do it. It was that determination that would cause me to become even more frustrated. Sometimes I think it would have been best to have not wanted any friends and to have just been able to take my life and accept it for the way it was. Why did I need friends so badly?

It was that Thursday evening when I made the surprising decision to come home for the weekend. Yes, I'd only been there one week, and I was going home for a visit. I thought this would just be a one-time thing, as I wasn't used to being away for too long yet. So I went to my 8:00 a.m. class on Friday morning and then came home to my apartment and loaded the car up. I left that morning. I would end up visiting and hanging out at the steakhouse quite a bit. This was strange to them and me, as it was only a couple short weeks ago that I couldn't wait to get away from Huntington.

I would spend Friday and Saturday night at home, searching for something to do or someone to hang out with. It was my lack of ability to find someone to hang out with while home that led me to spend most of my weekend at the steakhouse where I used to work. I didn't exactly want to hang out at my former place of employment when I wasn't working, but it was again a place in which I knew people and people knew me and were somewhat friendly to me. It was safe and comfortable when I wasn't working too because none of the other guys could beat me up and the girls couldn't try to take advantage of me by getting me to do their work for them.

Being home and sleeping in my own bed felt safe and comfortable. While there was still no one there whom I could connect with or really become friends with, for some reason, having the family around helped me to be more comfortable and relaxed. I didn't really do much that weekend except for hang out and see my cousin. He had decided to stay close to home and go to school at a local university. My family tried to understand what was going on. Since I didn't have a diagnosis yet, there was a lot of confusion as to why I was having all of the social problems I was having. They became very discouraged about everything and just couldn't understand me at all.

I took off to Bloomington late that Sunday evening. The drives for me were extremely peaceful. For some reason, I'd always enjoyed driving. It was because I was able to have a quiet atmosphere if I wanted one. I could turn the radio off and just cruise with the windows down in the summertime. I loved cruising with the windows down. There was nothing more relaxing than doing that on a bright, hot, summer day.

I made my way back into Bloomington at around 7:30 p.m. That seemed to be a perfect time to come in. Too much earlier, and you would catch the early crowd coming in; then, if you waited another hour or so, you'd hit the late arriving crowd. I didn't really have any trouble with traffic rolling in at 7:30. I had a bunch of unloading to do after getting back from that first weekend. I also had some laundry to do, and I'd need to take a look at a little bit of homework. I had a busy couple of hours in front of me.

That evening, before bed, I felt very anxious and depressed for some reason. There was just something that wasn't right. Something about being back there was bothering me.

Once again, going to sleep that night would prove to be very difficult. I was very nervous about school, as the social aspect was really starting to get to me. I just couldn't handle so many people all at once. I began thinking that maybe the school was just too big for me. It seemed like an easy answer as to why I was feeling the way I was.

I went back for a few days and began practicing with the ensembles. Things still weren't improving socially, and I was becoming more frustrated and hurt each day. The ensembles were great because I could just play my trombone, but the overall social aspect of campus life was bothering me. I tried hard to make friends in the musical groups but was unsuccessful.

Things only became more difficult during that week. When my parents visited that weekend, I indicated that I was very unhappy, but due to the magnitude of the situation, they didn't want me to just pack up and leave. I'd worked really hard to get to this point in my life at one of the best music schools in the world, and it's not exactly cheap to go to school, so being there for two weeks and then withdrawing isn't exactly a good thing financially either. After my parents left for the weekend, I broke down and started crying. I knew I couldn't stay and had to come home. My dream of going to one of the best music schools in the world was over, ruined by what I later found out would be a social disorder.

On Sunday, September 6, at around 8:00, I called my parents. They had just left my apartment about ten or fifteen minutes before, and I was still crying. I was scared to death. I begged my mom to let me come home and told her I'd try to go to school somewhere a little more close to home. After spending about ten or twenty minutes begging her, she finally gave in and told me I could come home. I had never felt so relieved in my life. I just didn't know how to fit in with anyone. The only thing that was connecting me with people was my music. Unfortunately, at that point in time, my interest in music would not be enough to keep me enrolled at one of the best music schools in the world.

After speaking with my mom, I loaded up some small items in my car and took off for home. I was saying good-bye after just two short weeks in Bloomington. I wasn't sure what I was headed home for or what I was going to do with my life once I got home. I just knew that Indiana University was an extremely uncomfortable place for me and I couldn't bear to be there any longer. I did a lot of thinking that evening on my way home. I wasn't sure why I had chosen to leave and come home because I remembered how miserable my social life was when I lived there for the first eighteen years of my life.

I had no idea what was going to become of my life. Now I was in a situation in which I wasn't enrolled in college anywhere and I didn't have a job. I had gotten myself into a huge mess. Little did I know that this was just the beginning of a journey, a journey that would involve many disappointments and tragic events. This was the start of what I call finding myself.

That evening it was extremely difficult to sleep. I couldn't stop thinking about the events of the day and how desperate I was to come home. I didn't understand why I had wanted to be home so bad due to how my school career went socially in Huntington. It made absolutely no sense to me.

My brief experience down at Indiana University taught me a few things. I learned that I wasn't able to adapt to change in a very positive way. My feelings of hopelessness were affirmed during my two weeks. I'd experienced other students staring at me, making fun of me, pointing at me, and ignoring me, and I didn't feel as if I belonged there either.

Today, I wish that I would have tried to stick it out down in Bloomington. If I would have been able to stay in Bloomington and go straight through school, I would have graduated in December of 2008.

# Big Mistake

The next morning, I awoke to a lot of pressure. I didn't have anything lined up as far as school or work went. I didn't even know where to begin. I had some ideas, though, and I wanted to quickly put them into action. Sometimes people with autism or Asperger's syndrome will often have great thoughts and ideas. Sometimes, when we get these ideas into our head, we want to act on them right away without thought.

This was always the case for me. No matter how small or big the idea, I had to act on it fast. Before I chose to attend Indiana University, I had strongly considered attending another university closer to home in northeast Indiana. Indiana Wesleyan University had been at the top of my list as far as a college choice.

There were many appealing characteristics about Indiana Wesleyan, as I had sort of grown up in a Christian background and I did believe in God. I had attended church off and on as a child, all the way up until my sophomore year in high school, when I started attending regularly. I was attending more regularly in my later high school years due to the fact that I was able to play on the worship team and use my special interest of playing trombone to communicate with God. I loved to play worship songs of all kinds, from slow, soft, and soothing to hard, fast, and crazy tunes.

Back in March of 2004, I had actually gone over to Marion, Indiana, where Indiana Wesleyan University is located, to play an audition for the music faculty there. I was awarded a full scholarship, which would help cover the cost of attending school at a private university. It wouldn't come close to covering the entire cost, but it did eliminate some concerns that I had financially about attending the university.

In April of 2004, I decided to go to Indiana University. When I made that decision, I was giving up my scholarship at Indiana Wesleyan. So, not only was I stuck back at home now with no job and no place to go to school; now I didn't even have any kind of scholarship to help cover the cost of attendance at Indiana Wesleyan.

Another reason I wanted to go to Indiana Wesleyan so badly was the fact that a gentleman by the name of Mr. Michael Flanagin was the director of instrumental music there. Mr. Flanagin was my old band director at Riverview Middle School.

Mr. Flanagin was always my favorite teacher. He was the one who would discover my talents in middle school and help develop me into an even better musician than I was. He put a lot of time and effort into developing my skills. The chance to work with him again in college was something that was extremely appealing to me.

That Monday morning, I sent out an e-mail to Mr. Flanagin. Indiana Wesleyan was located about forty to forty-five minutes away from my parents' home. I sent an e-mail telling him that I wanted to come to Indiana Wesleyan. I explained to him that Indiana University just wasn't the place for me. I asked if we could sit down and talk sometime, and he immediately invited me over that afternoon. I was excited to be presented with this new and amazing opportunity. I was hoping that it would be better socially for me there. I thought that being at a Christian school I would be around really nice kids and be accepted for who I was. To my surprise, even at a Christian university students have a hard time accepting someone who is different than they are. In fact, some things that happened at Indiana

Wesleyan were much worse than what happened at any public university I've ever attended.

Now that I had made a contact and possibly found another school to attend for that fall, I had another fish to fry. I had to find some sort of a part-time job. Luckily for me, I had worked for about three to four years at the Huntington steakhouse, and I was able to go in there and talk to the managers and get my job back. While I had never actually quit there, they weren't expecting me to come back and work until the following summer.

They told me I could have my job back and I'd start working part time immediately the following week, as soon as the next schedule came out. This was a huge relief for me. I had a job lined up and would have a source of income. I then had to worry about where I was going to live. I still had an apartment in Bloomington that was costing me almost $750 a month, and I wasn't going to be using it. Would I get a place of my own back at home, would I try to live on campus at Indiana Wesleyan, or would I just stay at home with my parents and drive back and forth for this year to Indiana Wesleyan for classes and ensembles?

I wasn't sure as to exactly which route I wanted to go, and I knew I'd have to do some thinking about it before making the decision. This might have been one of the last times in my life before I knew I had Asperger's that I was able to take the time and think through a situation.

It was on that Monday that I met with Mr. Flanagin. We discussed what my possible options were for me to go to school there at Indiana Wesleyan. I had a few options, as it turned out. I could try to sign up for classes and start school a week late, or I could just do ensembles and wait on the classes until the spring semester of 2005. I really wanted to start classes right away but felt as if I'd be behind and feel awkward in those classes. I didn't want to walk into a situation in which I had no idea what was going on. I didn't want to risk being made fun of or bullied by other students.

After talking with Mr. Flanagin for around a half hour or so, it was decided that I would just take ensembles for the fall semester and then sign up for classes in the spring of '05. I felt comfortable with this decision, and I was confident in my ability to be a great musician and contribute to Indiana Wesleyan's ensembles immediately. That same day, I was brought in for ensemble rehearsals. I was pretty excited about this. I was thrown into the duty of section leader of the trombones. This was something that would give me a little confidence boost, as confidence was definitely lacking for me those days.

This might have been another thing that attributed to some social anxiety down at Indiana University. When I got there, I was immediately a young puppy again. No longer would I be the best trombone player in my school. In fact, there were probably several trombonists who were playing at the same level or even better than I was. This was something that would cause some depression for me.

The one thing that was able to help get me through high school was my interest in music—not just my interest but how good I was at trombone. I had something that I was good at and could show to other people. This would always help boost my self-esteem. It was obvious to me and others that I wasn't the most socially aware kid in school. I definitely was never the coolest kid in school. But I could play the trombone like no other. This was a positive thing about me. Playing trombone was something in which I excelled, and being first chair was something I was happy with. It made me beam with pride. I had a smile on my face most often because I was sitting as section leader in band.

When I arrived at Indiana University, I was no longer the top dog. While I was still an incredibly talented musician, there were so many people in front of me that I would sit near the bottom of the trombone section in the ensembles. This was what depressed me the most. If I would have been sitting as section leader in the Indiana University wind ensemble or concert band, it would have been enough to give me the confidence I needed to succeed in school and stick around Bloomington for at least more than a couple of weeks.

Arriving at Indiana Wesleyan and immediately being thrown into the responsibility of playing first part and being the trombone section leader was just the confidence boost that I needed. I started to try to have more of a positive attitude. I began practicing more and more. I would practice trombone about as much as I did during my junior and senior years in high school.

Being put back into the realm of being one of the best musicians at a school bestowed me with a spark that I hadn't had in about a year or so. During my senior year, I had started to lose the drive to succeed in life. Once getting accepted into the school of music, I was kind of like, What more can I accomplish musically? Immediately after being accepted into the Indiana University School of Music, I would turn my attention back to the social scene or, in my case, the lack of social scene.

I started focusing all of my attention back into trying to develop friendships and becoming obsessed with every reason I could think of as to why I was struggling with peer relationships. I would lose all sense of time and organization as far as school and practicing trombone would go. I spent my days trying to figure out what was wrong with me again.

My lack of spark in life would continue all the way into the fall of 2004. In fact, when arriving at Indiana University, I noticed that while I was excited to be there, there just wasn't that musical excitement that there should have been for me. I mean, the excitement in possibly playing in some of the best ensembles in the country, if not the world, didn't hit me. I thought that I would be going crazy when I got down there. But I was still depressed. I didn't have any friends, and I had never had a girlfriend.

As I arrived at my first ensemble rehearsal at Indiana Wesleyan University, I was greeted with a warm welcome from the students. They seemed pretty friendly, and somehow, they had all heard about me. One student said, "As soon as you called Mr. Flanagin and told him you wanted to come to school here, he immediately started running through the halls, yelling with excitement." This made me feel good, as it's not too often in my life when I've felt like someone wanted me to be around. I thought maybe this was a different situation since these kids were supposedly all Christian students. I thought maybe I'd found my social home. I was excited to see how this year would unfold.

I immediately started playing the music that was before me and enjoyed it. I was able to sight-read almost anything that was put before me. I never seemed to struggle with a passage of music. I sometimes wish that my social life would have been this simple and something that I didn't have to work at so hard.

After a couple evenings of rehearsal, I was invited to go over to the college dining commons and eat some dinner with a few of the other students in the ensemble. They were trying to make me feel welcome, and I really enjoyed and appreciated this. It seemed like when I would be able to just sit there and not try to develop friendships with someone, people were more welcome to me talking to them or getting to know them. But for some reason, whenever I took a liking to someone and started trying to talk to them or get to know them, they immediately withdrew their interest and almost started to ignore me.

After managing to get myself all settled in at school over at Indiana Wesleyan, I decided that I would just live at home with my parents at least for this first year. I still had that apartment in Bloomington that I was trying to get rid of. I was anxious to start working again, as this would be something that I was very familiar with, and I thought I'd get back into the swing of things with little or no trouble.

A week after returning home, I was back at work. I started out working only a couple of nights a week, but due to the fact that a few people would quit or get fired, I'd immediately get back up to my usual forty hours plus per week. This would be great for my pocketbook, and at this point in time, I still had a pretty decent sense in my head about money.

I was able to save most of the money that I was making and build up a nice chunk of change in my bank account. I only needed to spend about thirty to forty dollars a week in gas and about twenty dollars or so in food. This was nice, as I was able to save up for things that I wanted and buy them. Eventually, I was able to get someone else to take over the lease on my apartment in Bloomington so I'd only have to pay about two or three months' extra rent for the time in which I didn't live there.

Eventually, I managed to become the full-time day hot buffet person at steakhouse where I worked. This would mean working forty to fifty hours per week with daytime hours on buffet. I was excited about this, as again I was doing something that I was extremely good at. I was learning how to cook more and more things and meeting more interesting people.

Eventually, I would be working so much that working and going over to Indiana Wesleyan for ensembles was taking up most of my time. I guess you could say that work became a nice home away from home for me. This was a good thing because I wasn't able to just sit around and mope about not having any real friends or not being as cool as the other guys were.

Instead of coming home to mope, I'd get off of work and just sit and hang out at work. I would order some food, which I got for half the price, and try to hang out with other employees. I never actually developed any friendships that really went outside of the workplace, but it was nice for me to have people, even if they were older adults that I worked with, to just try to talk to or connect with.

It was mid-fall of 2004, and I was becoming more familiar with Indiana Wesleyan University. This campus wasn't nearly as big as Indiana University, and I felt a lot safer. I was able to go and come whenever I wanted because it was so close to home. So whenever the socializing became too stressful, I was able to escape.

I would continue to drive back and forth just for ensemble rehearsals. I was in wind ensemble and jazz ensemble. Both of these groups would turn out to be some of the more fun groups I've had a chance to be a part of. The jazz ensemble played really well, and I just love jazz.

The wind ensemble at Indiana Wesleyan University had some interesting opportunities in it. As part of the wind ensemble, there was what was called the honors brass quintet. I was fortunate enough to be able to play in one of the greatest quintets ever that year. We had great trumpet players, outstanding French horn playing, and a great tuba player. The overall balance of the ensemble was outstanding.

Another interesting thing that the Indiana Wesleyan wind ensemble had the opportunity of doing was traveling to different churches throughout the Midwest. We had the chance to travel around and use our talents to teach about Jesus Christ to the rest of the world. This was wonderful, and as part of this, students would be given the chance to do testimonies.

The group usually toured two weekends per semester with an additional weeklong tour in the spring semester over spring break. I would really enjoy traveling and playing, and I'd often escape into imagination or find myself in the make-believe world as I was traveling. When traveling, I didn't engage in much socializing. Everyone else had their own group or their own cliques formed, so I was just quiet and kept to myself. Of course I wished that I was included in conversations and in social experiences, but I just stayed to myself and either slept or did a lot of thinking.

I had always thought that it would be awesome to be like the Glenn Miller Orchestra or some group like that and be a part of a traveling band. While I wasn't making any money to travel with the Indiana Wesleyan University wind ensemble, I found myself often imagining that I was with a group traveling the country, performing.

I would also imagine that I was the conductor of the band at times. For some reason, I never had to focus very much on my playing and was often able to drift off into the imaginative state while I was playing. I would imagine being the conductor of a prestigious orchestra. In fact, you could find me driving down the road and conducting an orchestra at the same time on occasion.

As the semester went on, I was able to use all of these musical experiences that I had to help ease the pain of not having a good social life. I began to stop thinking about it so much and was able to focus more on life itself and doing what I wanted to or needed to do to try to become successful in life.

It was during that late fall of 2004 when I would start to have more problems at work, and this time it was coming from the new management. Due to the fact that we had poor management and the steakhouse in Huntington, Indiana, was actually losing money, they were often forced to send employees home early in the daytime and leave just one or two employees around to handle the entire store. I would often be one of those employees who was left behind to run the entire store. It was quite often that the manager on duty would send everyone home but me.

I understood this, and I actually enjoyed it, as it was quite easy to handle when we weren't too busy. But there were those occasions when we would get extremely busy. Then I would be trying to do cash register, cook the steaks on the grill, tend to the food buffet, and help with delivering the customers' food, while trying to keep up on dishes all at the same time.

I was becoming very overwhelmed at times when we would get really busy and feeling frustrated. I had a million things that needed to be done all at once, and all of those thoughts were racing through my brain. But I was unable to organize them, so I often had trouble knowing what I should do first, second, third, and so on.

Unfortunately, this would be a situation in which I was being put every day at work. They knew that I was a good worker and wouldn't complain about it. Again, often people knew that I could be taken advantage of because I would take it and put up with it, as I thought that it was just a way of life and that in order for me to be alive and living in the world, I had to let people walk all over me and do whatever they wanted to me.

While I now had my life put together in such a way that I had a lot more activities going on and was less likely to be able to over-analyze social things, I was still feeling some emotional pain. At the end of the day, no matter how much I tried to do or became involved with, there was still this empty feeling. It's hard to describe it, but it's just like you're not getting any meaning out of your life because you can't connect with the rest of the world. This feeling was one of the most frustrating feelings that I've ever encountered.

I had several pieces of my life going, but there was this missing piece to the puzzle. This would be what those of us on the spectrum so often refer to as the missing link. It doesn't matter what you have going for you in your life; if one doesn't have access to the missing link and is unable to complete the puzzle, they will probably suffer a great deal of emotional pain and distress.

I had actually come up with the courage to attempt to make friends at Indiana Wesleyan. This is something that took a lot of courage and a lot of effort on my part. It seemed like I had to work harder at it than other individuals did. I would actually begin studying things on social friendships and self-confidence. I was reading as many books as I could that had to do with self-confidence and power of positive thinking, but unfortunately, since this was pre-diagnosis for me, I wasn't reading any books that had to do with Asperger's syndrome or autism.

I could read all of the books on self-esteem, power of positive thinking, and whatever else was out there; but without knowing and understanding that I was just missing a piece of the puzzle, it wouldn't matter how much research and reading I was doing. I wasn't starting at ground zero. I was starting on different floors surrounding ground zero, but I wasn't at the root of the problem.

Without fully knowing and understanding what the root of my problem was, it was almost as if I was going through life without knowing who I was. Unfortunately, as I've already discussed,

Asperger's syndrome is such an invisible disability that it's extremely difficult to see the root of the problem.

It was also at about this time, when I was only nineteen or twenty, that I really became even more interested in women. They say that some people are just late bloomers, and I was definitely a late bloomer. I began to notice girls everywhere I went. It was like I couldn't avoid them. It was like they were an advertisement that was following me around everywhere.

Indiana Wesleyan University had a male/female ratio of three females for every male. I thought surely with that kind of ratio it would be quite simple for me to get a girlfriend, and since these girls were all Christian girls, they would most likely be nice to me and treat me well. I was excited.

I tended to like girls who were a part of groups I was in, such as wind ensemble and jazz ensemble. As soon as I got to campus, meeting a girl named Bethany who was quite a bit older than me. She was a senior, and I was a freshman. She was extremely beautiful and a very talented saxophone player. She was very kind and easy to talk to, but she had a boyfriend and I think was even engaged, so she would be off-limits for me.

I tended to get really excited when I liked a girl and wanted to focus 100 percent of my attention on her immediately from the day that I met her. After Bethany, there were a few other girls within Indiana Wesleyan University wind ensemble that semester that I kind of formed a liking to. Once again, these wouldn't ever turn into anything more than acquaintances.

I was still a little timid and scared of trying to develop a friendship with a girl due to the fact that I was teased and ridiculed for it in my high school career. Anytime I would see a girl I liked, I would hear voices in my head telling me things that other kids told me in high school. They would be saying, "Travis, you're much too fat or ugly for her. She's way out of your league. You would kill her just by looking at her. She hates you." I heard all kinds of things, and these weren't just things that I was making up. I'd actually had people tell me these things in high school, and I believed them. I just thought that there was something wrong with me and I didn't have the right to like someone. So I had to pretend that I didn't like girls at all, even though I did.

This was extremely hard for me to do. I was one who, when I liked a girl, wanted to act on it right away and talk to her or ask her out. I would get all anxious and nervous and not know how to control all of my emotions. While I was able to control them without making too much of a fool out of myself, on occasion there would be times when I would have to go up to a girl and randomly tell her she was beautiful. I couldn't help it. I just had to express how I felt. I'm not sure why telling someone they are beautiful can be a bad thing, but trust me, to some of those girls, it was the end of the world for them because a guy so ugly as me was telling them that they were pretty. I think they felt insulted that a guy like me even bothered talking to them.

It was also at about that time that I would become really attracted to a girl whom I was working with at the steakhouse. This girl had a boyfriend too, but I was confused because every time I saw this girl she would complain about her boyfriend or complain about how he was treating her. This didn't make sense to me at all. I couldn't understand why a girl would be in a relationship with someone who wasn't treating her like she was a princess.

At that time, I had no idea how relationships really worked. I just knew that when I saw a girl who was really pretty, I would get this tingly feeling inside and want to talk to her. Of course, I didn't have the slightest idea as to how to go about talking to her, but there was the need and desire there, and I just couldn't do it. After struggling with this for a few years, I became frustrated, and I just wanted to know how to get a girl's attention.

This is something that I would think about time and time again, and it almost became an obsession in itself. I was bound and determined to figure out how to get a girl to at least notice me or say hi to me. I wanted girls to like me so badly.

Unfortunately, this is yet another area where failed attempt after attempt can lead to rejection and ridicule, which will immediately lead to ruining one's self-esteem. This was definitely the case for me. Attempt after attempt to develop a friendship or relationship with a girl would end in misery and the girl hating me or saying that I was dumb, fat, ugly, stupid, worthless, psycho, or creepy. Unfortunately, while I was and am a little socially unaware and naïve at times, I am very much aware of what all those words that they were using to call me names with mean.

But I wasn't trying to hurt anyone, and I couldn't understand why girls would feel this way. I never purposely said something or did something to the girl to hurt her. In fact, I tried so hard to be extra nice to her. I'd do anything she wanted. Basically, I would make myself available to her beck and call.

After several failed attempts, I was bound and determined to come up with a plan of showing a girl that I liked her. Since I was unable to communicate with her without her thinking that I was creepy or weird, I wasn't sure exactly how I was going to go about doing this. Well, one day, it all came to me; I had an idea. Unfortunately, this idea would cost me a lot of money, and it has never really worked in the way that I had hoped it would.

My idea was that I would send the girl flowers. I would send the girl flowers and write her a note on the card because then maybe it would be much easier for me to communicate what I meant in a non-creepy way. So, from that day on, whenever I liked a girl, before I even talked to her, I would try to figure out how to send her flowers. I would send girls flowers at school, at work, and pretty much wherever a girl whom I thought was beautiful was at. I knew that I would get made fun of or ridiculed for liking her or trying to talk to her, but if I could show her that I was a cool guy who was nice, then maybe she would want to talk to me.

In order for me to do this, I thought I would send flowers and a card explaining who I was and that I thought she was a perfect angel and that I really liked her. I would send a dozen roses to every girl whom I thought was beautiful to try to show them that I liked them.

Unfortunately, their reaction to this sometimes was also one of, "Oh my gosh. What is he doing?" or, "Why are you doing this?" but I didn't think anything of it. I just thought that it was yet another failed attempt in trying to show a girl that I liked her and that I would have to try again. So I would send the next girl that I formed a liking to flowers, and the same thing happened. I began to think, Surely one girl will like getting these flowers and want to talk to me and give me a chance, so I kept sending flowers.

The girl with whom I worked with was a very interesting girl. I liked her a lot, and since she was unhappy with her boyfriend, I couldn't understand why she was still with him. All she did was complain about him. Well, I thought that I would try to cheer her up by being her friend first. Since I'm not great at talking to people, I thought I would do this by sending her flowers.

She actually really enjoyed this for a while, as I think it was something different for her. She would actually say thank you, which made me feel really good on the inside. However, she still didn't really want to talk outside of work or develop a friendship or relationship with me. I was frustrated, and I just wanted her or a girl to give me a chance.

It became a routine for me to send her flowers at least once a week at work, if not more. Then, because I was able to come up with the thought that maybe she would think it was weird that I was sending just her flowers, I started sending flowers to more girls that worked there. I would just send them to them randomly and also attach a card saying have a great day or something like that.

The girl at work remained of high interest to me. There was something about her that I really liked. Well, I would often ask other guys working there what I should say to her or how I should talk to her. I would ask them how to get her attention and things like that. Well, as I started sending girls flowers, I was still taking advice from these other guys. I'll never forget that guy who told me some of the most bizarre things, but because I was so naïve, I tried them. I tried them because this was the same guy whom I would see having three or four girls around him at all times. He had to know something because he was doing much better than I was.

One day in the winter of 2005, I was talking to this guy about a couple of girls and wondering how to get their attention. I had already come up with the conclusion that since Valentine's Day was coming up in a week or so, I would send them each a dozen roses or something simple like that. This guy was very much aware of my situation and knew very well that I didn't understand girls or how to talk to them.

He pulled me aside one day and told me that if I really wanted to get a woman's attention that I would have to do something huge and something that would blow her mind. I thought, Yeah. He must be right, simply because he always had girls around him. He told me that if I wanted to get girls there to like me, I should send each girl who worked on Valentine's Day ten dozen roses. At first I thought, Wow, that seems like a lot of roses, but he proceeded to explain to me that girls liked flowers and the more they got the happier they were. He told me to send them to every girl who worked on Valentine's Day, married or not married, as they would simply see it as a nice gesture and I would get in good with the single girls. He told me I would definitely get some dates.

Getting a date was something that I had very much wanted. I just loved the company of girls so much more than guys. I thought that this guy must be right. I had to do something huge in order to get a girl's attention. So I went to the flower shop and ordered as many roses as I could. I bought out nearly every flower shop around. I took all of their roses. There were eighteen girls working that day, so I knew that eighteen girls times ten dozen roses equaled 180 dozen roses. Luckily, at that time, I had at least a little bit of money saved up in my savings account from working so much, so I went to the flower shop, ready to purchase all of these roses.

When I first went to the flower shop, I only took around $2,200. I knew that in the past, the roses I had bought for girls ran around $12 per dozen. I knew that twelve times 180 equaled $2,160. As I was checking out at my first flower shop with the first set of roses, something happened that put me into a state of shock. The roses were ringing up at a higher price than they normally did. I was wondering what was going on. Unfortunately, I'd never bought roses for Valentine's Day before. I guess that the price of a rose increases rather significantly on Valentine's Day. So now I had found out that each dozen was going to cost me $24.95.

Still very much wanting a girlfriend and believing that this guy who gave me this information knew what he was talking about, I knew that this was something I had to do no matter what the price was. I had to get a girl to notice me in some way. So I now had to recalculate my figures. After purchasing all of the roses, my total was $4,491 or so. This was a huge chunk of money, and then, after adding in the chocolate I bought for every girl, I was up to a little over five grand. Suddenly, my savings account had vanished, and I was now down to a little under $20 in there.

Well, after draining my savings account on flowers and chocolates, I was excited about the upcoming day. I woke up on Monday, February 14, 2005, with high hopes of having a wonderful day. Flowers were going to be delivered to work, and girls were going to have smiles put on their faces. Surely the guy who was helping me out knew what he was talking about. I really looked up to the guy because he was such a cool person not only with girls, but he was also someone that all guys wanted to be friends with.

I worked a double on that day, which meant I worked from 9:00 a.m. to 8:00 p.m. I would work hot buffet with one of the girls I liked. I had ordered around two or three dozen roses per girl from each flower shop, so that meant that at various times throughout the early to late afternoon, flower shops would be walking in with between thirty-six and fifty-four dozen roses. I couldn't believe how many roses were there when they came in.

After each of the individual flower shops had their delivery of roses completed, there was a restaurant full of flowers. I must say that it was quite festive scenery and an expensive one too. I was excited about how these girls were going to react.

As the girls started coming into work that evening, they would be sent into the banquet room to find all of their dozens of roses with their names on them. I was able to watch as a couple of them went in there, and the look on their faces was not what I was expecting at all. They looked terrified and like this was the worst day of their lives. I thinking, Wait a minute. You're supposed to like flowers. You're supposed to be happy and love them because Aaron said you would. Why aren't you smiling or running up to give me a huge hug? It almost looked as if a few of the girls were crying.

My feelings of excitement and happiness had immediately been replaced with feelings of sadness and horror, as I could tell that these girls hated me for getting them flowers and chocolate. I had done something horribly wrong again. I was so frustrated and thought that I was such a loser. Meanwhile, the rest of the guys in the kitchen were having a good time pointing at me and laughing. They would even make comments to me, teasing me. They told me that I didn't get them enough roses and that next time I needed to try at least twenty dozen. (I would end up trying this at a later date, and again, it would fail miserably.) I didn't get it. My wonderfully amazing day that I was hoping to be the best day of my life had just been turned into my worst nightmare. I was convinced that I was fat and ugly and that girls hated me. Why was I even born?

A few of the girls did manage to come over and say thank you, but even the ones that said thank you did it with such a weird look on their faces that I knew they hated me or thought I was stupid. Later that evening, a few guys who were boyfriends or husbands of the girls who worked there had called in and complained to the manager and said they were going to come find me and beat me up. I had numerous guys trying to get a hold of me, and I wasn't sure why, because I didn't like their girlfriend or wife. I was just sending them flowers because Aaron told me that I had to in order to get the girl I liked to pay attention to me.

So now not only had I made a fool out of myself and made girls hate me even more than they already did, but I had also managed to gain some male enemies. I wanted to give up. I went to Aaron and asked him what I did wrong, and again he told me that I just didn't get enough flowers and chocolate.

Again, for some reason, I was still gullible and desperate enough to try this. Aaron had all of the girls in the world talking to him, so I thought that he must be right. The thought that he would be trying to tell me false information on purpose didn't occur to me.

I went home that night feeling completely worthless and miserable. I was dumb, fat, ugly, stupid, creepy, and also a psycho. I was all of these things while all I wanted to be was normal and fit in with the rest of the people in the world.

The next day I had to work a double, as it was our senior night. I worked 9:00 a.m. to 8:00 p.m. I walked in that morning to humiliation and embarrassment, as there were lots of people who would just stare at me and ignore me. It was like they were saying, "What are you doing?" or, "Why did you do that?" I was so mad at myself, and I already hated myself. Why did they have to go and rub it in? I thought. The manager called me in to tell me that I couldn't get flowers for any of the girls anymore, as he was already fielding phone calls from upset boyfriends and husbands.

By telling me that I couldn't get girls flowers anymore, it really hurt me. You wouldn't normally expect a guy to tell you something like, "Not being able to give girls flowers anymore is very painful for me," but it was extremely harmful to me. Not having the ability to send a girl flowers with a card was detrimental to my self-esteem and would lead to more depression.

For me, sending a girl flowers and a card became a way of communicating how I felt about her. Since I didn't have the proper social skills to be the biggest flirt in the world and really get her attention like other guys could, I had come up with an alternative to replace that. I thought that by giving girls flowers or a card, I would be able to connect with them more and they would want to talk to me. At least, maybe they would know who I was and say hi to me on occasion.

Now I was even more helpless. I didn't have any source of communication with girls. I didn't have any way at all to connect with them or tell them how I felt about them. I was rejected, depressed, and miserable. How was I going to talk to girls now?

Eventually, after trying so hard to not want to connect with a woman so bad, I was able to quit worrying about the work scene so much and became more fascinated by the scenery over at Indiana Wesleyan. I had an "aha" moment. I was like, Wait just a moment here. There are around two or three thousand girls that go to school at Indiana Wesleyan. All I have to do is try to meet them and start talking with them.

I could have girls to talk to, interact with, and send flowers to. I wasn't going to die because I couldn't send flowers to girls anymore. I just had to do it at another place. There were already a few girls whom I was interested in over on campus, ones I'd never even talked to, and I immediately sent a couple of them flowers and a card. They were a little freaked out, as they had no idea who I was. Again, I couldn't understand how they could have been freaked out. Needless to say, I was upset with myself and still wondered why girls hated me. I wanted to get to the bottom of this so desperately. How was I going to get there, though?

# Buying Love

I was ready to get back into the swing of things as far as classes were concerned. Or was I? After sitting out and only taking music ensembles my first semester at Indiana Wesleyan, I had started classes in January of 2005. I was actually taking real college courses, and getting a degree at this school would be much more difficult for me, as there were many more required liberal arts courses.

I had a pretty significant music scholarship lined up that was ready to kick in during that spring semester. All I had to do was make myself go to sign up for classes in mid to late November. For some reason, though, I struggled with making myself go over to the registration office. I wasn't sure why, but I was afraid to go to school. I was afraid of being made fun of even more and ridiculed for trying to make friends. I knew that it was a Christian university and all, but I still had a difficult time with trying to trust these other students.

After everything that I had been through in the previous few years in my life, building a trusting relationship with peers was going to take a lot of time and work on both my part and their part. I was bound and determined to beware of predators and people who would just try to take advantage of me and hurt me on purpose. I didn't want to be used again or be taken advantage of in any way.

It was close to the end of November, and I was petrified of the thought of January and school coming around. The thought of going to classes and being put on the spot and possibly being called on to give an answer to something I didn't know or, even worse, to answer a question that I didn't even understand was enough to make me wet myself. I was so nervous that I just couldn't come to grips with it and go to the office to sign up. I knew exactly what classes I wanted and needed to take, but I just couldn't risk putting myself back out there yet.

As the fall semester of 2004 was coming to a close, people were asking me if I was excited to be taking classes next spring, and I'd just kind of blow it off and say, "A class is a class," or, "School is school, you know. It is what it is." I didn't want to make too big of a deal out of it because I didn't want them to know that I was scared of signing up for classes or that I hadn't signed up for classes yet.

At times, during the months of November and December, my parents would ask me if I had signed up for classes yet. I would, of course, just say, "Yeah. Of course I have," just to keep them off of my case and from getting mad at me. I was already being put through enough stress and anxiety that I couldn't handle any more from anyone, including my parents.

While I understood their concern with wanting to make sure I was in school, I also knew that they didn't understand what all I was going through. They couldn't possibly know of all the trouble I was having with fitting in and making friends. They couldn't possibly know of all of the bullying and ridiculing that I was put through throughout my entire life. It seemed like it was impossible for them to even comprehend how I felt.

So with the end of the fall semester drawing near and all of the Christmas concert preparations, I was able to "accidentally" forget to sign up for classes. Unfortunately, this would be the start of a nasty pattern of running away from my problems that would last for about two or three years. I thought I could just kind of disappear off into space without anyone even noticing I was gone and hadn't signed up for classes. I didn't think any of the other students would realize that I wasn't there until after ensemble rehearsals started up.

In the process of running away, I'd try to bury myself in more work at the steakhouse. I didn't talk much at work at all anymore, as I just went in there to do my job and go home. I was starting to hate my job there, as people were so often mean to me and didn't seem to care about people at all.

I was beginning to become more and more depressed about my life, as I just didn't feel like it had any meaning to it at all anymore. After all of the social failures, not even the musical successes were enough to keep me motivated. I was struggling more so than ever before with self-confidence. I retreated to my make-believe world, only leaving to go to work and over to Indiana Wesleyan to finish up ensemble rehearsals and the Christmas program.

After finishing up the Christmas extravaganza, I would have three weeks away from school. I thought that over these three weeks I would be able to overcome my fear and anxiety and force myself to sign up for classes. I knew that it would be hard, but I also knew that I didn't have much of a choice. During much of that Christmas vacation, I was often found in my room, watching movies or trying to connect with someone on television. Yes, I was now nineteen, almost twenty, years old, and I still had a make-believe world that I could create and retreat to almost instantly to help me deal with the pain of being bullied, teased, and rejected. Again, retreating to the make-believe world was a safety net. Nothing can go wrong in the make-believe world, especially if it's a world that you've created for yourself.

I did manage to invite myself to a New Year's Eve party that year. This was really the first New Year's Eve party that I had ever been to. I knew of someone having a party, and somehow I talked them into inviting me. I'm not sure how exactly that was able to happen, but it worked. But when I was there, I felt so left out. Most people attended the party with their significant other. I felt like the third-party kind of guy, as I most often did throughout my life. I watched all of these kids drinking and playing drinking games that didn't seem very interesting to me, but they looked like they were just having a ball and the time of their life. I wanted to be included in the games, but I didn't want to drink. I wanted to be one of them so much, but it was impossible for me. I had a mental block that wasn't allowing me to connect with them on the same level as they would connect with each other.

It was right around this stage in my life when I started to notice a dilemma. Instead of one-on-one socializing going on, you could be at a party such as a New Year's Eve party, or any type of social gathering for that matter, and people would be standing in groups and talking with each other.

I remember back in my life when I first noticed this happening. I was thinking, *What is going on?* How can these people be having a conversation of sorts when they are in a huge group of individuals? They would trade turns with talking almost as if it was scripted. I didn't get this at all. I wondered how each person knew when to talk or how they knew what to say. I wondered how they just knew how to do things and react so quickly. It was almost as if they didn't even have to think about what they were going to say or when they were going to say it.

I can remember watching and analyzing these kinds of situations in which groups were involved for several years. When I would eventually have enough self-esteem and courage to try to get involved with some of these groups, I would at first enter the group as an observer. I wanted to observe exactly what it was that was going on so I could know what to say. I really tried to pick a guy who was in the group who seemed somewhat confident and popular. I was looking for the leader of the pack, so to speak. I wanted to try to be like the leader of the pack.

After I would hang around in these groups for a while, I quickly realized that I had no idea what was going on. It seemed like a game. One person says something, and then another person says something; then there's some laughing, and people look away; then, boom, within a second or two, someone else has started talking. It seemed like it was just a social game going on.

I wanted to know where they learned how to play the game, and I wanted to find the game itself because I wanted to read the instruction manual. I quickly became frustrated with trying to figure out this social game at times and would move on to something else. I would float around from group to group at these social meetings/parties, just looking and hoping for a group to include me into their obviously exciting conversation.

This is where I came up with my yo-yo theory, because I literally would feel like a yo-yo after going to a social event. After trying to find a place to fit in, I really felt like I was being pushed away and toward a different group, only then that group would pass me along to another group because no one wanted to include me in their group because I wasn't cool enough for them or I was different.

Being bounced around from group to group can be pretty emotionally draining. Not only is it tiring, but it's also frustrating. I just wanted to be included in the fun. I didn't see why it was such a big deal that I wanted to talk with other people my age. I mean, didn't most other people my age want to connect with others their age too? Or was I weird for wanting to connect with people my age?

It was after that party on New Year's Eve that I had to return to the awful scenery of making myself try to go sign up for classes for the spring semester. This seems like such an easy thing for someone to do, yet for me, it would be one of the most difficult things in my life. I was scared of other people my age, and I didn't want to hurt them anymore. I also didn't want to get hurt anymore myself. I was becoming more miserable by the day. *Something has to be done*, I was thinking and hoping.

The day had finally come and gone for the first day of classes, and I wasn't present. I had decided that I just couldn't do it. I went to work and stayed at work all day. Once again, I was missing out on a chance to go to school. I was miserable because I was starting to really hate my job and everything that came along with it. I would continue to be taken advantage of while working at the steakhouse both by girls and guys. I just wanted some relief from pain, but I wasn't getting it. I was still left wondering what was wrong with me. I wanted to fix it, but in order to fix a problem, one must first know what the root of the problem is, and I had no idea.

Eventually, Mr. Flanagin contacted me to see why I hadn't shown up for the first day of classes. I tried to explain to him that I just couldn't do it, and I also would try to explain to my parents about how I just couldn't make myself go. I couldn't tell them that I was afraid of going to class because of other kids because at that point in time I still had not really opened up to anyone about any of my problems. I was still holding everything in, and this was not good or safe. I was just waiting to explode because of all the emotional and physical pain I had built up on the inside.

Eventually, though, it was decided that I must go back to school. There was no way around it because if I wasn't enrolled in classes my student loans were going to immediately start coming due, and I would not have a good enough job to pay them. So I was forced to go back to an uncomfortable setting and try to fit in somewhere in which I just didn't feel like I belonged.

Once again, though, due to the fact that I had held out and was late, I was unable to get into any education classes, and I would be forced to take all music ensembles. While this was something that I really enjoyed and that was tremendously easy for me, I wasn't getting anywhere academically.

This would mean that I would have been in college for a whole year now without successfully completing one academic credit. I didn't have one academic credit completed because I was unable to keep myself in class. I was not able to face other students by going to class. It was just too much for me. There had to be a way for me to overcome this. I tried quite often to just not think about it and/or try to think that I was just as good as the other students were, but this was a task that was above my cognitive ability at the time. I had never had any social success, so how was I supposed to feel like I was as good as these other students?

I managed to get myself over there and face the music. I was back at a place where I felt uncomfortable and was a little scared of my surroundings. It was just hard for me to get used to people by this point because I was so on guard about them doing something mean to me. I spent a lot of time that spring semester thinking about how the other students seemed to be able to laugh about things in a way to which I couldn't relate. They seemed to understand different jokes than I did, and our senses of humor weren't the same at all.

It was a custom for the Indiana Wesleyan University wind ensemble to spend their spring breaks touring the country to provide a testimony of just how amazing God can be. It was during these weeklong adventures that we would perform nearly fifteen to twenty times in six to seven days. We would leave on a bus on a Friday evening and often not return home until Sunday evening before school was slated to begin.

These would often make for extremely long weeks with a lot of social interaction going on. During the tour, we would perform in churches, and then they would host us by feeding us a most generous meal before our concerts. They would have volunteers from their church take a couple of students from the group home with them for the evening.

During this time, it would be a custom to spend your evening socializing with the family that had taken you home. More often than not, the family would also have kids. Knowing that this was going to be the situation, I had a huge dilemma. I still had the occasional bed-wetting problem at the age of twenty. It was no longer an every night thing, but it was something that would pop up every once in a while. At the time, I was quite frustrated with this, as you could imagine.

I was so worried that I would have an accident while on our spring tour. Not only did I not want to have an accident because I didn't want to ruin any beds or sheets of the family's that we were staying at, but I also was worried because I knew that I would be staying with other students who were close to my age, and there was no way I wanted them to find out or see that happen. I had a huge dilemma. Not even Mr. Flanagin knew of this problem I had, so I couldn't just come right out and say, "I can't go." I didn't know what to do, and I was scared to death about the entire situation.

Eventually, I had enough courage to talk to my parents about it to see what they thought I should do. We decided that maybe it would be best to consult the director of the group, Mr. Flanagin, and see what he had to say about the whole situation. So I decided that I would have the courage to talk to him about it, and my mother might have even called him to help explain the situation.

Mr. Flanagin suggested that maybe we would find two of the most mature students in the group and possibly let them know of the situation so they could be at least somewhat aware of it. When he first suggested that, I wasn't too sure about how I felt about his idea. I had seen and heard way too many horror stories where other kids or students had found out that someone had a bed-wetting problem and then basically proceeded to destroy their life. I didn't want to deal with that on top of everything else I was also trying to deal with at the time. I wasn't sure if I could handle that.

On the optimistic side, I thought, What if maybe they really are mature students and have a good heart and won't share my secret with the rest of the group, which would then get spread to the rest of the university when we get back, which would then eventually get shared with the rest of the world?

After debating this for a couple of weeks and really cutting things close by waiting until the last minute to decide, I decided that I would go. I decided I'd go and I would room with these two guys who seemed somewhat mature, and I would take a chance on trusting them not to tell anyone about my problem. I knew if they were to tell anyone about my problem, my already-miserable life would get much worse.

I let Mr. Flanagin know that it would be okay to call those two students in and let them know of the problem I was having. He informed the students of the problem and then immediately informed me that they reacted very positively to it and were willing to help in any way that they could.

I was still a nervous wreck about the entire situation. I just didn't know what would happen if I had an accident and they found out. I was scared out of my mind.

Meanwhile, back at the steakhouse, where I was working, I was having trouble with them not wanting to cooperate with my school schedule anymore. They decided they didn't want to schedule me around it anymore and were very mean about giving me the week off to go on the spring tour. On the Tuesday night before we left for the spring tour, we had a concert on campus over in Marion. Well, usually I worked 9:00 a.m. to 8:00 p.m. on Tuesdays, so this was a change in my schedule, as I'd need the day off, or at least the evening. I originally requested the entire day off because on concert days you have rehearsals and then have to quickly eat and take care of all sorts of other little things. It was nice to have the entire day off of work on the day of the concert so I could really focus in on the music as well.

So after having to put up a huge fight just to get off of work and go to the concert, I now had to drive forty-five minutes to Marion and get there as quick as I could. Everything was becoming such a hassle, and it made life even more difficult to deal with at times. I was really starting to dislike the steakhouse, and I wanted to find something else. I knew that I'd have a week to think about the experiences I was having at the steakhouse while I was on the spring tour with the wind ensemble.

After making it to the concert in the nick of time and enjoying a great performance, I was able to relax for a couple days before we left for vacation. I guess you could say it wasn't really a vacation, as we would be so busy that we didn't have too terribly long to enjoy ourselves. However, we would get one day off to spend at the Mall of America in Minnesota.

I was still very skeptical and nervous about my whole situation, and I didn't know what was going to happen to me if I had an accident. I was so anxious that I was a complete wreck. But I was ready to go on tour, and I had to suck it up and move on. I had to be willing to take the chance of an accident happening and my little secret being revealed to the entire world.

That Friday, I would spend the majority of the day packing. I made sure to pack my medication. (At the time, they had me taking some medication that they supposedly thought was going to help with bed-wetting issues.) I packed everything up, including my trombone, and went over to Indiana Wesleyan for a little picnic/meeting on Friday evening before we were to leave. I was still nervous about things, but I had a little bit of comfort in knowing that these two guys were people that Mr. Flanagin trusted.

The picnic was spent as a socializing hour or two for the group to become more acquainted with one another. There would be plenty of time in the coming days to become even more acquainted with one another. I still had problems socializing and making friends. But at this point I'd become accustomed to it and tried to play it off like it didn't bother me. I just tried to get through each day. I felt very alone and left out. After the picnic was over, everyone returned to their dorms for a little rest and relaxation. Unfortunately for me, I had to drive all the way back to Huntington and then sleep for a couple of hours before making the return trip to Marion bright and early. We were to be at school around 5:30 a.m. so we could depart, as we were heading for Cedar Rapids, Iowa, for a Saturday afternoon/evening performance. I was excited about the performing aspect, but the long bus ride would not be something that I was looking forward to. These bus rides weren't nearly as horrible as the bus rides I had experienced in elementary through high school and then again on the bus down at Indiana University.

This bus ride would be different because there was a seat for everyone, so I wouldn't have to expose my poor sensory motor skills by wobbling all over the place and running into other people or, even worse, falling and knocking everyone, including myself, over. I managed to bring a set of headphones, and I listened to music most of the trip. I sat next to someone I really didn't know too well, and there was little or no interest on his part to get to know me, so I thought I would save my breath of embarrassing myself and looking like a fool socially. I didn't try to talk to him too much. It was a very relaxing bus ride. I think it took us about seven or eight hours to get into Cedar Rapids from Marion.

On the bus ride it seemed as if everyone was sitting with their good friends that they had made, and they were all quite capable of carrying on a conversation. Even between seats, in the front of the bus and the back of the bus, there could, at times, be a conversation going on.

There was so much noise going on that it was hard for me to even tell who was saying what. I couldn't quite make things out, and I had a difficult time concentrating and comprehending what one particular person in the huge crowd on the bus was saying. This is another trait of Asperger's, as people will often have trouble organizing all of the cluttered noises they hear.

As we came into Cedar Rapids, we came to a small church in which we'd perform. I was getting more nervous, though, as night was drawing near. I was excited for the performance, and I knew that we would play well as we always did. There were really some really great players in that group. While we were a little bigger than your standard wind ensemble, it was because at Indiana Wesleyan, no one was cut. There was really no audition to say if you made the group or didn't make it.

After that first performance, we were to head back to the host home with the family and enjoy some fellowship together. Again I made some effort to socialize with my peers and the host family, but the other kids in the group seemed to naturally know how to converse with the new people and make acquaintances or friends with them. I was getting really nervous because of the whole sleeping situation and the problems I had with wetting the bed. I was praying to God that I could just go one week without having an accident and make it home. I was so anxious and nervous that I didn't sleep at all that night.

I purposely tossed and turned so I could stay awake to go to the bathroom when I had to go. I wasn't about to take any chances of having someone find out that I had a problem. The next morning, I was extremely exhausted, but I knew that I couldn't sleep. I was going to try to stay up the entire trip because I was afraid of the consequences of what would have happened if I would have fallen asleep. Even though the people I was with knew about this problem, I still didn't want to have any issues or take any chances of ever being made fun of.

The next day, we had a performance in the morning, and it went extremely well. I was still tired due to the fact that I hadn't slept at all that night. After the performance, we would then have to load everything up and travel off to another city.

The rest of the tour went pretty well musically. I still had a very difficult time fitting in on the bus. People would talk to me, but I could just tell it was in a different manner than they were talking to someone else. That's one of the things about high-functioning Asperger's syndrome. You're able to see and recognize the level of social interaction between two neurotypical individuals, and you can tell that it's different. You can't tell what they're doing different that's making their interaction go so much more smoothly. No matter how hard I would try to analyze situations and figure out what they were doing that allowed their social interaction to work, I just couldn't get it.

I managed to enjoy our day off at the Mall of America, and I was able to be a tag along with a few different groups. I tried to divide my time up between different groups for a couple of reasons, one of which was to try to avoid overstaying my welcome. The other was because I'd quickly become uncomfortable with the social situations, as I wasn't able to contribute to them, so it was just like I was a robot sitting in on a conversation with a group. Eventually, I became lost and confused anyhow, so I would decide that it was time to move on to the next group of people I could find.

Of course, there were often times on the trip when I just wanted to be by myself. I was suffering from what I've named people over-kill. This is something that happens for me when I'm around huge crowds of people. Now, there are some individuals on the spectrum who just have to have their alone time, and some want more alone time than they do time with others. It's just a personal preference thing. I am one who doesn't like alone time very often. I would so much rather be out playing putt-putt or bowling with a group of friends, or going to the movies, or even better on a date with a gorgeous young woman. There wasn't much alone time at all on this trip. We constantly stayed at host homes in a group of three or four peers or were traveling and performing. I was able to relax every now and then, but the whole week was socially and emotionally exhausting.

Once we returned to school after a long and exhausting trip, I had to head right back to work on the following Tuesday. Work was becoming very stressful, as we had all sorts of problems with management. The steakhouse in Huntington suffered from some of the poorest and most immature management that I've ever seen. I mean, it was ridiculous some of the things I'd see them do and get away with.

I saw male managers making out with their female employees in the restaurant's banquet room. I'd walked in and seen managers smoking pot in the office only to try to cover it up as I was walking in. I may have Asperger's, but come on, dude. That stuff smells from a mile away.

The steakhouse where I worked went through five to ten managers per year, it seemed like. It was frustrating for me because I had such a hard time adapting to change. Each time a new manager was there, I'd become frustrated and just want to quit.

Eventually, I would get put into some situations at work in which I was getting taken advantage of by the managers. After working at a place for almost four to five years, you can get a pretty good understanding of how things work. I knew how to do everything in that store. I even closed many nights with a manager who was lazy and couldn't do anything. He'd sit at a table in the dining room and smoke all night long.

He'd always drag me along into his office with him after closing and tell me that it was my job to do paperwork and all sorts of stuff that a manager should be doing, and I was told that if I didn't do it he'd fire me and hire someone else.

Eventually, it would get to the point where the closing manager would just leave before everyone else was done closing their positions. They'd just leave and tell me to lock up as I left. At first I thought this was cool because I was getting the chance to act like I was someone who had a significant role in something, but after this was happening night after night, I quickly started to wonder what was going on.

I started to think, *He's leaving, and I'm staying to do his job that he's still getting paid to do, and I'm not making the salary that he's making to do his job for him.* I thought that there was something wrong with this, but I never said anything to anyone because, again, I hated conflict, and I didn't want to cause a huge scene.

That particular manager ended up being fired and I stayed on as a regular employee. Life became a little easier there for a while. I worked there and went to school at Indiana Wesleyan. I loved playing in the wind ensemble at school.

Eventually, I found another girl who was in the wind ensemble at Indiana Wesleyan University whom I liked, and I started to try to talk to her. Talking to her was hard for me because she was so pretty and I was afraid she would hate me and ignore me too.

It was at about that time that the social networking site Facebook was coming on the scene for college students. At that point, it was a social networking site for college students only. Now, just a few short years later, it's one of, if not the biggest, social networking Web site for anyone in the world. People of all ages, shapes, sizes, and colors can now join the site.

I was thinking that maybe it would be easier to talk to her on there, so I added her as my friend on Facebook and started sending her messages just asking her how her day was or what she was up to. I'd also send her random messages saying, "Have a good day." I loved to be nice to a girl and show her that I cared about her. Unfortunately, it was a common thing in my life for girls not to like me and even hate me. At times, it felt like they hated me just because I was being so nice to them.

I would continue trying to get to know a girl I liked. Eventually, I would become frustrated because it just wasn't going anywhere at all, and she wasn't even really wanting to talk to me anymore. So I went to another guy whom I worked with and asked him how to get a girlfriend.

He told me that you had to go out and buy them some jewelry and flowers. He told me to get a diamond ring and about twenty dozen red roses and have them delivered to her in a class at school. He seemed very genuine and like he was being honest and really wanted to help me. I never even thought twice about it because he was always talking to girls and seemed cool. So I took his advice and immediately went shopping for a diamond ring. Since I was still working at the steakhouse and making a pretty good chunk of money, I was able to open a line of credit at a local jewelry store. The ring that the gentleman at the counter helped me pick out came to around $750 on sale. It looked like a big ring, but I'd told the gentleman my friend said to get a diamond ring for her, and that's what he gave me. I then went to the flower shop and ordered her twenty dozen red roses.

I had the ring and the red roses delivered to her at school in her world changers class. I wasn't there, so I have no idea how this went down in the classroom, but knowing what I know now, I can only guess that it didn't go well at all. In fact, I never heard from that girl again, and when I saw her, it looked like she was trying to get as far away from me as she could. I couldn't understand why girls reacted like this when I was trying to be nice to them and get them something that they liked. I didn't get it, and I still don't.

After that whole situation went down with her, I immediately felt rejected and embarrassed again. There was something wrong with me. I knew there was. I went through the whole cycle that I'd always go through when I would get rejected. I thought, I am a stupid, worthless piece of trash. I was really hard on myself every time I did something wrong and messed up. I didn't know what it was that I was doing wrong, but by the way people were reacting, it was really bad. I didn't belong here. I belonged on a different planet or something.

I retreated to my home and my make-believe world as much as possible. Again, this was a much safer place—at least in my mind, although I don't believe that the make-believe world is necessarily a good place for someone on the spectrum to stay in. I kind of gave up hope on girls for a while except for my imaginary friend, Cameron Diaz.

I struggled with being able to get motivated to do things. I would go through one of the most difficult summers in my life that coming summer. I didn't understand what was wrong with me. All I knew was that I was always tired out and didn't want to get out of bed in the mornings and couldn't sleep at night. That summer was spent pretty much by myself, as I would go to work and then come home and watch television and play trombone. I didn't try to socialize outside of going to work. There was no socializing for me at work, as I was beginning to feel taken advantage of by management and other employees, so I kind of just wanted to keep to myself while I was there.

That summer, I continued playing in the Blue River Big Band as well as in a couple of summer concert bands in the area. Something that I did notice during that summer is that I had an easier time talking to and being accepted by older adults who were in their thirties and forties. I had no idea why this was, but I felt more connected with them than I did my peer group. These older adults would be much nicer to me and wouldn't judge or tease me or take advantage of me like some of the other kids my age would.

It was toward the end of that summer that a situation developed at work. I was having a typical morning at work with little or no socializing going on, and the daytime cook and prep person were picking on me constantly. They were both complaining about their jobs and how they hated working there, and I tried to join in that conversation.

Eventually, it got to the point to where they were daring me to walk out and quit, and they were teasing me and making fun of me. I felt like I was being harassed. But they kept teasing me and saying that I'd never walk out because I was a dork and I loved this place. They said I was going to work there for the rest of my life because I liked it so much. They told me I was a wuss because I wasn't man enough like other guys to just walk out and leave the job. They kept saying that I was a chicken and a wimp and that I'd never get anywhere in life because I didn't have the balls to just walk out and leave the job. I just couldn't take it anymore. I was tired of being a pushover, and they were right. I didn't usually have the balls to do something like this, but I didn't want to be around them to be getting teased and made fun of anymore. To this day, I can still see and hear those voices in my ear. "Travis, you're such a chicken. You'll never have the guts to walk out." I just had to get away, so that's what I did.

I had no intentions of quitting my job on that day, but the fact that I was getting made fun of and told that I wasn't cool because I wasn't willing to walk out on them really hurt and upset me. I wanted to be cool because I wanted to be accepted and liked by my peer group.

Shortly after that event at the steakhouse, I met a guy on Facebook, a guy who seemed like a nice guy with good intentions, and I was drawn to this. We talked on the Internet for a couple of days and then decided to hang out. I had resorted to using sites such as Facebook or MySpace to try to make new friends because meeting new people in person was very hard and overwhelming for me and they nearly always made fun of me. This guy would talk to me online for a while, and then, eventually, we'd meet up. I was so excited because I thought I was making a friend.

We met up at Applebee's for dinner to chat, and I found him to be interesting. He was going to school to become a doctor and had a lot of knowledge about things. When it came time to leave and pay the checks, he told me that I would be paying for both him and myself. He said that this was a custom. I told him how I had a hard time making friends and was hoping that he'd be able to give me some good advice. He said that in order to make friends, you have to buy their meals every time they hang out with you, and you might have to pay them. He told me that he would hang out with me as long as I bought all of his meals and his drinks, along with paying him $100 each time we hung out. This didn't seem strange to me at the time at all. I was smart enough to figure out that I was different than other people were. I didn't know why at the time but felt that due to being different I owed people to coexist in the same world that they did.

He also introduced me to a few of his friends, and I was excited because I thought I was going to be a part of a group of guys for a while. I was excited about this for many reasons. I wanted to learn how to be a cool guy, and I felt accepted by them.

They told me that in order to be a part of their group I'd have to go through a little group initiation. It was a custom for new people who were joining their friend circle to go through this initiation all the time, they said. The idea was that they wanted to know and see how tough I was and how much pain I could handle before I could be a part of their group. They said that I'd have to get beaten up by one of the guys in the group to see how I handled myself.

I was tied to a tree, and the guy spent about ten or twenty minutes hitting me. To this day, this event causes me many painful memories. The guys took turns hitting me and bullying me. They were also laughing and acting like this was one of the best parties that they had ever been to in their lives. They were drinking. I felt hopeless as I stood there but wanted their acceptance so bad. I wasn't sure why I had to go through this just to become their friend or whatever, but I was willing to do whatever it took to make friends. I wanted that friendship and peer acceptance so much that I just had to put myself through the pain so I could become a part of the group.

During the rest of the summer of 2005, I would continue to try to hang out with the group of guys who would physically push me around and abuse me. I knew that they were doing this to me, but I wasn't able to convince myself that I needed to get away from this situation because my need for hanging out with people and having what I thought were friends to hang out with was far greater than my need for avoiding physical pain.

I would continue to pay this guy $100 per month and would still have to buy his meals and pretty much pay for him in whatever we did. I really just thought that this was normal, that when you are meeting new people and you're not as cool as they are, you have to do whatever they tell you in order to become their friend. I thought maybe it was just a custom, that when the less cool person wants to become friends with a cooler person you must buy their meals and drinks as well as pay for anything else that you do. I also truly believed that it was a custom that you would have to pay the person a price to hang out with them. This had happened to me quite a bit throughout my life already, even in high school. The amount of money that I had to use in order to hang out with someone in high school was far less than it was at this time, but still, even at such a young age, I was tricked into believing that the only way you could have someone want to spend time with you is if you were paying them and allowing them to do whatever they wanted to you, such as beat you up and take advantage of you.

Whenever I was away from that individual during the summer, I was at my house either escaping into imagination in my make-believe world or practicing my trombone. I didn't try to do much else, mainly due to the fact that I didn't have any more money.

Toward the end of the summer, as I was getting ready to head back to school officially at Indiana Wesleyan University, I became really nervous and once again had to debate on if I would be capable of going back or not.

After taking an entire year off, I thought getting back into school and actually taking real classes would be a pleasant change. Unfortunately, after taking so much time away from school, it was kind of like, How do I go back to school? I think it's a proven fact for anyone—and not just people on the spectrum—that the longer you take off from school, the less likely you will be to go back.

# Try Again

After leaving my job, I returned to school. This time, I would be taking real academic classes instead of just the music ensembles. This would provide a little bit of spark in my life once I got past all of the anxiety that starting school led to.

I was taking about sixteen credit hours this particular semester. While the majority of them were still music courses, I also had to take some challenging general education courses. I wasn't able to concentrate very well in my general education classes due to the amount of social anxiety that I was having. It seemed like every attempted approach to make a friend was a disaster and would lead to bad things.

Once again, music would be the thing that kept me motivated and trying to succeed in school. I was once again named section leader of the trombone section, which was something that I could be proud of. As section leader, I was also eligible to receive grant money for each semester in the amount of $500. I wasn't able to tell if other students in the group liked me too much or not, but after reflecting back on this a year or two later, in talking with Mr. Flanagin, it was decided that they all liked me but just weren't sure what to make of me at first. They thought I was a little strange.

I was once again a part of the Indiana Wesleyan University Honors Brass Quintet. There were two outstanding guys in the group—not only outstanding musicians, but they were just all-around good people. Phil Wiseman is one of the coolest guys I'd ever met in my life, and he actually talked to me and made me feel a little bit included. Paul French was another outstanding musician and another guy who would take me under his wing for a while and kind of lead me along.

As I went through the semester, I would experience some interesting things. I often wondered about certain social situations and how to develop them and study them. I became fascinated with studying friends. I guess I needed to know exactly how to interact with someone, so I was willing to put a lot of time and effort into figuring it out, which would cause my grades to slip and classes to become increasingly more difficult.

I became a little more depressed, but it was this fall that I was introduced to a high school band director who would quickly become someone I looked up to. I was highly recommended to work on this gentleman's summer marching staff, teaching the low brass/trombone section how to play the music for their fall 2005 marching show. I was already busy with school and homework, but I decided that taking on something like this would be good for me because it would look good on résumés and it would help to keep me busy and hopefully less depressed.

I worked their band camp in August, just prior to school starting, and this was something that I really enjoyed. They asked me to stay on staff during the fall marching competition season to continue working with the low brass. I graciously accepted their invitation. Teaching was somewhat frustrating for me, as I had to try to use a lot of social skills that I did not have. Luckily, the type of teaching I was doing required me to lead by example more than talking.

I ended up spending quite a bit of time over in Monroe, Indiana, that fall. I would drive back and forth two nights a week for rehearsals. It was about an hour's drive from Indiana Wesleyan University.

I always looked forward to every day and opportunity that I had to travel there to work with those kids. When I was helping kids learn something that I was very passionate about, it made me feel important and like someone appreciated my talents and wanted me around. Even if I was twenty and they were high school kids, it still meant something to me to be wanted and included.

My drives back and forth to Monroe on those evenings were sort of therapy sessions in themselves. I would often put on some of my favorite music and just relax and enjoy the drive with the windows down. I loved listening to marching shows and jazz music in the car. There is nothing more therapeutic for me than listening to music.

Some of the best times of my life were spent on the football field both in high school and then again when I was doing support staff for high school marching bands. There is nothing like standing on a football field on a Friday night during halftime of a football game, performing a show or even standing on the sidelines, watching the younger kids play their hearts out.

I would travel to Monroe on Tuesday, Thursday, Friday, and Saturday nights, which would help keep me busy and not thinking about negative/depressing thoughts over that fall.

School in itself wasn't too bad yet. I was taking basic, intro-level or freshman-level courses. Due to starting college over basically, it was like I was still a freshman who had to take beginning-level classes before I could get into the real stuff. I was exceptionally talented at music theory and ear-training. I was always one of the students who knew what the interval was or what the rhythm was. I just hated to be the one student that the teacher would choose to call on, though. In fact, there were often times when I would want to avoid eye contact with the teacher completely. Whenever I was called on, I asked, "Why me?"

The fall of 2005 would also include going on a couple of weekend tours as an ensemble. I had tried to ensure that I had the same roommates, but due to circumstances that I couldn't control, the other guys who had roomed with me the previous year wanted to room with someone else. This was another circumstance in which I felt neglected because I must not have been good enough or cool enough for them. I wanted to room with them, and when I had gotten around to asking them if I could, they both said that they were already rooming with someone else. So that left me to do a roommate search.

Eventually, I got to know a drummer in the jazz band who also played percussion in wind ensemble. He was looking for a roommate, and we decided that we would give each other a try. He was a really cool guy and probably one of the nicest guys that you could ever imagine. It seemed as if he saw something in me that most others didn't and was willing to at least be nice to me.

It was in about October of 2005 when I was trying to find people to connect with and be friends with online that I met a girl. I had joined a dating Web site in hopes that I would be able to meet a girl and feel more comfortable talking to her online before meeting her in person. I had finally met a girl and had gotten to know her, and we decided to meet.

She was from Cincinnati, Ohio, so I decided that one Saturday afternoon I was going to make the drive down to Cincinnati and meet her. I was feeling so excited about meeting her. She had e-mailed me and had instant messaging conversations with me. We texted back and forth, but I never did talk to her on the phone. I just got in the car and drove to meet her after a couple of weeks of texting.

When I got there, there was no woman in sight. It turns out that this person posing as a woman was actually a man, a man who was desperate for interaction with other men. I was so stunned and disappointed that I didn't even have a clue as to what to say.

I thought, I've got to get out of here. This is so weird, and I feel uncomfortable. I have a hard time telling people how I really feel sometimes, though, because I'm afraid of hurting someone's feelings. I will try to refrain from telling someone the truth if I think it's something that could offend them.

But I certainly didn't drive nearly four hours from my home to Cincinnati just to meet a guy. I was thinking I was meeting a beautiful woman. I was tricked and fooled into doing something I didn't want to do. This just goes to show you all of the things that are out there and how you can get yourself into trouble quickly. I've seen and heard of things happening to neurotypicals, but imagine when it's someone on the autism spectrum who could be a little socially naïve.

As the fall semester of 2005 was coming to a close, I was proud of myself for accomplishing something that I had not done before. This was something that I should have done a year earlier, but due to other problems that got in the way, this would be my first time actually completing a semester of college and getting college credits. I was excited to have some sort of a record on my academic transcript now. Because my classes were mostly introduction courses that semester, I did pretty well in them, so I really set my grade point average high. My GPA was a 3.7 or something close to that.

During the fall semester, I had accomplished a lot of great things and some not-so-great things. I had managed to stay in my classes without withdrawing. I also was able to use my special interest and play in many musical ensembles. I was in wind ensemble, jazz band, and orchestra, and pretty much anything that was musical and included a trombone part, I was in it.

However, there was still this big social situation that was just looming over my head. I still hadn't managed to learn how to develop these peer relationships, and I was becoming more and more desperate to find out by the day. I was getting to a point in life in which I realized that any meaning I had in life with my music and trombone just wasn't enough. I soon began to discover that the only thing that can provide true meaning in life is having great friendships and being accepted by people around you. Just having someone to say hi to goes a long way toward providing meaning in my life.

The other really bad thing that hurt my feelings during that semester was this guy I had met online from another school. He had said that he was going to be my friend as long as I did his homework for the entire semester. I did every single homework assignment that he asked me to do, and come the end of the semester, he didn't even take the time to say thanks. Needless to say, I never met this guy or hung out with him.

Toward the end of the fall semester at Indiana Wesleyan, the music department hosts an event that they call the madrigal dinners. This is a formal event where people from the community purchase a ticket and are then treated to a formal dinner and show by the Indiana Wesleyan University Chorale.

As part of the show, the IWU Honors Brass Quintet opens up for the chorale by playing a few charts. These charts are originals written for madrigal dinners.

It was during this show that I would experience what I now know was probably a classic Asperger's moment.

As part of the madrigal theme, the brass quintet was all wearing tights. Now this was pretty embarrassing. Five guys in white tights. However, somehow or another, after the first evening's show, I managed to lay my tights down somewhere.

Come about 6:30 p.m. on Saturday evening, as I was going to get dressed for the concert, I realized that I couldn't find my tights. I thought maybe, just maybe I was going to get out of wearing tights that night. They managed to find me something even better than the white tights. Somewhere, the costume people came up with a pair of black tights for me to wear. This was pretty entertaining to the audience I'm sure, and the other guys gave me a heck of a hard time about this. Looking back on it now, I actually find it to be pretty humorous and I am able to laugh about it.

I've learned that people on the spectrum will often be very unorganized. I did manage to find the white tights a couple of days later, buried under a big pile of stuff in my trunk. I guess I had just thrown them in my trunk after taking them off on Friday evening.

After the madrigals, it was time for me to go into my last full week of the college semester. This was going to be finals week, and I wanted to ace all of my finals so I could have an awesome GPA and just relax and enjoy my winter break. Studying for tests and finals was something that was really difficult for me. I've always had a hard time sitting still long enough to study for a test.

Luckily for me, in my first semester, the tests were simple. I managed to get A's on all of them except for one, for which I received a grade of a B. I had just finished up my first semester in college without dropping out due to anxiety or depression. I was happy and couldn't wait to head back in January.

During the spring semester of 2006, I would continue on my academic journey. I was excited to have passed some classes and be moving onto a few higher-level classes. I continued my studies in music and tried to play in as many ensembles as possible. Once again, I didn't do a whole lot outside of school. I began really trying to get to know good-quality people through the Internet. This is something that I wouldn't recommend someone with autism or Asperger's syndrome do unless they are aware of what they are getting into.

I, for one, was very unaware of what I was getting into. I thought that it was a safe place and didn't see why there would be any problems with it. I would continue to try to make new and good Facebook friends during that entire semester.

Once again, I was still having issues with making friends in real life. I really liked a couple of girls that I was going to school with. They were so pretty, and I thought they seemed nice, at least to others. I wanted to talk to them so badly. I thought that maybe this would be the year in which I would be able to talk to a girl and get her to go on a date and possibly date her.

There was a girl in wind ensemble whom I liked as well. Since we would spend a tremendous amount of time together performing and going on tours, I thought I would be able to get to know her. However, my attempts to ask her for coffee were always turned down with her saying some sort of line about being busy or something. The funny thing was that she'd say that she was busy at that particular time, but then during that time frame, I would sometimes see her at the coffee shop on campus, grabbing coffee herself. This made me feel betrayed and lied to. I felt as if she thought that I was fat, ugly, stupid, worthless, pathetic, and dumb.

That year, the wind ensemble was scheduled to travel to Florida for the spring tour. Most everyone was pretty excited about this, as it meant warm, southern weather instead of the cold, arctic weather that we had endured the previous spring up in Minnesota and Wisconsin.

In the weeks leading up to spring break, I was starting to get a little lonely and depressed. It was really hitting me that I didn't have any real friends. My friends were people whom I saw on television, such as Cameron Diaz, and they were also people whom I would see on the news, particularly local news anchors. Up until about this point, I had been able to deal with it a lot easier, but as I began getting older, there was something that set off an alarm in me that was trying to tell me there was something wrong with me. I just began to become more aware of the situation. I could tell just by observing social interactions how different mine were from everyone else's. They had to know something I didn't. I would keep on searching, as I was still bound and determined to find out exactly what it was that they knew. I needed answers, and I needed a solution to my problem immediately.

On the Saturday we were leaving for Florida, I had mixed emotions. I loved to travel and was glad we were going somewhere warm, but I was starting to feel overwhelmed by spending large amounts of time with big groups of people. I wasn't sure what was causing it, but I did know that it was uncomfortable. Sometimes, when we would perform on these tours, I would feel crowded because the venues in which we played were so small that the members of the ensemble would practically have to sit on top of each other.

The bus ride down to Florida would prove to be a long one. We left the school at around 4:00 a.m.

It was one of the more interesting bus rides of my time. The first bus driver was somewhat of a crazy driver. I looked up to see him talking on his cell phone, smoking a cigarette, and driving the bus all at the same time. I was thinking, *Wow. This guy's a really talented person.* Then the other thought was, *What if he's not a talented person?* I wonder *what would happen.*

Eventually, we made it to Florida all in one piece. One of the guys I knew pretty well, Paul, had to drive the van that had a trailer full of our equipment on it, and he followed the bus. Paul drove all night on this trip and had some company in the van.

Paul was talking to a girl named Abbi, who had become fond of him during the fall and spring. They would ride on the van together during this spring tour. Then, on top of that, there was another girl who just happened to be named Abby who really liked Paul too. This was fascinating to me, as I saw Paul becoming quite the ladies' man. I was wondering how he did it.

I was in a room with Paul, Phil, and Justin, and that week being full of girl talk, like they were just talking about girls and their situations constantly in the room. While I loved this, I felt a little left out because I never have had a girl interested in me like that, and I didn't really know a whole lot about girls. I just kind of let what they were saying go in one ear and out the other. I knew that if I listened to them talk about the girls over and over again it was going to drive me nuts.

That particular tour was a lot of fun, and I had a chance to see some awesome things. I took my digital camera with me so that I could hopefully capture some of the scenery. We were down South, and there were hills and mountains. The weather we had was perfect.

There were a few nice days in which we would have a half hour or so to enjoy ourselves and relax. One particular place in which there was a huge lake nearby, and I thought it would be a good idea for the group to take a picture together in front of the lake. I was and still am big on getting pictures taken whenever I'm with someone.

I want to have pictures taken when I'm in a group because I want something to remember the people by. Since it isn't very often at all that I get the chance to hang out in a group of people, I wanted to have some kind of memory of the event. I wanted to be able to see the people whom I considered friends many years from then. In fact, I still have several pictures from way back then and try to look through them quite often.

I also really wanted to have pictures of me taken with a couple of girls. I wanted to have a picture taken with me standing in between two girls. I'd often see pictures of guys on Facebook standing in between two girls, and they had their arms around each other, and I thinking that that guy was the coolest guy in the world. Girls wanted to be in a picture with him. I was often going around the group during that spring break and trying to ask a girl if we could take a picture together, and they acted pretty funny about it. I guess I was doing something wrong by asking them to be in a picture with a guy like me.

After trying to get them to take pictures with me and failing, I was able to manage talking Mr. Flanagin into getting a group picture taken in front of the lake. Again, this made for a great background to an incredible picture, and I still have the picture of the 2005-2006 Indiana Wesleyan University wind ensemble hanging in my room.

Toward the end of the week, we were getting ready to do our last few performances. We were on the bus ride in between one church and another. As we were getting closer to the church we were going to perform at that evening, one of the section leaders in the group who played flute lost her eye contact and we couldn't find it.

So everyone on the bus was looking for her eye contact, and I, being the musician I am, was going crazy because not only did she not have an eye contact to see for the rest of the trip, but she didn't have an eye contact to see the music at that night's performance. I'm sure she probably had every piece of music memorized, but still, it's nice to have the ability to see a passage of music sometimes just to make sure you've got it down.

After several people had spent several minutes looking for her contact and everyone had pretty much given up hope and returned to what they were doing, I thinking that I'd try one last place. There were several empty Walmart sacks on the floor of the bus due to the fact that all of us liked to have snacks while on the bus. After looking down and checking through a couple of bags, I eventually came to a bag that had a small contact in it. I had saved the day. The girl could see again, and I was happy. She was happy too. She said thank you, which meant a lot.

On the way home, we stopped to perform at a church in Alabama. There was a valley right next to the place in which I stayed at that evening, and I was amazed at just how wonderful the scenery was. It was great to be able to look out into a valley across the mountains and see for miles.

After returning home from our spring tour that year, we only had about a month and a half of school left. Since I had walked out of the steakhouse the previous year, I would have to try to find some sort of a summer job to keep me busy and try to make a little extra money. I actively began searching for summer employment.

Meanwhile, back at school, we were doing some end-of-the-year things in wind ensemble. The honors brass quintet, along with the saxophone quartet and various other small ensembles throughout the group, had a chamber music series concert right after the spring break. We performed some music that had been composed by the person I was working for, whom I thought was a friend but turned out wasn't. We enjoyed our last official performance together.

# The Rebound

The summer of '06 was probably one of the most interesting summers. In late spring, I decided to apply for a summer job at General Motors. I thought this would be a great opportunity for me to meet some people and also make a lot of good money because they paid college kids to come in as summer help and gave them twenty dollars per hour.

In May, I had to spend one Saturday afternoon in Fort Wayne doing some testing. They would bring all of the college kids in for testing. If you passed the test, then you'd be put into a pool to wait to see how many college kids they needed for the year. I was kind of excited and hoping I would get the job at General Motors. I didn't have anything else going on for the rest of the summer, and I thought that maybe I could even work second shift, which would allow me to sleep in and make even more money.

One afternoon in early June, I got a phone call. It was General Motors, and they were asking me if I would be interested in working at GM for the entire summer. I said of course, as I was pumped to make a lot of money and save it. I thought that maybe I could get myself a nice thing or two at the end of the summer and save the rest to live off of for college.

I had never been so excited in my life—probably because I'd never had the chance to make so much money while I was working. I mean, I was going to college so I could make this kind of money, but to have a chance to just make big money all summer long and bank it was something I would cherish.

In late May, I met a girl on an online dating Web site. She actually went to Indiana Wesleyan University, as I would later find out. At first, she was kind of mean and skeptical; then she started to really get to know me and thought that possibly we could hang out or I could take her shopping or something of that nature. So a couple of weeks later, we would hang out for the first time. We went up to Fort Wayne and did some looking around and had dinner. I had a great time, and I was hoping that she did too. In fact, it seemed as if she did, but then, later on, she kind of blew me off and wanted nothing to do with me.

When I asked her out again, she said that she couldn't because she didn't want to ever get married or have kids. She told me this, but yet she was on a dating Web site. This really confused me. So I just kind of let it go and tried to move on like I always did, thinking that every girl would hate me for the rest of my life. At least I had the job at General Motors lined up and could make some money and get ahead during the summer. At least that was the plan.

So, on June 12, I would report to General Motors for my first day of work. The first two days would be spent training, and on the third day we would go out to our jobs and try to start training on them. Working on the assembly line was one of the coolest things that I've ever had the chance to do. I really enjoyed the pace of things and was able to work on my own and not have to do anything with anyone else, even though it was one huge team. I tended to work better in one-on-one situations.

I was very nervous during the training sessions, though, as they were in the mornings and there would be a lot of people all in the same room and even some big shots from the company. I was always afraid that I wouldn't be good enough to do the job that they wanted me to do. In any job I've had, I've never thought that I would be great at it because I have some sensory issues. The problem is that when they don't know you're having sensory issues, they don't know how to help you. So since I didn't even know I had Asperger's syndrome, there was no way I could get help on any job that I was doing.

We would often get a little break during the meetings because all we were doing was sitting there and watching videos about the job. During these breaks, I noticed that not only were the other people going to the bathroom, but they were also standing around and talking to each other outside of the room. This was interesting to me because I wasn't able to do this like they were. I immediately felt left out and just wanted to go back into the room and get on with the rest of the class.

After spending the two days of training basically locked inside of a classroom, I was ready to get out and start my job. While I was nervous that there was a chance I wouldn't be able to do it and others would make fun of me, I liked being active more than sitting in the classroom. I had to be doing something to keep my mind off of things, and this was the perfect opportunity to do something productive that would keep my mind away from the negative in life.

They ended up drafting me to work in a section of the facility called trim four. This was where much of the detail work was done to the inside of the trucks as they passed down the line. I was put into the position of being the person who had to put the middle console in the truck. Along with this, I was supposed to peel off two stickers and place them inside the truck's glove compartment. I had anywhere from thirty to forty-five seconds to accomplish all of this, which wasn't too bad.

I would, however, have some trouble with putting the stickers in the glove compartment. This was the easiest part of the job, yet I was having trouble with it. I thought I was just stupid. I couldn't get the stickers to peel off very easily, and once I did get them off, they were bent and I had to try to force them to stick to the glove compartment. This is also a job that needs to be neatly done, and having Asperger's usually means that you're not the most neatly organized individual.

Other people couldn't really see me performing my job, so even if I was doing something wrong, they wouldn't get the chance to laugh at me or make fun of me. This I was grateful for. My job was pretty easy, and I quickly caught on. With the exception of the sticker problem, this would be a job that I'd become a master at. I actually got to the point in which I started to look forward to going in to work at around 4:30 p.m. This was something I truly enjoyed. There were a few people that I would get to know on this assembly line. There was a guy in his thirties and a few others who really seemed to like me and think that I was a good worker. I enjoyed their company and appreciated their thoughts.

As my life was going on and I was still not having any success at all in social relationships with talking to girls, I began to brainstorm and try to come up with some reasons. I mainly focused in on the reasons as to why girls didn't like me. I didn't care so much about the guys not liking me, and I don't even to this day, to tell you the truth. I mean, it would be great if they could or would, but it's just that there have been guys in my life who have really taken advantage of me and used me as well as physically abused me. This is something that I just can't get over. There is no trust there for guys.

I thought that maybe my problem with girls was that they thought I was really fat and ugly. I couldn't think of any reason as to why they wouldn't give me a chance to even get to know them. It had to be me or how fat I was. Due to the fact that I thought I was very unappealing to girls in the way of looks, I would go down a very dangerous road for a while.

I decided that I was going to do something about the problem. I wasn't even fat really, as I was only around 166 pounds at the time and I was five feet eleven inches tall. But it wasn't based off of what I thought of myself. The decision to start doing some of these things were based off of what I thought girls thought about me.

I decided to up the number of crunches I was doing per day from a thousand to two thousand. I then started walking for one half hour every day. Eventually, as I would encounter more situations with girls, I would decide that I must not being doing enough or I must not be trying hard enough. I would up my crunches to three thousand every day and walk the half hour and then start running a half mile every day. I couldn't miss a day of this because I had to lose weight so girls would like me.

On top of all of the extra hard working out I was doing, I decided that I had to stop eating. Girls hated me because I was so fat and ugly, so I had to lose some weight. My goal was to get down to 120 pounds so that girls would like me or think I was at least cool to talk to. There was no way I was going to live my life like this anymore by sitting around waiting. I had to make a change and become more attractive to them. Something had to be done.

I started to go through phases in which I would not eat for three or four days at a time. I didn't want any part of having food because I knew food equaled me becoming fatter, and that would mean girls hating me even more than they did. The goal was to lose fifty pounds and not gain. I couldn't lose fifty pounds by eating. After going three or four days in a row without eating, there were times when I became pretty exhausted and a little sick. I thought this was a normal thing, so I didn't really let it concern me too much. There was no way I was going to start eating again. I had this big goal in my head at times that I wasn't going to eat anything ever again until a girl at least would talk to me for five minutes.

I had lived at home, but I wasn't home very often. Therefore, not even my parents noticed that I wasn't eating, and they had no idea why I was running so much or working out so hard. I just don't think the thought that something could have been wrong crossed their minds because they knew nothing about Asperger's and neither did I.

Now that I was working at General Motors and was bringing in a little more money, I quickly joined as many dating Web sites as possible, as I just so desperately wanted to meet a girl. I joined several of them. I was on them for about two or three weeks before I met a girl. Her name was April.

When I met April, I began talking to her at about the same time as my two-week vacation was getting ready to begin. I didn't receive a paid vacation from General Motors, but being summer help, I did get two full weeks off. General Motors shuts down for the first two weeks of July every year. I wasn't sure what I was going to do with myself for these two weeks. I didn't have any social activities planned because I didn't know anyone really and I just wasn't quite getting it. I was on the outside looking in.

Friday, June 29, was our last day to work at General Motors before the two-week shutdown. We got out a couple of hours early that night due to the fact that they have to completely shut the line down before the company officially goes into shutdown mode. So there I was, with two weeks' vacation and nothing to do.

It was on that following Saturday morning that I would meet April. April was from Michigan. She lived about four hours north of Fort Wayne, Indiana. She was twenty-four years old at the time, and she had just gotten out of a relationship. That last part about her getting out of a relationship meant absolutely nothing to me at the time. It wasn't until later, when it was too late, that I'd begin to understand the significance of that.

April and I immediately began talking and getting to know each other. We talked for about three hours on an instant messenger that's associated with a dating Web site, and we seemed to get along, so she gave me her phone number and told me to call her the next day.

I was immediately excited and had high hopes. I was thinking, Could this be the first time I get to hold a girl's hand or kiss a girl? I called her up on that Sunday afternoon and talked with her for a couple of hours. She was getting ready to leave town to go on a trip with her church. She was headed off to Oklahoma for a week, but she wanted to meet up for dinner when she got back to Michigan, so I said okay.

It was on the Sunday evening before she left when we talked on the phone for about ten hours. I had never had any kind of experience with a girl in my life—not even talking on the phone or texting a girl too often. This was a whole new experience for me, so I wasn't sure what to think of it. She talked a lot about her past and how she had just gotten out of a relationship in which she was engaged and the guy cheated on her. I let her vent because I felt like it was the nice thing to do. It was easy to talk to her because all I had to do was listen.

Obviously, I liked having the attention from a girl. After talking on the phone that evening, she left for Oklahoma but continued to call and text me all day long. That Monday, I bet I had around two hundred text messages from her, and we talked on the phone that night. I was still excited and couldn't wait to meet up. She continued texting me and calling me. I would guess that I would get anywhere from three hundred to five hundred texts per day from her and a few phone calls. It was like she really liked me.

I quickly became interested in her since she was willing to pay attention to me. She started e-mailing me these things called e-cards and sending me random text messages and was really great. However, later on in that week, I noticed a red flag, but at the time, with my social unawareness, I had no idea what was going on.

It was about Thursday of that week when I thought it was a little strange and I wasn't sure if I was really ready to be texting a girl five hundred times per day and calling her ten or twenty times. But I thought this was normal. On that Thursday night, I tried to talk to her about it by telling her that I wasn't sure about this and if it was going to work because it just felt kind of weird or awkward. She immediately freaked out and started to beg me to give her more time and another chance. She had been through a lot in the past and just really liked me, she said, so I thought, Okay. I'll try to give her more time and another chance.

The rest of the weekend continued like the first half of the week. She might have tamed her texting down a little bit.

The rest of that weekend was spent relaxing around the house. I continued my running and my working out with three thousand crunches daily. I was walking a half hour and running a half mile as well. I wanted to be sure that I was in perfect shape when I met her.

As the weekend went on, we would continue to text back and forth quite frequently. Again, thanks to my lack of social awareness and due to the fact that I'd never even been on a real date with a girl, I would have no idea of what was supposed to be normal or abnormal behavior for a girl in a dating experience.

Finally, after a long-awaited week and a half, she would arrive back in Michigan. She came into town late Sunday, and we planned on hanging out on Monday. I was so excited about this because it was going to be my first date.

Finally, at the age of twenty-one years old, I was going on my first date. Of course, I had to drive nearly four hours to experience my date, but I was about to break the ice and have my first real date.

I woke up bright and early on Monday, and I began to work out. I did my normal routine, and then I showered, got in my car, and hit the road for Michigan. The ride up to Michigan was a peaceful one, as I listened to music. She did call me and text me a few times during the ride up, updating me of her day, as she had some errands to do in the morning.

Finally, at about 12:00 p.m., I met up with her. I was quickly amazed and impressed with how beautiful she actually was. We then sat and talked for a little bit before getting a picnic lunch prepared and heading to the park to enjoy it. The park was amazing, as it was a picture-perfect day. The temperature was nice, and the sun was shining.

We spent about seven hours together that day before parting ways. Both of us had a good time. We had gone to a picnic in the park, a movie, dinner at Applebee's, and finally to get some ice cream. It had been a very busy but productive day.

I left and headed home feeling the greatest that I have ever felt about myself. I had finally experienced a successful interaction with a woman. I was excited and nervous all at the same time. I didn't know what to think of this whole girlfriend thing or the possibility of having a girlfriend.

It was decided that we would hang out again on that Friday. It would be such a long week for me, as I was even more excited to see her the second time than I was for meeting her the first time. I couldn't wait until Friday. I was so happy. When I arrived home, I immediately wanted to start telling everyone about her.

The rest of that week we spent talking on the phone and texting back and forth. We were starting to get comfortable with one another, and this was making for a good time. Meanwhile, back at home, I was continuing with my workout routine and trying to avoid eating as much as possible. Just because I had finally received some attention from a girl, it didn't mean that I could let up. No. I had to work even harder to make sure that I was in shape and she wouldn't think I was fat or ugly.

On Thursday, I had a wonderful idea pop into my head. I thought that I would make the four-hour drive to Michigan just to drop some flowers on her doorstep and come home without her even knowing that I was there. So I got in my car and drove up to Michigan. I had done some research and learned of a few great flower shops around the area, so as I got there, I immediately started searching for them.

During my entire drive up there, she was texting me constantly from work. She had just started a new job and was at training for it. She was apparently bored at the training, so she started texting me.

I went to the flower shop and was able to find a dozen roses. I picked up the dozen roses and went for her place. I left them at the doorstep to her apartment, and then I got in my car and proceeded to come home. I thought that just by doing something this simple you could really make a girl's day.

About twenty minutes after I'd left her place, I got a phone call from her. She said that she came home and was surprised to find some flowers sitting on her doorstep. She read the card and was calling to thank me.

I arrived back home that evening with enough time left to once again talk with her on the phone and tell her goodnight. Then I proceeded to relax. I watched some television and did a little bit of reading. For the first time in a really long time, I was feeling happy and wanted to keep it this way.

On Friday, I went up to Michigan to see her again and spend most of the day with her. We had another picnic in the park and then watched a movie. I helped her with some baking she was doing, and we just hung out and relaxed. It was a wonderful afternoon, and I was learning to enjoy myself in a woman's company.

Then I would have to go a week or so without seeing her, which wasn't a big deal at the time. It was during this week that I would learn more about her. I learned that she expected me to take her shopping and buy her expensive gifts. Luckily for me, this wasn't going to be a problem since I was working at General Motors. So, as time went on and we continued to talk on the phone and communicate with text messaging, we were drawing closer to meeting again on Saturday, July 22. I was excited, and I had bought her a necklace so she could have some jewelry to wear.

She had also told me she would like some new clothes to wear. So I immediately started looking for clothes I could get her. She had a lot of wants, and she wanted me to get everything for her, so I was bound and determined to make her happy and very willing to do whatever it was going to take.

Unfortunately, my plans of saving all that money that I was making over the summer at General Motors had quickly gone out the door, and I began spending instead of saving. I wanted her to know that I liked her, and apparently it was going to take buying her nice gifts and giving her money to show her that I liked her. It was just like the other girls I had met in my past; I had to buy them stuff or give them money just to get them to think about having coffee with me. At least with this girl it would be a little different in that fact that she did hang out with me more than once.

After a really long week, I was done with work. I went home to get a little bit of sleep on that Friday evening before waking up early the next day to travel to Michigan to spend the day with her. The fact that I was dating someone or at least had more than one date with them was an accomplishment that would make me feel extremely good about myself.

I woke up bright and early the next morning, ready to go. I did my three thousand crunches, walked a half hour, and ran a half mile. I was ready to go and excited to give her all of her gifts that I had gotten for her that week. She said that she really loved getting gifts and that the only way anyone could be her boyfriend was if they kept buying her stuff. I didn't want to screw up or lose her, so I thought, The more I buy, the better chance I will have at her liking me long-term and wanting to date.

I was finally on my way up to Michigan to see April. It had been about eight days since we'd seen each other, so I was kind of excited just to see her again. I had planned a rather eventful day around Michigan that I thought she would enjoy, plus I had all of these gifts with me to get to her. I was particularly excited about the necklace that I was giving her. It was 10-karat gold. I spent about six hundred dollars on it and couldn't wait to show it to her and have her try it on.

When I arrived, I was surprised to see that her mom was still at home. I hadn't exactly planned on meeting anyone's parents as of yet, but she surprised me by introducing me to her mother. Then we sat around a talked for a few minutes, and I was able to give her some of her gifts. I was glad to see the delightful smile on her face when she opened up the necklace.

After she had opened all of her gifts, we decided to go out for lunch. We spent the day going to lunch, doing some shopping at the mall, going to a movie, going out to a nice dinner, and then getting some ice cream. The day was most enjoyable and relaxing. I loved the fact that I had someone to spend time with. I enjoyed it so much that I really hated to say good-bye when the day was over.

That day, it was suggested that we make up a song, a song for us. So we began listening to some music, and we really fell in love with a Stephan Curtis Chapman song called "I Will Be Here." To me, the song said so much about how a guy should treat a woman. I liked the song, and being a music person, it was important to me that the music be of good quality and taste. This song fit all of my requirements, and she liked it, so "I Will Be Here" became our song.

That evening, after departing Michigan, I played the Stephan Curtis Chapman CD all the way home. I was so excited that I even listened to the song over and over. After getting home, I proceeded to upload it to my computer. That's how important it was to me.

Later on, as time would go by, I would even try to memorize all of the words. I thought that it would be a really nice gesture if I were to memorize every line and then call her one day and sing it to her on the phone—or, even better, sing it to her in person sometime. Now, I wasn't anything close to the world's greatest vocalist. I played trombone. Singing was a stretch for me, but I wanted to show her how special she was and just how much I cared about her.

I wanted her to know that I was going to go above and beyond to do great things for her to make her happy and feel appreciated. I even wrote her little cards and sent creative messages. Life was great. I was getting to communicate how I felt with a girl, and she was getting to feel appreciated. What could be any better?

After spending the whole week practicing the song and going shopping to get her some gifts as well as going about my other daily activities, I was ready for yet another weekend. I was ready to go hang out with her once again.

I had bought her a couple more outfits and even a pair of earrings. I was so excited. Part of it was the excitement of just having a girlfriend.

On Saturday, July 29, I left very early in the morning. I was ready to spend the day with her and show her all of these great things. It was another nice day, and there was not even a cloud in sight. I listened to our song all of the way back up to Michigan and thinking that it was a really special song.

I arrived in Michigan, and she was ready and looking very gorgeous. We went about our normal routine. I gave her the gifts, and she loved the earrings. It was wonderful. Great things were happening, and I was feeling like I was on top of the world. I couldn't wait to introduce her to my family.

We again went to lunch, then shopping, then killed some time at her place in the afternoon. We went to a movie and dinner before heading back to her place again. It was an amazing day, and I enjoyed it more than anyone could imagine. Just being accepted by someone was a huge breakthrough for me, and I loved every moment of it.

Once again, after spending the day with her, I was thrilled. I got a hug at the end of the day, and life was going so great. I wanted to cherish every moment of this, and I took as many pictures as we possibly could. I can't tell you how meaningful it is to actually have a positive social experience with someone, even if it is a very brief one.

The following week continued about like the other weeks had. She kept calling and texting, wanting to talk. I kept talking to her and listening to what she had to say. Toward the end of the week, she had received phone calls for a couple of teaching interviews. She had a bachelor's in elementary education. She finally had a couple of interviews and was excited about that. On a particular Friday afternoon, August 4, she had one of her interviews, and I told her to let me know how it went as soon as it was over. Well, she happened to call as I was walking into work, and I was going through a small area in which I had no service. She left me a frantic voice message saying that I was supposed to answer the phone when she called and kind of made me feel bad. I thought she was upset that I didn't answer, but I didn't answer because it never rang, as I had no service in that tunnel.

I was so excited for her having the interview and then having yet another interview lined up on Monday morning that I decided to do something a little extra special. I decided I would drive up there right after I got off of work and surprise her. This was planned out perfectly on my part. At least I thought so at the time. I thought I would leave work, go home and shower, and take all of the gifts that I had gotten for her that week and hit the road for Michigan at around 4:00 in the morning on Saturday, August 5, so I did. My goal was to arrive at around 8:00 a.m. or 9:00 a.m. and surprise her in some way.

During the drive up there, I thought that it might be cool to get her some flowers. I stopped at Walmart to buy some flowers, as that would be the only place that would be open at that early an hour. I had a bunch of daisies, and then I thought I would stop at McDonald's and get her favorite breakfast meal and then take the flowers and the McDonald's breakfast and leave them at her doorstep. I thought I would wait until she woke up and send her a text telling her she better look outside. I thought that it was going to work out perfectly. I loved it.

When April awoke that morning, she began texting me, and I explained to her that I thought she should go look out of her front door. So she did, and what she found were several daisies spread out surrounding a sack of McDonald's food. It seemed as if her first thought was, What is this? or Why did you do this? or even, This is weird. I didn't understand the delay in her response, but after several minutes, she eventually replied with a, "Thank you. That was really sweet."

I thought that this was sort of strange, but I attributed it to the fact that she was still tired from just waking up. After she got ready and I got over to her place, everything was good. We shared some food and talked, and then we decided to go about our day. We decided to just take the day as it came to us, without really planning too much. We ended up doing a lot of the same things, such as lunch, shopping, dinner, and a movie. We also managed to stop at a store in the mall for her to get a manicure.

That evening, back at her place, things seemed a little strange to me. She just wasn't very talkative like she usually was. I was exhausted because I hadn't slept all night, so I decided to head home as early as possible. I left at around eight that night because I still had a four-hour drive ahead of me. That night, while driving home, I was doing some more listening to our song. I loved the song, and I really liked this girl. I was so exhausted while driving home, though, that it was hard to stay awake. I was nearly falling asleep while driving home a few times. It was a pretty adventurous drive.

April was someone that I liked and wanted to get to know some more. Little did I know that Saturday, August 5, would be the last time I would ever see her.

It wasn't until later the next day that things started to happen. She told me that she was no longer interested in me and wasn't sure exactly what she had wanted. She wasn't sure what she wanted in the first place. I had already ordered some more flowers that were going to be delivered to her apartment on that Monday. I wouldn't get a chance to cancel them because of the fact that I was finding all of this out on a Sunday night. I was devastated, and I couldn't understand what I'd done wrong. I wanted to know what happened, but she just said she was no longer interested.

Knowing what I now know today about relationships and girls, I now realize that I missed so many red flags and signs about getting involved with someone of this nature. April was twenty-four years old, and she had been dating a guy for about two or three years. In June of 2006, April found out that this guy had basically lied to her about his entire life and existence and about who he was. She was completely devastated and ended the engagement.

That all happened in June, and I met her on June 30. I knew very well of all of this. She told me everything. In fact, that was one of the reasons why she said she had liked me so much, because I was a sensitive guy who was very willing to listen. She had stated that she'd never had a guy let her complain about a previous relationship for so long.

When we first met and she started texting me and calling me constantly, she was quickly ready to move on and get some attention from another guy. It was during this first week that something else happened that should have been a red flag. I'm sure that it would have been a red flag to any neurotypical individual. Before we even met each other in person after talking on the phone for a little under a week, the words "I love you" came out of her mouth. Wow. I'd never heard such amazing words from a woman.

This could have been tragic, telling a neurotypical individual that she loved him before meeting him, although he most likely would have told her to take a hike because he would have known what was going on. Unfortunately, as someone with Asperger's, I'd have no idea what was going on. I thought that this was how dating worked and this was how girls operated. I was just along for the ride and enjoying it.

I now know that as soon as she said the words "I love you" before ever meeting me in person, I should have been running away myself, and running fast. Unfortunately, I was unaware of this.

I had a cousin who was trying to explain this concept to me, which I couldn't understand. I was telling him what had happened. I shared with him every little detail of the month or so that I had known her. My cousin first introduced the term rebound to me. I had no idea what a rebound was. I mean, to me, a rebound was when someone shot the basketball and missed and someone grabbed the ball as it came off of the rim. I couldn't get a grasp as to what the word rebound meant when dealing with dating and women.

My cousin eventually proceeded to explain to me and try to get me to understand that April had been hurt right before I met her by another guy and that she was doing what's called a rebound. I had no idea, and I still don't understand why someone would do this.

What happened after April had pretty much picked me up, chewed me up, and then spit me out, I compared to an aftershock of a magnitude 7.0 earthquake. I was immediately devastated and distraught, and I didn't even know where to begin. I needed help immediately. I needed someone to talk to, as I just couldn't deal with all of the pain.

My body started shutting down. I lost the desire to eat again and became weak. I didn't sleep well at night, but once I did get to sleep, I didn't want to get out of bed the next morning. Any motivation that I had in my life was gone. I needed to pick up the pieces and move on so desperately, but I had no idea how to or where to start. I was a lost young man searching for answers once again. I had thought I had finally solved one of my problems of figuring out how to get a girl to like me, but as I was finding out, I didn't solve it at all.

That following Monday, I had to go back to work at General Motors. I had a hard time with this, as I was so depressed that I was unmotivated to do anything at all, let alone go spend eight hours a day at a place where several people would be and work all at the same time. I needed to be alone, locked in my room, where I could cry and talk to my best make-believe friends in the world. Cameron Diaz and Lisa Winter were two of my make-believe friends with whom I would try to connect while I was locking myself in my room.

Yes, even at the age of twenty-one, I was secluding myself in my room and turning on the television set to try to talk to or at least listen to Cameron Diaz talk and watch her act, as well as watching Lisa Winter play basketball.

I quickly redeveloped the horrible habit of secluding myself from the rest of the world just because I felt so hurt and rejected. The one time in my life in which I really thought that someone was giving me a break or the benefit of the doubt and going to actually get to know me, it ended up all being a big joke.

Going to work at General Motors became increasingly difficult. I just didn't want to be there. I was so depressed. I don't think I had ever realized quite how serious my situation was at the time.

As time went on, I didn't get any better. In fact, I would get worse and become more depressed. I was ready to give up on trying for good. I had completely quit eating because I thought I had to be fat and ugly. Why else would she just all of a sudden up and say, "You're too nice for me. This isn't working out"? I knew that she hated me and that I was worthless. This would be the beginning of my fall.

The following is a journal entry that I wrote about four days after April said that I was too nice for her and we were done. This was written on August 10, 2006.

> I don't understand what happened. What did I do wrong this time? I thought that things were going perfect. I did whatever she wanted me to whenever she wanted without complaining. I don't get what happened. Why do I feel so hurt right now on the inside?
>
> I don't understand why girls hate me. I know that I'm pretty fat and stupid and ugly, but I just don't know why they want to hurt me and be so mean to me. What did I do wrong? I've never hurt them or done anything to them. Why do they hate me? Please, please someone tell me what I did wrong. I want to fix it. I just want to be the perfect guy for a girl to like.
>
> I don't understand why April wouldn't keep getting to know me and give me a chance. She really hurt me. What did I do wrong? I am going to go jump in a cave and never come out. It seems like it would be so much safer in there. The only people that pay attention to me are my imaginary friends that I've created. They make me feel good and don't judge me or anything like that at all. I wish that others could be more like them and treat me nice.
>
> I want to be like everyone else. I just don't understand what it is that people hate about me. Can you fix it please? Please give me the answers so I can go fix it and be the perfectly cool person everyone wants to hang out with. I want to be someone else because being Travis isn't working for me. Lisa and Cameron are the only two people in my life that treat me nice and give me a chance. They're on television, though, and I wish so much that they could be real. Those are the type of people that I want to have around me because they don't talk about me or make fun of me or steal things from me. They are just cool people with a great personality. I wish more than anything that I could meet them. Please someone take me there and let me meet them. Just let the pain go away. I'm tired of it hurting and want it to

> leave me. Leave me far alone and never come back. Please go away.
>
> I want life to go on, but you won't leave me be. Please, pain, go away and never come back. Why do you stay here with me? I want real friends with real feelings, and there are none like that here. They are in Hollywood and other various places, and I cannot get to them. Please, pain, go away and don't ever come back. I need hope, happiness, and peace, so why are you still here?
>
> I don't know what to do next, as I feel I'm about done trying and out of time. Please give me hope and courage to keep on fighting. Where has the happiness gone? It's no longer here. Please come back and never go away. Pain, go away; happiness, come back and let's never lose each other again. I want a new life, with real friends, and I want to be cool and want everyone to like me and be my friend. Please give me that. If not I don't know if I will stay.

I wanted to move on with my life and maybe even start a new life. I hadn't ever felt pain like this. As the weeks went on and it became time to go back to school at Indiana Wesleyan, I was starting to dread going to work more and more. As they found out that I was going to be quitting and going back to school instead of staying there to work full time, they started to put me in different areas and tried to make me do jobs I didn't know how to do. I couldn't handle this with all of the emotional stress I was going through. I needed a break and I needed out. It was on the last Friday in August that I was put on a job that I really didn't know how to do, and I couldn't figure it out. As time went on, I started to get made fun of and teased, and I couldn't take it. During one of our breaks, I just kept right on walking out the door and never came back. I was done, and I couldn't take any more pain from people. I needed to be alone.

I spent the last week before school started at home, pretty much keeping myself locked up in my room, with the exception of going out to walk and run. I didn't want to eat family meals, and I didn't really have the desire to interact with anyone after all of the pain that I'd just been through. For a while that summer, I had been really looking forward to going back to school, but after this event happened, it was kind of like, Why bother? I was getting sick and tired of the same old story: I try to make a friend or girlfriend, and then I fail miserably, only to have my heart ripped out, cut into pieces, and then sewed back in.

I was tired of feeling depressed and hopeless. I was tired and hurt as well as stressed out, and here came another semester in school in which I was going to be taking harder classes than I had to the year before.

# Lost

I quickly realized that it was time for me to start thinking about going back to school. This was not something I was looking forward to after experiencing what I had over the summer, but I knew it was a must, and I certainly had to find something to keep myself busy and occupy my mind.

I was glad to be back in Marion and on campus.

I went over to visit campus about three days early just to see some familiar faces. At that point, I was really struggling and feeling pretty worthless and miserable. Just to find someone to talk to would provide a huge relief for me. At that point in time, it didn't matter what we talked about so much. It was just the fact that someone was there to listen.

As it became time for me to start classes on the Tuesday after Labor Day, I was still a mess. I was able to be a little bit hopeful of the fact that maybe something positive would come out of it, and I would be able to talk to someone about it and have them understand me and possibly even want to be my friend. For the longest time in my life, I was able to hold on to just the slightest glimpse of hope. However, as time went on that semester, any hope that I had slowly diminished.

After trying to get everything in order and get my classes situated and figuring out what day I had what and when I was going to study, I was able to calm down a little as far as anxiety, but the depression just wasn't going away. I didn't know what to do. I had been on this path for about four or five weeks, and the pain wasn't getting much better. It was magnifying at times. I couldn't even function sometimes due to the intensity of the emotional pain. It was interfering with my abilities to do my studies as well as anything else I wanted to do. The depression that was sinking in due to being rejected so much was unreal, and it was quickly destroying my life.

As the semester began, I had many obligations. The first, of course, was to my studies. Then I also had the obligation of playing in as many ensembles as I could so I could help out the music department and enjoy my life. Then there was also the fact that I needed some kind of income. I needed to have money to pay some bills as well as provide for gas to get back and forth to school. No gas, no school. I had to get some sort of a job, and it didn't have to be a high-paying job, but it had to be a job that I could do. And I knew that doing any kind of a job that was going to require a significant amount of concentration probably wouldn't be a good idea for me. I had to find something simple, something I could do with ease and that I was good at.

Eventually, after quite a bit of searching, I was able to find a nice little job in the music department on campus. It was actually a job that I received through the school.

This would prove to be the perfect job for me at this time. I obviously had very poor social skills, so whenever I was forced to work with other people, my working skills suffered due to my poor social skills. This was a job in which I would be allowed to conduct my job alone, without anyone else being around. I was doing mostly work with computers or filing papers. This was something that I could handle, even with all of the stress and pressure I was under.

The amazing job that I had secured proved to be a lot harder for me than I originally thought it would. I thought that because there would be no one else around to tease me or bully me that it would make working a lot less stressful and more enjoyable. But, to my disbelief, it didn't really help a whole lot. It actually created a lot more anxiety and caused me to become quite depressed. When I was sitting inside working all alone on some things, I was really anxious because I was sitting inside, working, while there were thousands of other students running around the university, hanging out with each other. These other students were out playing basketball and volleyball, going to lunch or dinner with each other, and getting coffee at Mcconn, which was the on-campus coffee shop. But the point here is that these other students were out running around everywhere and hanging out with one another and it was something that I couldn't do and wanted to so badly. This caused me to think about it a lot while I was trying to work, and I'd become more and more anxious and less able to concentrate on the important tasks at hand.

It was so bad that I would just stress out and shut down. I had to get up and walk around every ten minutes or so, as I just couldn't sit still. I had to go outside and see what the other students were doing and see if I could become involved in whatever activity they had going on at the time. I really wanted to be included, and I never really was. I just couldn't handle it anymore. Going to school and work was so stressful, mostly due to the amount of anxiety and depression that was being caused by my poor social skills.

As time went on, I was beginning to realize more and more that something was wrong with me. That in itself would continue to depress me even more. I was searching for answers and had no idea where to start. I couldn't figure it out. I was lost in a world in which I didn't even exist.

# Reaching Out

September of 2006 was finally here. I had been struggling with a lot of emotional pain for about a month, but I was finally going to get a chance to go back to school and get away from the pain. Within the first couple of days, I was able to make myself busy with preparing audition material for ensembles as well as trying to find and get used to all of my new classes.

At the beginning of the school year, there was a girl who played the piano who was a freshman. She was extremely beautiful and had all of the markings of an amazing musician with lots of talent. I knew that she was very good at piano as well as very smart in all academic areas. She was an amazing and wonderful young woman. I wanted to get to know her so bad, so I tried.

It was at a music major picnic/gathering at the end of the first week of school that I would try to get to know her. I asked her what she was doing that weekend, and when she said she didn't know or hadn't planned anything yet, I asked her if we could go on a date. She looked at me like I had just ruined her day or shocked her to death, and then she was telling other people that I had asked her on date. It seemed like before I knew it I had a crowd of people laughing at me and pointing. I was definitely the joke of the evening, and

I didn't understand why. I didn't realize what I had done wrong, and then they just all started making fun of me.

That evening I immediately took off and started to drive home. I cried all the way home. Once I got home, I was going to be secluding myself in my bedroom and trying to connect with my friends in the make-believe world yet again. They seemed to always be there for me when I needed them to be. Thanks, Cameron and Lisa. They probably helped save my life at times when I wanted to kill myself when I was just going through such a hard time and couldn't handle any more pain. I was able to find some relief in watching them on television and connecting with them.

During the entire fall semester, I struggled with many things, including academics. It seems kind of odd, but when one little thing is off in your body, it can have a huge impact on your entire life. Just the fact that you're depressed can impact all of your daily interactions. My advice to anyone now is if you're feeling the slightest bit of depression, make sure you talk to someone about it. If you bottle it all in, it's only going to get worse, magnify, and intensify until it forces you to explode. So to anyone who might be on the autism spectrum out there, please talk to people when you're feeling down on yourself.

As we got into the middle of October, I would begin crying nearly every day. No one knew what was wrong with me, as they all (including my family) just thought I was crazy. I was crying when I woke up, crying in the shower, crying on the drive to and from school, and then crying some more at night when I came home. I couldn't shake the crying, and I was starting to wonder why I was alive.

As time went on, classes became increasingly difficult, and I didn't really have the desire to socialize. I started to lose some desire to even make an attempt at social situations. I had lost any confidence that I had, which was already very low. I just couldn't shake all of the negative thoughts and feelings, and I was seeking help in any way that I could get it.

During this same time period, the Indiana Wesleyan University wind ensemble was slated to go on a couple of fall tours. I was having a really difficult time, and my mother was scared that I was going to hurt myself and asked that the band director keep an eye on me as we were touring. I just wasn't right. I had been hurting for too long, and it was starting to have permanent effects on me.

When we were on the first tour of the year, I just sat on the bus alone and stared out the window. I'd developed a blank stare, and I didn't want to really look at anyone. I felt that if I looked at them I was going to get hurt emotionally. I thought that I wasn't good enough for anyone anymore and that the only reason I was even there was because they thought I could play trombone pretty well.

I was just a mess on the trip, and people knew it. I sat in the group during the Sunday morning rehearsal and then again when we were at church, and tears were just running down my face. I knew I had a problem, but at that time, I still hadn't heard about Asperger's syndrome. I was sad and lonely, but no one knew why.

After a few weeks of moping around, not wanting to get out of bed, crying constantly, not wanting to eat, and not being able to concentrate on my academics at all, I decided that I needed help. I quickly began searching for ways in which I could get the help I needed. Luckily for me, there was a counseling center on Indiana Wesleyan University's campus. As soon as I found that out, I quickly began researching how to get in contact with them and become a part of their program. I wanted counseling. I was able to sign up with Mr. Herr, and we immediately began talking about what I was going through. I kept struggling, and I didn't know why. I told him about not being able to talk to anyone really, told him I just felt out of place, and he was as puzzled as I was.

I went in to see the counselor thinking he was going to be the person I had been waiting for my entire life. I was thinking that I'd go in there for an hour and come out with all of the answers to my problems. I thought he was going to be like a Superman who could fix any problem that I was having. All I had to do was open up to him and tell him what was going on, and surely this man would have answers, right?

Well, unfortunately, it just doesn't quite work like that. Counselors don't just have that superhuman power that we all want and desire. With anything in life that involves a problem, there is a root to the problem that we have to find. This can take some time, and it certainly takes more than one counseling session.

The counseling I received from the Altersgate Center at Indiana Wesleyan University wasn't really that beneficial for me at this time. It did help just to have someone listen to what I had to say, but at this point, what I was telling them was that I was depressed and everyone hated me. I'm sure that everyone involved in my life just thought that I was blowing this entire problem way out of proportion.

After going to a few counseling sessions on campus, I felt a little better for a brief period of time. I was able to push myself to get through the rest of the fall semester. It wasn't easy, and I had to withdraw from one class because I wasn't able to focus on balancing all four of my classes along with everything else that was going on. I wasn't happy at Indiana Wesleyan, and I thought it was because everyone hated me and that if I went somewhere else to get away, then I might have a chance at developing real friendships with real people.

I began looking to make another change in my life. I was still convinced that it was something to do with the environment that I was in. I had convinced myself that all of the pain that I was experiencing was because of where I was going to school, and if I could just get away and attend a different university, then maybe the pain would go away, maybe I'd be more accepted. I was searching for answers.

When I was thinking about other places that I could go to college, I immediately thought about Indiana Purdue University, Fort Wayne. IPFW is a great school, and it was fairly close to home, which would again be convenient because I would have to commute back and forth yet again. In the middle of December, I decided that I was going to try IPFW.

I was going to take music education classes at IPFW. I was also going to double major in trombone performance. I was really looking forward to it, as I was going to be studying with a teacher whom I studied trombone with in high school. I was excited for the opportunity to make new friends.

Classes started out fairly easy. I loved music. It was like a special interest for me. I didn't have any trouble. My hardest class was a geology class. If I didn't like something, I hated learning about it, and it bored me to death. Classes were fine, but once again I wasn't making friends in them. Sure, I could go to school and could get good grades and play the trombone pretty well. But what did all that mean? It meant nothing without having friends and being allowed to connect with other people. I would make it through that semester with all A's and B's. But that didn't matter to me. That was the last semester of college I've actually completed, spring semester 2007.

I met a fellow trombone player named Tom. Tom was kind of a cocky kid, and he was pretty good at trombone. I had wanted to live on my own but wanted to live with someone so I could have more of a social life. I thought that living with someone who was somewhat popular would help me to make friends. So one day Tom and I were just talking, and it ended up that we both wanted to move out. However, he couldn't afford to pay me anything until August. This was in April. We agreed to move in during the month of May and I'd just pay the full rent until he could start splitting it in August. This was the only way that he'd move in with me, so I had no choice but to say yes.

I didn't really know him, just knew that he was a trombonist and was pretty cool. I hadn't really developed any kind of a friendship with him and hadn't hung out with him outside of school. As soon as we moved in together, all chaos broke loose. He started having big parties every night. He would invite people over, and they'd be really loud and drink a bunch of beer. Meanwhile, I just managed to lock myself in my room and try to ignore everything that was going on. It was really frustrating because at the time I was paying all of the rent and just wanted a little peace and quiet every now and then. Yes, I wanted that social life, but this wasn't the type of lifestyle that I was after.

I wanted friends; I didn't want a bunch of people over in my apartment partying and trashing the place. I was hoping that he would calm down, but things got worse. One day when I came home from work, I found him in my room using my computer. It turned out he was using my AIM and talking to Kecia, a girl I'd met on Facebook. We'd developed an online friendship. But he was talking to her pretending to be me. He was telling her that I thought they should meet up and hang out because he'd be good for her. He was making all of this stuff up and saying that I was trying to fix them up.

I have to work really hard to get people to like me as it is. Now here he was trying to tell her something that wasn't true. I immediately texted her to tell her it wasn't me, hoping that she'd understand and not hate me. Luckily she did, and she told him off and wasn't upset with me because I'd told her what had happened.

There were times while at the school in Fort Wayne that I was taken advantage of by people who didn't even realize they were taking advantage of me. People would sometimes invite me to hang out and then vanish and not be where they were supposed to meet me at. There were a few instances in which I found out that they were doing this on purpose. I tried to just let things like that go because I was so used to it, but there was one evening in April of 2007 that really bothered me.

I had met this girl on Facebook who went to school at the same place I did. After talking for a couple of weeks, she told me to come over to her place, so I made the half-hour drive. When I got there to hang out with her, the place she said to go wasn't the right place. I called her, and she was on the phone saying, "Well, go knock at this door and go knock at that door." Basically, I played a game of tag with knocking on every door I could. I kept holding out positive beliefs that the next door I knocked on, the girl I had been talking to was going to answer. That was never the case.

The rest of this semester at the university in Fort Wayne was spent trying to fit in. I was trying to be like everyone else no matter what it took. My OCD characteristics took over, though. I started becoming more obsessed with working out and walked and ran farther and farther each day.

By the end of the semester, I was at another low point and fighting to stay alive. I had been rejected so much that I believed I was nothing but a stupid fool. I knew deep down that I was a good person, but somehow and someway no one else could find any good in me. I had no idea why people hated me. It seemed I could do nothing right. The harder I tried, the worse things became. Any attempt to show interest in a woman was quickly denied, and I was ridiculed and made fun of. I believed that me looking at a girl was going to kill her. I went about my days trying to avoid girls so I couldn't hurt them. I felt ashamed of myself for liking another person. I started to think that being born onto this earth was a huge mistake. I believed I wasn't good enough for anyone and quickly withdrew from society. I couldn't bear to go to classes or work or anywhere because I just knew that no matter where I went or what I did I was going to hurt someone just by being in the same room as they were. I became very suicidal. I can't say that I was ever actually going to do it, but I do know that the thought of I wish I wasn't here or I wish I was dead went through my head constantly during these days. I couldn't take too much more pain.

Late in the semester, I met a girl who would be a huge influence in my life. Her name was Kristen. Kristen was a nineteen-year-old college student who had a three-year-old child. She would be the first girl to really try to help me out instead of make fun of me.

I also met Kristen on Facebook, as this had become the way for me to meet people since I would always get rejected in person. I was afraid to try to talk to anyone in person. Kristen ended up giving me her number and meeting up with me. I was so excited. I bought her some flowers and took her to a Comets hockey game. She seemed to enjoy it a lot. We even held hands at the hockey game. Throughout the course of the next week or two, I tried to get to know her. The positive attention I was getting from her made me want even more, so I kept calling and texting her.

Eventually, she didn't respond and asked me to leave her alone too. I thought, Oh no. I messed up again. After allowing her to cool off for a couple of weeks, though, she finally answered a text and agreed to hang out with me again.

We met up at nine o'clock at night and went to Steak & Shake. Then she came over to my place and we watched a movie. She took some pictures with me and even smiled. It was amazing. She had on this cute hat, and I pulled it off of her head. I would say that if there was ever a time that I felt comfortable with someone that it was that night with her. After I pulled it off, she made a confession to me. She told me that what I did was really cute and that it would have been a good time for a first kiss. She knew I didn't have any experience in dealing with girls, so she was trying to help. I asked her if I could take her hat and try it again, but she said no, that the moment was gone.

Another week went by, and then we went to a concert and watched a band. I got to dance with her a little, but this would be the last time that I ever saw her in person.

I had also met another girl online, and we are still friends. Kecia was reluctant to meet me in person but was okay talking online and texting. To this day, we have only hung out three times in person. We text a lot and talk on Facebook periodically. She has also been a huge inspiration for trying to get through all of this.

It started out with me trying to get her to go out on a date with me. I wanted a girlfriend. It was something I'd seen other guys gain with ease, but I'd never had a girl want to get to know me or talk to me. I was so scared to talk to anyone in person, so I started adding random people, mainly random girls, to my Facebook friends to try to talk to them and ask them to hang out with me. At first, of course, she thought I was a major creep. She was very resistant in the getting-to-know-you process. Basically, she was cool talking to me online, but she didn't want to meet me in person. She became a great friend online for me. She gave me some amazing advice and helped me through some tough times. She was there to help me through situations with other people like Kristen.

One night in late April I tried to have a party. I lived in an apartment by myself and wanted to have a bunch of people over. I invited about two hundred people on Facebook. I spent about $100 and bought a bunch of food and soda. The party was supposed to start at seven. I waited anxiously for people to arrive. Kecia was actually going to come and meet me that night. She gave me her number and texted me. This was a good feeling for me because I had now moved from online conversation to texting. I was making progress in a friendship. As the clock struck eight, eight thirty, and then nine, the reality that no one was going to show up to my party was starting to sink in for me. I was sitting in my apartment on my couch crying, wondering why no one had come. Again, thoughts that people hated me and that I was just a fat, ugly, worthless piece of crap went through my head.

Kecia ended up texting me to see what was going on and if anyone was at the party. She was only going to come if someone else was there. Sadly, I had to tell her that no one had come. I thought that my chances of meeting her were over. But she then invited me out to Applebee's to meet up with her and her guy friends. We had a good time talking, and it was cool for me to be around people. But I was so nervous and awkward. I wanted to be cool like other people, like the guys she was with.

Kecia and I talked online quite a bit. I loved hearing stories about her life. She had a lot going on. She joked that boys she liked were trolls, and I just thought it was funny. It wasn't funny that they were mean to her, but it just felt good to be able to comfort someone else and talk to them about stuff. Kecia helped me a lot during the spring of 2007.

It was in late May that I sold my trombone for $400. This was a professional trombone that was worth well over $2,500 that I just gave away for $400 because I thought that was the reason why no one liked me. Once again, that feeling of being a band geek was stuck into my head. I had to change majors and become a business major because that was what the cool kids were doing.

After selling my trombone, I became even more depressed. This showed me that music was a way of therapy for me. When I had my trombone, I was able to get away and escape into a make-believe world and play music. I couldn't get hurt there. Without that, there would be no escaping, and there were many chances to get hurt.

# Meltdown

I continued getting to know Kristen. However, my intensity level would eventually push her over the edge. I wanted to talk every day. I wanted to text every day, and I wanted her to come hang out with me every day. I didn't understand why there had to be a week or two in between hangouts. This is common for someone with Asperger's, as we've never had friendships before and aren't sure how they develop. For example, I just met someone else who is twenty-four who has Asperger's syndrome. I gave him my number and told him he could text me. The texting went like this:

Him: Hey, what's up?

Me: Not much, you?

Him: Nothing. Would you be my friend?

Me: Yes.

For people with Asperger's, that's how it works. There are no shields to get through and no boundaries to cross. It's that simple. However, when making friends with someone who is neurotypical, there are plenty of rules to follow and plenty of boundaries to cross. Unfortunately, to the person on the autism spectrum these rules and boundaries are invisible.

One night in June, I ended up trying to get a hold of Kristen. I had texted her; I had called her. At this time I wasn't even working due to all of the depression I'd been through. I just couldn't focus on anything other than making friends and socializing. I even had my phone turned off at one point, so there was a time when I'd walk a mile or two just to get to a pay phone to try to call her.

One night when I really needed someone to talk to, I called her. No answer. Called again. Still no answer. To the normal person this means something, but to me and to most on the autism spectrum, this means try harder. So I called again and again. Finally, after thirty times, she answered. She wasn't happy, and as I look at it today, now I know and understand why. She basically told me to "f" off and never talk to her again. That sent me into a meltdown and led to me being very suicidal and depressed. I didn't understand how my want, need, or desire to have a really good friend could be hurting someone so much. Today I look back and am sorry that I put her through all of that. I'm also sorry that I had no idea what was going on and put myself through all that. I wish I could have had the diagnosis of Asperger's syndrome at that point. It would have helped me handle that situation.

The suicide attempt itself was spontaneous. I felt as if I was hurting Kristen by being here in this world and liking her. So I knew that I couldn't keep hurting her and had to try to step away. Most people would be capable of walking away from the situation completely, but with having Asperger's, it's so difficult to make yourself walk away from someone who was nice to you. It's hard because you could spend another ten years trying to find someone else to be nice to you like she was to me.

On June 17, 2007, I had had enough and couldn't take it anymore. I was communicating with Kristen and Kecia and letting them know I was sad and wanted to kill myself. I had set up a place to hang myself on my balcony. I'm not sure if I would have actually gone through with it or not, but I was very unstable at the time. Luckily, the two of them got together and called someone, and they got there just in time. I spent the next week trying to recover from that situation. I was in a behavioral unit at a local hospital.

During the hospital visit, I spent most of my time lying around doing nothing. The hospital is nothing but a waste of taxpayers' money for someone who has Asperger's syndrome and is suicidal. If it had any effect on me at all, it made me more suicidal and depressed. You have to spend the night locked in there. It's so stupid. I never understood why you can't just go home and sleep in your own bed. The other frustrating part about this whole situation is I feel like they are just trying to remove a person who is suicidal and depressed from society. In my perception, it seems as if they want to punish someone for being depressed, and I don't quite understand this concept of putting someone in a behavioral unit for depression or suicidal thoughts.

You may spend a total of one hour per day actually getting help or talking to someone. I found that I'd see the psychologist for about ten to fifteen minutes to talk about my feelings, and then I might see a psychiatrist for two or three minutes so he could give me the medicine he thought I needed. That psychiatrist didn't know me from Tom. To him I was just a computer program that he was trying to fix and prescribe medicine for, which is often why meds can backfire and don't work for people with Asperger's syndrome. The problem I have with medicine and Asperger's is that there is nothing medically wrong with me. To this day there is no medicine that automatically makes someone who is socially awkward less socially awkward. Asperger's is different in every person. In my opinion, the only medication that is needed for Asperger's syndrome is education and awareness. At this time I was being treated mainly for bipolar disorder and/or depression, which is common for someone who has Asperger's syndrome to get diagnosed with at first.

I was allowed to have visitors for one hour per evening. My parents and some other family members came every night. But to my disappointment, not one single person my age would ever come to visit me in one of these hospitals. It's not that I don't like family because I love them. But when you're in your twenties you want and need connection from peers. You so desperately want to have friends your age. I think that most people my age were afraid of visiting me because they thought I was crazy, creepy, weird, psycho, stupid, and pathetic. I also believe just the thought of visiting someone in a behavioral unit of a hospital like that is scary for most people. There was not one single thing that helped me in these hospital visits, and I truly believe that I was hurt more by the hospital visits than helped.

During that week where I was supposed to be receiving help and encouragement, I met a kid who was in there for drug abuse. I told him my story, and he said that it was crazy and he was going to show me how to be cool and not get taken advantage of. So he gave me his number and told me to call him when I got out of the hospital. I thought it was cool and maybe I was making a real friend.

When I got home, I was recovering and trying to become happy again when I gave him a call. He said to meet him somewhere and that he was going to introduce me to a really hot girl. When I got there, he said he needed to do some shopping but had forgotten his wallet at home and told me if I paid for his stuff he'd pay me back when we got to his place, so I did—over $300 worth of new shoes, new clothes, and some other stuff.

Then he said he was going to run inside and grab some stuff and he'd be back and we'd go meet the girls. He had me park in an alley because he said he didn't want anyone to see we were there. He walked away. After an hour and a half, he wasn't back. After two hours, I finally gave up and left feeling used and abused again.

The next few weeks were spent trying to regroup and feeling depressed once again. My roommate was in and out of town, so the apartment was pretty peaceful. He came back around the fourth of July. I just couldn't stand being hurt anymore, and on the third of July, I had another suicide attempt.

I got in the car thinking I was going to run away and die somewhere. I ended up in Fond Du Lac, Wisconsin. When you are so misunderstood, you have no one to go to and/or nowhere to go. I thought that I was pretty worthless and no one wanted me here and thought possibly someone in Wisconsin or somewhere else might want me. If they didn't, then I'd just kill myself there. I left with only $75 in hand and was just going to go live out my last days. I thought I'd just run out of money and then starve myself until I was dead. No one liked me. Everywhere I went, everywhere I turned, I was just the weird, psycho, or creepy guy that wanted to be friends with people. No one understood me and wanted to be my friend. So after this trip, I ended up in a hospital again.

After this hospital stay, I moved back in with my parents for three weeks. At this point my parents were at a loss. They were beyond frustrated. They didn't know how to help me and couldn't afford to keep helping me. They were sad, scared, and concerned but didn't know what to do for me. They tried to help as much as they could. People kept saying that I had to get through school and I had to work. But none of this was going well for me because of all of the rejection and depression. People couldn't understand that I needed to have normal friendships and relationships with people before I could even begin to concentrate on anything else.

By the first of August, I had met yet another guy who said he would befriend me and move in with me. He told me if I paid for an apartment he'd pay me, so I believed him and moved in. This guy never ended up paying me a dime and, in fact, ended up in jail. I got stuck paying for the entire apartment. I was only there two days and had to pay $3000 just to get out of a lease. Once again, I was lost and confused and had no idea what to try or do next.

By the time the middle of August rolled around and it was time to go back to school, I was still in a lot of emotional pain and didn't want to go back to Fort Wayne to go to school. So I switched schools and went back to Indiana Wesleyan for the fall semester of 2007. I was going to live on campus this time and have roommates who were Christians. I thought that this was the cure. This was the solution for all of my problems. Even though I'd been there before, I thought that it would be different this time. Just maybe after escaping and getting away for a semester and the summer, things would automatically be better. There would be new students there who might appreciate me and like me for who I was. Maybe some of the students who didn't like me before would change their minds and like me now. All of this was, of course, a dream, a dream that I'd made up in my head.

As the school year started, things were calm and I was having fun. No one was being mean to me yet because they didn't really know me yet. During the early fall, the group of guys from the unit I lived on would go play volleyball with a group of girls. These were normal college students doing normal things with other college students, and I was actually being allowed to be a part of something like this for the first time in my life.

I actually felt like I was fitting in. I wasn't the coolest kid playing sand volleyball, but at least I was fitting in. We would go grab pizza or something almost nightly after we played. It was great. However, as the semester went on, I became more and more frustrated. It was hard for me. Yeah, I was able to play volleyball with these kids, but I still wasn't able to connect with them on a level to be able to be good friends with them. Again, it's the friendship/acquaintance ratio. I was an acquaintance to them, but I wanted them to be my best friends.

Schoolwork was hard—not because I didn't know how to do it but because I was so focused on social interactions that I just couldn't even concentrate on schoolwork. By mid-October, I was struggling socially again because it was getting cold out and the sand volleyball stuff wasn't going on anymore. I became more frustrated and depressed. After attempting to get some counseling several times through that university and being pushed away, I didn't have anywhere to turn.

On October 30, I ran again. This time, I ran to Indianapolis. I ended up in a mall parking lot in Fishers, Indiana, which is just outside of Indianapolis, and had a pair of scissors with me. I was sure that someway or somehow, I was going to end my life and get away from the world of pain. The funny thing is that sometimes people, especially girls, start paying more attention to you when you feel this way. They actually texted me and wanted to know where I was at.

I sat in the parking lot with the scissors in my hand most of the evening. I was just thinking about how bad my life was and what a horrible person I was. At this point I wasn't even able to argue with myself and say, "Wait a minute, you're a good person." I needed evidence to show me that people liked me, and I hadn't seen any. My life was a waste, and I wasn't sure why God put me here. I was crying. People often tell me that grown men don't cry. I'm not sure if I believe it. I cried a lot back then and still do now. I felt hopeless. I wanted something that I could never have. I didn't know I could never have it at the time, but after being diagnosed with Asperger's syndrome, I realized that what I was wanting was something that people with this syndrome or disorder don't typically have. I was fighting a losing battle because I was never going to have 100 percent normal friendships and relationships.

After about five hours of waiting in the mall parking lot, I was finally able to tell someone where I was at, and they came and got me. This time when I got back, I was forced by the university to go to a hospital.

Being put in the hospital for having Asperger's syndrome is such a waste of time and more depressing than being out of the hospital. It's funny that they think they're helping you by keeping you cooped up somewhere for a week. I wish they could come up with a better and more user-friendly way of helping people in need.

After I got out of the hospital, it was like we were back to the drawing board. I ended up taking the rest of the fall semester off. I decided to go back to IPFW for the spring semester, and this time, I would live on campus there.

# Finally, an Answer

At about the same time I was being put in the hospital by Indiana Wesleyan University, my parents were receiving the news that would change my life. I was scheduled to see Dr. Jay Fawver in Fort Wayne on the morning of October 30. That morning I woke up after the previous night in Indianapolis in shock. I was still just as confused as ever and didn't feel much better about life. As they were putting me in the hospital, my mom called to tell me that the doctor had told her that they tested me and were ready to diagnose me with something called Asperger's syndrome. At the time she didn't remember the name of the syndrome; she was just able to tell me it started with an "A." I told the counselors at Indiana Wesleyan that they had found something and were diagnosing me with what my mom called a learning disability. The counselors didn't have much interest in learning much about it, as they wanted to rush me off of the campus and get me to the hospital. At one point one of the counselors told me that they wanted to get me out of school because they didn't want to have to end up counseling a bunch of other students in a dorm about how someone committed suicide. I can understand their concern with that but still feel there was a better way to go about it.

This was the moment of truth. After spending a few days at the hospital this time, I was aware of the fact that I had this thing called Asperger's syndrome. I wasn't sure what to think of it but was relieved to know what was going on with me and my life. After spending an entire summer going to counselor after counselor with no answers, I was able to receive this diagnosis. At the time, I had no idea what Asperger's would end up meaning to me and my life, but I knew it would be significant.

I was promised by Indiana Wesleyan that the counselors there would come visit me and bring me my homework. But that promise was never kept. After being dropped off at the hospital by a university counselor, I would never see him or any other counselors from the university again. They then proceeded to set up a meeting with my parents. What happened at that meeting is extremely sad. This meeting took place on November 2, 2007. The counselors and the university staff informed my parents that they felt it best to give me a medical withdraw from classes. They told my parents that the last day to drop any classes for the semester was that day. But actually the last day to withdraw from classes and receive a "W" was November 9, 2007, one week later than what the university was willing to tell my parents. With me being in the hospital, I was unable to stick up for myself, and my parents knew nothing about the dates, so it was decided that I'd take a medical withdraw.

I finally got out of the hospital on the following Monday, November 5. I still had stuff in the dorm rooms at Indiana Wesleyan, so I needed to go back to get it. I drove over there one evening just wanting to pick up my belongings and get out of there. But what I ran into was a huge mess of discrimination. I was stopped by law enforcement and told that I was no longer allowed to be on university grounds. They told me to leave and that if I came back I would be arrested. This troubled me, as I wasn't sure what I'd done. The only thing that happened was that girls at Indiana Wesleyan thought I was creepy, psycho, or even weird. I find it very troubling that you can get into such trouble for being creepy, psycho, or weird.

I understand that it may make people uncomfortable, and of course if there is a person who is trying to be these things purposely, then yes, action should be taken. But again I have to ask, what if the person is being creepy, psycho, or weird by complete accident?

At this point and time in my life, I felt like just the fact that I existed was hurting people. I felt horrible about myself, and I felt like I hurt everyone that I interacted with by just wanting to be friends with them or trying to be included in the group. This inspired the following journal entry.

> "I Don't Mean to Hurt You."
>
> Ugh, I'm so tired. I didn't sleep well last night. I must begin my day. The dreaded thoughts start just as soon as I open my eyes and I get out of bed. The first thought that goes into my brain is, I'm creepy. I look in the mirror, and I see a guy who is creepy. I've been convinced that I'm creepy and I have to live with it. Of course, now I know that this creepiness comes from the fact that I have Asperger's syndrome. But I start my day in fear of social interactions with other people, not because I don't want to interact with them, but mainly because I don't want to hurt them. See, to me, when someone tells me I'm creepy, I feel like I'm bothering them or that I'm hurting them in some way. I can't get it out of my head. I feel that in socializing and making friends there is only one way to not be creepy and there are hundreds of thousands of ways to be creepy. Unfortunately, I've found that having Asperger's makes it significantly more difficult to find the one way that won't make someone think you're creepy or that won't allow you to hurt someone.
>
> I wake up with the harsh reality of knowing that my desire for friendships and relationships with other human beings has the potential to hurt them. I have to think extra long and hard about my social interactions with people. But I don't much enjoy waking up knowing that just the sheer fact that I exist or the fact that I like someone or could be interested in getting to know them is going to possibly hurt them. It can hurt them because I don't know how to like them in the way

> that they are used to being liked. Maybe it's because I don't understand all of these unwritten social rules. I don't intend to hurt anyone, but I think by breaking these rules it's really hard to not hurt someone. Most people are used to people automatically following these rules and not even thinking about how to follow them. For me, it takes a conscious effort to just get through my day and try not to hurt someone by doing something creepy. It takes a lot of energy out of me. Therefore, anything else I might want to do throughout my day, such as go to school or go to work, becomes more difficult, and I don't have the energy left to focus on it.

As January 2008 came along, I was living with a random roommate I had never met before, which was a horrible idea. I let myself get bullied again. Campus policy is that no significant other is supposed to be living there. Well, this guy had his girlfriend living with him, and it was just a two-bedroom, one-bathroom. I ended up being late to class in the morning quite a bit because of his girlfriend. She would just go shower whenever she wanted before she had to go to class, and I was too afraid to say anything to them. I ended up doing pretty bad in most of the classes from that semester.

I learned a lesson that semester. I am not a drinker, so I didn't really know much about this at the time. Well, there was this girl whom I danced with one time, but at that time, she was drinking. So I started to try to dance with her again at another time because I thought she liked dancing the first time, and she flipped out and got mad. She then explained the whole saying-things-when-you're-drunk-versus-not-drunk situation. She told me that sometimes when people are drunk they say and do things that they wouldn't do when they're sober. This made absolutely no sense to me. I still can't comprehend why someone would do or say something differently when drunk as opposed to being sober. It's like having two personalities.

The rest of the semester at school was spent coping, or should I say just dealing with, what life had dealt to me. It was in this time frame, January 2008 to June 2008, that I would really start to try to make some discoveries about girls. In May of '08, a girl told me that she would go on a date with me if I did her homework. She had three final papers that had to be turned in and told me if I wrote them she would go out for coffee or drinks. So I immediately started working on them. I ended up doing two of them because I was busy with my own stuff. It turns out that she never intended on hanging out with me. She just wanted someone to write her papers for her. Little things here and there happened like this off and on for about a year.

After surviving the summer without any social interaction again, I was ready to go back to school. In August of '08 I was planning on attending IPFW to major in accounting. I was also offered a job and took it, working with the YMCA. I ended up being afraid of going back to school. I couldn't do it because I knew the other students would hate me and make fun of me. So I ended up dropping those classes and never going. The same thing happened in the spring semester of 2009. I signed up and then couldn't force myself to go. It's so painful to be made fun of and rejected all of your life. I just couldn't do it anymore.

In the fall of 2008, I was so frustrated about my inability to connect with other people and especially girls that I Googled a phrase. I Googled, "How do I get a girlfriend?" I ended up spending about $5,000 buying books or programs that I found on Internet Web sites telling me how to get a girlfriend or how to attract girls. One of the more memorable programs that I got was a book containing text messages to send to women that would make them attracted to you. My favorite one was the one that it said to use when asking a girl out. I was told to text a girl this. "Hey. I need to do some shopping. You should come along, and if you're nice, I'll even let you carry my bags for me." So I tried some of these things out for a few months and found that nothing really worked. I was one of these people who thought that anything and anyone, no matter who they were or where they were from, would be out to help people in this world.

I've had a few people who are helping me out tell me that the people I bought that stuff from were just wanting to make some money off of me and had no intentions of helping me.

In October of 2008, I met a guy by the name of J Nasty at a club who wanted to help me out—or so he said. I started talking with him, and I told him my story and about how I wanted friends and wanted to learn how to talk to girls. He said he was a pro with girls and could teach me anything I wanted. It did seem like he knew how to talk to girls and had a lot of success with them. He told me that I could hang out with him and his friends on weekends if I paid him a few hundred bucks a month. He said that he was doing me a huge favor because I was paying thousands of dollars for material that I bought from professionals on the Internet and that a few hundred a month is cheaper than a few thousand. So I took him up on it and tried it. It lasted for a few months. Basically, all I learned from him was that I had to be drunk and drink all the time in order to talk to girls.

He told me that if I wanted to learn how to act around girls, I had to be drunk. He also said I had to be cocky and arrogant and not care about what they thought. It seemed to work for him, so I was willing to give it a try. I'd watched him walk up to women at Pieres Entertainment Center numerous times and say to them, "Spank my butt, baby." And they would do it without hesitating or thinking about it. He'd walk up to random girls and just grab their butts like there was nothing to it. These women wouldn't even get mad. In his words, "Women respond to a man who doesn't care about them or what they want, a man who puts himself first and takes care of himself first and makes them feel like a piece of meat." I'd seen this guy with some of the most beautiful women, and I really believed that it must work for him.

I would never get to the point to where I had enough confidence or courage to just walk up to a woman and do some of the things that he did. I could never bring myself to just grab them or slap their butts. I couldn't do it. Part of me thinks it was because I didn't really want to do that or act that way around them. Maybe deep down I knew that acting that way wasn't in my belief system or a part of who I was. I believed that a woman should be respected and cherished and not treated like some sex object or a piece of meat.

I was very confused about interactions with women at this point in my life. My original concept had gotten me the label of being "creepy nice." No girl would ever give me a chance to get to know her. I was confused. I wanted acceptance from women so badly and wanted them to like me for who I was. I was so hurt by the fact that it seemed like guys got girls to like them by being mean to them. I couldn't understand this. Out of my want to have a girlfriend, though, it was something I'd try.

I would continue studying books about being a bad boy and learning how to be mean to girls. Today as I look back I find it pretty sad that I devoted about a year or a year and a half of my life to learning how to be mean to women so they could like me. It doesn't seem logical, does it? But that was where I was at. I was so hurt and tired of getting the response, "Oh, you're such a nice guy, but..." or, "You're creepy nice. Get away from me, loser." I had to try anything and everything I could to avoid be called "creepy nice" anymore.

During the months of January and February 2009, I would go out with this guy, JNasty, and his friends every weekend. I thought that was my chance to finally learn how to get a girlfriend. Friday night would usually start with me having to go to the liquor store to buy him and his friends some alcohol. At first I didn't drink anything at all. But I'd spend about $100 a week buying them alcohol so they could do what they referred to as "pregaming" before they went out.

Then we'd go to the clubs. We'd get to the clubs, and the first thing he'd say was to go buy them all shots. So I had to go down and get shots. He said he could get girls to dance with me but I had to buy him shots all night long. Oftentimes I'd buy the shots and he'd end up disappearing with a girl without ever helping me out. But being so determined to learn how to get a girlfriend, I continued to buy him shots and do things for him and his friends for a couple of months.

Eventually he told me that in order for me to get a girlfriend I'd have to be drunk before we went out. He said, "You're so retarded that the only way a girl will ever say more than hi to you is if you are drunk by the time they meet you." So I believed him. We went over to his buddy's house and "pregamed." The first time we did this they made me do about ten shots of Patron, I believe, which for someone who's never drank before seemed like a lot. I was more confident at the club, though, and was able to talk to a few girls. But it didn't go anywhere. There was one time when I did get to dance with a girl, and she even kissed me, but later she told me that he had paid her to kiss me. I was so hurt and frustrated. I was becoming more lost. Not only was I lost as to what to do and how to act around people; I was just lost as to who I was. I had spent so much time trying to learn how to be someone that I wasn't that I had lost who I really was. Not only that, but I was out of financial aid money and couldn't pay JNasty any more money to hang out with him and his friends.

I was frustrated with life. No matter what I did I just didn't feel as if I belonged in the world. It seemed people hated me. I kept trying things time and time again, and still my want and desire to have friends was made fun of and ridiculed. I wanted to be normal. I wanted people to know that I had feelings, and I also wanted to have friends and be included. I wanted to be a part of life. I wanted to be allowed to make friends and have a girlfriend.

The friendship with him ended in late March or early April of 2009. I didn't have the money to keep paying people, and I wasn't getting anywhere with girls or life. In March 2009, I was feeling really depressed and wanted to kill myself again. I stopped caring about everything. I didn't even go to work because I felt like no one liked me. There was a young teacher that worked at the school I was stationed at by the YMCA that I really liked a lot. I thought that a teacher might understand that I had Asperger's and possibly like me, so I sent her a card and flowers to tell her I liked her, and I think she got mad. It was around that day that I ended up visiting the hospital again due to suicidal thoughts. I never went back to the YMCA after that.

After leaving the YMCA, I began a journey, one that would lead to the writing of this book but more importantly one that would lead to me finding out who I really was. I started down a road of learning to accept myself. This road was a bumpy road, and it was never with ease that I accepted myself. I used to believe that I had to be accepted and loved by other people before I could accept and love myself. But as some of my friends would show me that wasn't the case.

The summer of '09 was pretty quiet for me. I was emotionally drained from trying so hard to make friends that I didn't go out and do much. I was also unemployed and didn't have a lot of money to do anything. During the month of May, I began writing this manuscript. There were times throughout the summer when someone would offer to hang out with me if I gave them something or did something for them. I sometimes fell for it and took them up on it. However, I was mainly focused on writing.

At one point during the fall of '09, I was at a dance club called Early Birds looking for someone to hang out with. I used to go out by myself because I so badly wanted to make friends. I ran into two girls who were in a class of mine in a previous year. They knew a little about my situation and approached me to talk to me. I asked if they wanted to dance, and they asked me how much money I had. With desperately wanting that connection from someone, I didn't even think twice. I pulled out the wallet. I had $54 left. They said they'd both dance with me for $50, so I got one dance. The song went fast, only about four minutes.

The holidays came and went, and all of a sudden it was 2010. To be honest I was pretty down and still in a rut. No longer did I want to kill myself when I was depressed. I knew that it was just an easy way out and there was no coming back. I also knew that it would hurt the people who did care about me. But I did ask God quite a few times to take my life for me. I couldn't bear the pain of social rejection from my peers anymore. It was hard for others to understand how I was feeling mainly because they didn't live with Asperger's or experience its effects on a regular basis like I did. To me it was like being trapped in a glass ball with no way out. Before meeting my friend Mandy I was ready to give up. I wasn't thinking about killing myself at this point. Instead I thought every day about how I just wanted to sit around and wait on God to take my life. I was hoping to die soon and that somehow or someway something would kill me. I was in a lot of pain and didn't foresee things getting any better anytime soon. Meeting Mandy and Mary would change my way of thinking. It changed my life. To be truthful, it saved it.

At first I thought that getting to know them would be just like it had with any other person I'd met. I'd become interested or fixated on their friendship and text them too much or show them too much attention. I thought that I'd lose them because they too would think I was creepy. I thought they'd run from me and I'd have the same thing happening with rejection. I wasn't ready to deal with that much pain again. But I was determined to give it one last effort in order to make a friend and save my life.

I was determined to get someone to understand me and how I was feeling. I was a very good writer at times and liked to journal. The following journal entry was written as an attempt to explain my feelings.

> After having the chance to hear a great presentation by Dr. Stephen Shore yesterday, I wanted to share some of my feelings about autism and in particular living with Asperger's syndrome. Much of my life has been spent living within this little ball of glass. Of course, Aspies, this is not to be taken literally like we so often would, but it's more an analogy that I've been learning. See, I've had to teach myself even little analogies like that, something that it seems most people just naturally pick up on. What exists inside of this glass ball I'm in?
>
> Well, it's my world. I call it my Aspie world. The Aspie world is a wonderful place, except for it can get quite lonely inside

this little ball sometimes. There is a door that opens on my glass ball, but it remains locked and I don't have a key for it. Only other people have a key to open it from the outside. You might ask, "Well, how or why do they open it, and why can't I open it?" That is simple.

I have Asperger's syndrome, which can cause me to be a little socially awkward. When I try to leave my glass ball and interact with the neurotypical world, I can be lost and confused, as I'm not able to understand all of their nonverbal cues and hints in society. Because of this I can often be called names such as creepy, psycho, or worse. Inside of the ball is a safe, safe place, but I would like to live outside of the ball a little more often or even permanently.

The reason I say it is a glass ball is so I can see outside of it. It's fascinating for me to see and observe the neurotypical world. I am astonished at how they pick up on easy social skills and norms. The simplest task socially that they perform is likely to be so hard for me to learn. At times it can get really frustrating being stuck inside of the ball and seeing people that I like as friends outside of the ball going about their lives doing everyday normal things, such as going to a movie with a friend, going putt-putt golfing, going to a school dance, going out to eat for dinner, or going to a dance club in the evening, or even I saw sometimes where college friends will go on a trip over spring break together. It's extremely sad to watch these things happening outside of the glass ball.

I've spent my whole life trying to jump outside of the ball. But it seems the walls are so hard to bring down. I often try to leap out of it but run into the side of surface of the ball and it doesn't open up or pop. Sometimes it will stretch out or expand, but it's never quite popped and let me out. The easy way out, of course, is to be let out the door. How do I get let out? Well, it's real simple. If I send someone a text message and they reply, then the door opens a little bit. Or if I call someone and they call me back, the door opens a little wider.

Even if I ask someone to do something with me and they say yes, the door opens more. However, for most people, it would be quite easy to open this door from the inside. You see, most have the key to the lock on this door within them. They can open it from the inside and the outside. What is that key?

I believe the key is social skills. Yes, social skills are the foundation for life, both on your professional life and on a personal level. After being stuck inside of the ball for twenty-two years not knowing why I was in there, I was finally able to figure it out at age twenty-two. The doctor looks at me and says, "You have Asperger's syndrome." After hearing that, I was like, "What is that?" Of course, I began reading and studying from with inside my little ball. I would say I've grapsed a pretty good understanding of Asperger's now. I so often feel like I'm misunderstood by people that are NTs, or neurotypicals, and I do know that it's not their fault at all.

Over the past three to five years, I began trying to learn how to get out of the ball. Well, I can't remember exactly how it happened to me, but I found out over time that there was a way out of the ball. Or at least I thought. One day when a girl said to me, "I'll give you my phone number if you give me five hundred dollars," the concept of paying someone to give me their phone number didn't make any sense to me at all. Of course, I didn't really give it much logical thought because I so desperately wanted out of the ball. I wanted her to open the door and let me out. So I paid five hundred dollars to have a small door opened. Sure, I got a phone number and was let out of the ball for a little while, but I was quickly returned to my ball. So I guess you could say I spent five hundred dollars to get out of the ball and into the real world for a few hours. Or in this case to be able to send a few text messages to someone who I thought was pretty and I was interested in getting to know.

Then the next time a girl would offer the same type of thing. She might even offer to have lunch or coffee for around five hundred dollars. I wondered how other guys were able to hang out with girls for free. I was convinced that I had to give them something to spend time with me. What happened?

Eventually guys started offering to open the door to my ball and let me out, but not without cost.

Sometimes I'd try to explain what was going on to an older adult who was outside every day, and while it would seem they'd hear my cry, they couldn't quite fully comprehend the magnitude of someone charging me to hang out with them or someone telling me I could sit next to them in class if I gave them money. This was in a college setting, and it seemed they were in shock when I'd tell them this. I remember one time when I was twenty I was let out of the ball only for a friend initiation, an initiation in which I was told by these guys I worked with all people with the group of friends get tied to a tree. Then each guy takes turns swinging baseball bats and throwing punches. That was one of my more painful trips outside of the ball. Situations like that are reaons why I have a hard time even trusting a guy or wantintg to make friends with a guy today. Guys have physically hurt me, and they've also told me I can't be their friend until I have a girlfriend or I'm not a man until I've done such and such with a woman. So, therefore, I step aside and try not to get hurt by guys.

Right now, however, I'm in the process of what I feel is my first real journey outside of this glass ball. I feel like I might be being let out of the ball for free this time, and let me tell you what a great feeling it is. It's amazing when I find someone young or within my peer group who's willing to accept me as someone with Asperger's as being a little different. I was in the right place at the right time I guess you might say.

It was on one of my paid journeys outside the ball when I was paying to be somewhere with someone that I met Mandy. Mandy isn't a typical college student that I've met at like IPFW or anything like that. She goes to a different school. She also has some friends, Mary, Ayriel, and Audrey. Well, to tell you the truth, I am kind of nervous and afraid to talk about this, but I feel I need to thank them and for letting me out of the ball for free.

Mandy has been really good with talking to me and texting me as well as even taking me out to go dancing. I've also just recently gone to a hockey game with Mandy, Ayriel, and Mary, and I feel this was the first time in my life where I've been let out of the ball and allowed to join the real world for free. It was the best experience in my life.

There aren't really words that can say or show appreciaion for the fact that they are letting me out of the ball and helping me. One day I hope to hold the key in my hand that will let me out for free, but for now the key is in others' hands. But let me tell you where I think that key is to let me out of the ball. When I was paying people to let me out, I think the key was coming from someone's ego saying, "Sure, we'll let you out of the ball and come out to join us in the real world, but it's going to cost you." I've had my door opened with that key many, many hundreds of times in my life. But for Mandy, Mary, and Ayriel so far, it seems as if the key to open the door to the ball that I am in has come from somewhere different. I think it comes from the heart or a place where real people in the real world are able to have some compassion.

There's not enough appreciation I can show to these girls who are going above and beyond what nineteen- or twenty-year-old girls do in this country. They are helping to show me some boundries to friendship but also are able to understand that I can't see the boundaries like they can or other guys can. I wish there was a better way to thank them, and in time I may come up with a way. For now, though, I try to be careful because I like to have my door opened for free. I like to be allowed to join the real world for free. I'm still trying to convince myself that I can be let out and into the real world for free by peers. But at the same time, because I've been locked up in my ball for twenty-five years, I still have to try to think hard and remember that these girls already have their lives established. And I can't expect them to hang out all the time

> or let me out for free every day. So right now I'm just appreciating being let out for free whenever they can, and I try to be the best friend to them that I could be. I love to be in the real world and not stuck inside of the ball. It makes me feel like a person and not a thing, like I used to think I was just a thing.
>
> In conclusion, my ball is not a bad ball on the inside. Sometimes I just need out. Being an Aspie doesn't make me a bad person; in fact, I'm really a very good and compassionate person. I may show it differently than neurotypicals, but I'm very caring. While being an Aspie is great, there are still needs for neurotypical friends and to do activities that neurotypicals participate in. Mandy, thank you for reaching out. Thanks for allowing me to feel like a real person and not a thing. And to your friends, thanks for helping her help me. One day I hope to learn the skills to let myself out. But for now I keep trying to practice social skills and know that I'm lucky that some people are willing to stand up for someone different and make them feel included.

You noticed a few names in that journal entry above: Mandy, Mary, and Ayriel. These women aren't just three ordinary women you'd find in any city or at any college campus across the country. When I first met Mandy, in February of 2010, you might say I was in a place where I was ready to quit. As I mentioned above, I was just waiting on God's timing to take place. No longer did I have the courage or the desire to continue to try at anything in life. The only thing I was worried about was friends. I needed a friend. By a friend, I mean someone who could understand me and try to accept me for who I was, someone who understood that I was Travis Breeding and not a syndrome or a disorder.

Mandy would be the first person to let me in the door to developing a real friendship in my adult life. I'd had other encounters with adults in my life, but they often cost me lots of money. The ones that were free only went on for a couple of weeks. As of this writing, this has gone on for three full months and hasn't cost me anything other than investing some time in the friendship, which is all a friendship should cost someone.

Mandy is pretty young, just turned twenty as a matter of fact. But she has by far been the first person to really understand me and how I work. The things that she says and does to interact with me are on the maturity level of another planet. I've never met anyone who understands what I need in a friendship as well as she does. I have to be honest. It does take a little more effort for someone to be friends with me at first. We know that the traits of Asperger's are to appear a little clingy and needy at first. So I needed that comfort of constantly knowing everything was all right. She provided that. We've shared some great experiences, and she's even introduced me to some of her friends.

Just having a group of people to call friends has been a huge breakthrough for me. I now have someone to talk to and someone to enjoy activities with, such as going to the hockey game or going to the zoo. It's great to have someone to text or to talk to.

Something that shows the maturity level of Mandy is this text she sent me. "It's not hard to be your friend. It's all about communication. I find you very interesting and intelligent." When I read that I shed a few tears, not because I was sad, but tears of joy. I knew I had my first real friend since being in fifth grade.

I'd never had a real friend as an adult before. I wasn't sure how to act. I found myself locking into those typical Asperger's tendencies of texting too much, calling too much, or sending too many gifts. I was glad that Mandy had a few friends who would take me in and accept me for who I was too. I found that it's a little easier not to overwhelm one person with the attention when you can spread it out between three or four people.

A myth about Asperger's syndrome is that those who have it don't generally care about other people or don't have the capability to be compassionate or show affection. As someone who is on the spectrum, I have been deeply hurt and offended by this. I, for one, have a tremendous amount of passion for caring about other people.

I am able to feel other people's feelings a little easier than most are. The problem I have is knowing why they are feeling those feelings and how to fix them. As someone with Asperger's, I just have a strange way of showing my compassion and affection for other people. That doesn't mean that it's bad, but it's different, and society as a whole isn't used to it. I've often been ridiculed for sending friends flowers, cards, or balloons. It has hurt me that they don't understand what I'm trying to communicate. I'm trying to say I'm sorry you're having a rough time but I do care about you and hope you have a better day. It's frustrating to me that a lot of times people seem to take my actions of compassion and affection out of context. But I must realize there's nothing I can do about that, and I have to try to modify the way I show affection for people, even the way I show them I appreciate them. I am often too intense with this. I think this is where they would say that they think I don't care about other people, because I don't see these unwritten social rules that say you shouldn't do this because it means this and so I do it. Most assume I'm just that strange, crazy, weird, creepy, psycho person.

After finally forming friends with a few neurotypical individuals, I've made some interesting observations. For me, being diagnosed with Asperger's syndrome was a life-changing moment. What I thought would help me ended up hindering my growth as an individual. After being diagnosed I was told to do this or do that. Get help there and go there to see this person. Basically I was pushed through a sequence of events that our professionals are taught works best in dealing with someone who has a form of autism.

Being pushed through this same system as most people on the spectrum are, I learned that it was a hindrance to me. I was quickly given a label. I was no longer Travis Breeding. I was a man with Asperger's syndrome. Once I was labeled "autistic," I was quickly told that I couldn't do a lot of things. A psychologist said, "You'll never have friends. You'll never work. You'll never get married." It's troubling to me that I was often told I couldn't and never told I can. Most psychologists are neurotypical. It is with great respect that I feel that while they are very book smart and do have degrees in their field, they are not very experienced in what they are trying to help someone with autism go through. Unless you've lived with it or at least lived with someone who has it, it's going to be hard for you to fully grasp what is going on. For example, a professional in the autism field once told me I should only try to make friends with other people who have autism or Asperger's syndrome. She said no normal people would ever want to be my friend.

The problem with this is it's simply not true.

You've probably heard the phrase "You become what you believe you are." After some recent experiences with people, I really believe it's true. From the time I was diagnosed with Asperger's syndrome in 2007, I was no longer Travis Breeding. I was the guy with Asperger's. What they said I couldn't do I quickly started to believe I couldn't do. Once I believed I couldn't do it, I behaved like I couldn't do it. It's all about a belief system. I've even met a psychologist recently who focuses in cognitive behavioral therapy. He thinks that Asperger's is overplayed by professionals. He doesn't feel like people with it are at as big of a deficit as most professionals in the field. I don't fully agree that this is the case, but I do believe there is something to be said for this. I know for me when I'm brainwashed that I am autistic I start to think more autistic-like. I become more clingy and needy than ever. When I'm around neurotypicals and learning from them, I'm able to behave more in a neurotypical-like way. Will I ever be completely neurotypical? Probably not, and that's okay. For me, if I had it to do over again, I wouldn't have thrown myself into all of those autism support groups right away and wouldn't have listened when all of the doctors said I couldn't do this or that. Instead I would have began seeking out ways that I could do what the others are doing and be included with them and accepted as Travis Breeding, not the guy with Asperger's syndrome.

Being an Aspie is difficult. It's also a little frustrating at times. I'm fighting a battle that many people will never understand. There are people in this world who do bad things to other people all of the time. But when you have this thing called Asperger's, it's different. There's no desire to be mean to anyone at all. In fact, it's quite the opposite. I want to give everyone the royal treatment and please them. But for some strange reason, that alone can end up hurting those I care about most.

With the conclusion of this book, there are just a few things I have to take care of. I started down this journey of writing a book for many reasons, one that may seem a little selfish if you don't understand it. When I first started writing, I had been told that people would be my friends if I was able to give them money or buy them nice things over three hundred times in my life. I still have text messages and instant messaging conversations to document this. I was convinced and believed I owed the world money to exist.

I started writing the book hoping to share my story with the world in hopes that people would understand what I was going through and like me for free. But I also was writing with the intent of trying to educate the world about what Asperger's syndrome is and how it can affect those of us who have it. I have to say those of us who are lucky enough to have Asperger's syndrome can be some of the kindest people you'll meet in the world. I think it's that kindness that bothers people. We have a real appreciation for some of the simplest things in life. We are just lacking social skills, and that hurts us and those around us.

As I come to the end of the project, I am thinking about autism. I thought I'd close with one last journal entry.

> My Life with Autism
>
> Everyone is born with a gift. Someone can be a good basketball player, a great artist, a musician, or even just a plain good person. Others are born with conditions, such as Down syndrome or autism. I was born with autism. Some people would say it's a blessing. In some ways they would be right. However, unlike any other disorder out there, autism affects the way you interact with the social world. Therefore, my

happiness has been left to be determined by my peers and how people my age treat me and accept me.

People will tell me to be who I am and make no apologies for it, but sometimes—well, most of the time—these are the same people who make fun of my autistic characteristics. I cannot lie to you today. Many will argue that autism is a blessing or a gift. But it's not that. It's far from it. I guess some who have it are okay with mediocre treatment and not being like the rest of their peers, but I am not. I'm tired of not being good enough to be friends with someone because I'm autistic. I'm tired of not being good enough for a girl to date because I'm autistic. The truth is it's discrimination for a girl to reject me because I have autism, and there's no way around it. She'll tell me it's not because I have autism, but deep down you know it is.

Like it or not, once diagnosed with autism, your life will never be the same. In many cases your family's life will never be the same. I've tried everything. My goal for life is to be as neurotypical as everyone else, but it's just not possible. I've been called creepy, psycho, retarded, dumb, fat, ugly, stupid, worthless, lazy, and many other names my entire life, and it's frustrating. Creepy is so hurtful. No one intends to be creepy or is purposely creepy, but yet in most cases women are quick to jump to creepy. While it's true some people who are creepy do hurt people and you should be very careful and aware of this, being judgmental and thinking everyone is creepy is just not fair. To be honest, the fact that women call me creepy is killing me. I have very little feeling left because I've been told I'm creepy so much. I just think that I'm a thing and not a person anymore. I hope one day I can overcome this, but I'm just not sure it's possible. Until society has the ability to open up and understand people who are different, my life and all of the successes of life are in the neurotypical society's hands. They control how my life goes and who I am.

And so the story ends. It may not be the best written story in history or not even a story that follows proper grammar rules. I'm not trying to accomplish all of that. I'm not an author, just someone with an unfortunately sad story to share with the world. What dreams I ever had of becoming a professional trombonist or band director have been crashed. My life is kind of at a standstill with the only positive thing going for me right now being that I met my two friends Mary and Mandy.

A lot of times I meet professionals in the field, and they want the sugarcoated story: "Life is okay with autism, right?" Or I'll meet that parent of a child on the spectrum who will ask me, "Is life going to be okay for my child when they grow up? What's your life like?" My natural response is to want to give them the real answer. But I want to give them hope. I know they're looking for that sugarcoated answer. They want the answer, "Yes, your child is going to be just fine. He's going to grow up and be very independent and function in society. He's going to have lots of friends and will have an outstanding career. He'll even get married and have kids." I want to give them that answer so badly. Sometimes I have. Unfortunately, I can't say that it's the truth. I have given the sugarcoated answer to parents or to family members on the spectrum a few times. But they too deserve the truth.

You'll meet a lot of autistic individuals in your life who will for whatever reason pretend to be okay with the situation they are in. Some have been brainwashed by the autism community since they were diagnosed that it's okay to be different. It's okay to be autistic. This is great; it really is. But they forgot to educate the rest of the neurotypical world and tell them that it's okay for someone to be different or for someone to be autistic. I know people on the spectrum who will say they are just fine being alone and autistic, but then I read status updates on Facebook about how they wish they could be like everyone else. The truth is everyone longs for connection, belonging, and importance. There isn't any denying that. While some of us have been taught by professionals or our moms and dads or even other family members to accept what we've been dealt and realize it's a part of who we are, some of us, for whatever reason (maybe because we were diagnosed at a later age in life), are not okay with it. In fact, we are far from okay with it.

I want to be neurotypical. There's absolutely nothing wrong with having autism. The only problem is that it affects the way that I make friends or go about my social life. Asperger's syndrome is such a unique disorder because unlike a lot of other disorders where someone may seem different and get made fun of for it, people with Asperger's are very smart people. They are socially naive but very smart. So the person with Asperger's who is being called names or being made fun of knows what's going on. They know the person is laughing at them or making fun of them for something they did in a social interaction. They may not understand why, but they know.

It's rough being different. Every day I wake up wanting to be like everyone else. I want to be able to text a friend at will without worrying about texting them too often. I want to be able to go to the movies with friends or to the zoo or anywhere. I want to be normal and not have autism. But I can't. I pray every day for a cure or just for plain acceptance from my peer group. It's a lot to ask for, but I know it can happen someday soon. So for the reader who has an autism spectrum disorder, try to keep your head up. Realize there is hope. People are fighting for you. But beware of whom you surround yourself with. Some professionals have their best interest in mind and not always yours. Just be careful. Live your life like you belong here because you do. Be strong and fight for equal rights. Remember you are special in your own way, just like everyone else in the world.

*Today, I would like to pursue another major in communications and travel around and speak to people about autism and Asperger's syndrome. If you're interested in contacting me you may do so by e-mailing travis@travisbreeding.com.*

*A big thanks to everyone who read I Want To Be Like You and learned a little about what it might be like to live with AS.*

# Afterword

By Mandy Herrington

Travis Breeding. One name, so many meanings. Travis is not your typical twenty-five-year-old male. Travis has a kind heart, an excitable personality, and a type of genuineness that you don't find in most men. It's true that Travis has Asperger's, but this title does not define, describe, nor limit him. It's simply that, a title. Travis has made huge progress in just the short time I have known him. If he wouldn't have told me he has Asperger's, I would have never known. This could be due to the fact that Travis has tried so hard to be "normal" that he truly has mastered "normal" characteristics and behaviors. Travis calls me a neurotypical, or a "normal thinker." A neurotypical person is someone that does not have Asperger's, someone who is "normal."

When I first met Travis he was outgoing and very informative. He approached me and my friend and invited us to an event. After we got to talking I was very intrigued. He knew a lot of cool and interesting facts. He told us how he was working on being less "creepy," and he asked us to point out guys in the room that seemed creepy. I and my friends loved that; we had a blast pointing out all of the guys that seemed creepy or scary to us. Travis went on to tell us why we subconsciously thought they were creepy and what signals they were sending out with their body language that made them appear scary. Now, after getting to know him, I will never again assume someone is scary or weird. They could have a disorder that makes them appear that way. Travis was very informative, and we enjoyed talking to him.

The next weekend we actually went to the event just to see Travis. There was a photographer there taking pictures. She was charging per picture, though, so we decided to take our own since we brought our own camera. I and Travis posed and took our first picture together. I was astonished to hear what he said next. He told me that that was the first picture any girl had ever taken with him for free. I was so confused. Why would anyone ask to be paid to take a picture with someone, let alone actually accept the money? This, however, was the harsh daily reality of Travis's life. I went on to learn that that wasn't the first time Travis paid someone for their friendship. It was so sad to me that he was actually conditioned to think he had to pay for someone to even talk to him or be his friend. That night was the start of our friendship.

Travis has made huge progress. Though he has never once seemed creepy to me, he has struggled with knowing when things are too much. Although Travis struggles immensely internally with trying not to be too overwhelming to people, on the outside he is doing just fine. He does a lot better with personal space and neediness than he thinks he does. Travis thinks I am a blessing in his life and that I have done so much to change it. Little does he know he is affecting me just the same. He thanks me so much for being his friend, but really I should be thanking him. Before I met him I knew little to nothing about his disorder. Travis has enlightened me and broadened my mind. I find myself secretly diagnosing people who may seem a little "off" now. I always say in my mind, "Well, maybe they just have Asperger's." I'm not saying to just trust anyone, but before you rule someone out or make fun of them for being different, you need to become aware. Ignorance is not bliss and can hurt and be painful to those who are different.

Travis is my friend. His disorder will not come between us. Sometimes I may get frustrated with him, but there's nothing that communication can't fix. I learn just as much from him as he learns from me. It's so refreshing to know someone is so excited just to be friends with me. The littlest things make his day, and that's so awesome. I feel special to be Travis's friend and feel even more special knowing how much he values our friendship.

# Appendix

In the following section, you'll find an appendix of terms and explanations of things dealing with Asperger's syndrome. These are topics that were introduced throughout the chapters, but due to the flow of story, I wanted them be expanded upon more at the end of the book. This is a great source for a greater explanation of Asperger's syndrome.

### *The Reason behind the Special Interest*

There are a couple of reasons as to why the special interest develops to such an intense level in an individual on the autism spectrum. I should note that this is only my opinion and you should always consult a professional, but I do believe that getting advice from someone who's experienced this can be very insightful.

### *Reason Number One*

The child on the spectrum doesn't have a normal level of social skills that is up to par with their peers.

I formed a special interest in things because I didn't have the capability to carry on a conversation about things that other kids might have wanted to talk about. This caused me to be excluded from any group of students who was ever congregating or sitting around, talking. When one is excluded from a group, what's left for him to do?

Throughout middle and high school, I would often sit at home and just think about music, practice my trombone nonstop, and listen to jazz recordings to the point to where it became an obsession but also a way to not feel so lonely.

For me, music—and in particular the trombone—was my best friend. I had pretty much lost my best friend, Austin, from the fifth- and sixth-grade years at Andrews Elementary, and to tell you the truth, I think Austin was the last boy or guy that I've ever been friends with. That was in 1998-99, going on eleven years now.

The special interest is also something that doesn't go away. People come and go, but things are usually always here. For a person with autism or Asperger's syndrome, losing a friend who's a person can be devastating—not only because we become attached to the person but also because of our lack of ability to make friends. So when we lose a friend, we have to try to make new friends, and this is very stressful for us. I cannot speak for all people with an autistic disorder, but I can tell you that I'm one who wants friends. I've always wanted to be included in the group. I know that there are some people on the spectrum who don't have an interest in having friendships at all or interacting with others. Then there are some who do but can't talk or communicate in any way at all, which would be extremely frustrating.

To sum things up, the special interest forms because the person with the autistic disorder is excluded from basically all forms of social interaction by their peers. Without having any social interaction at all, they have a lot of time on their hands, and they spend that time doing something they like. It's just that they spend more time with the thing they are interested in rather than being around other people, which causes the interest to become a friend. In my opinion, the special interest is something that someone on the spectrum uses to cope with not being able to build successful relationships with other people. Because they can't have a friend, they replace the friend with the special interest.

*Reason Number Two*

Communicating with the special interest is easy and much less stressful than communicating with an NT.

A lot of people just don't realize how stressful and tiring talking to people can be for individuals on the spectrum. It's extremely hard to talk to someone. Just trying to look them in the eye and say hi is a challenge for most of us. Therefore, it is stressful. It's also so much work that it can become tiring. People with an autistic disorder often report being tired after even just a brief social exchange with someone. This is happening because of the dysfunction in their central nervous system.

It is my opinion that because communication with people is very stressful, challenging, tiring, and, yes, frustrating for us on the spectrum that autistic individuals form a special interest. Think about it. It's so much easier for us to communicate with an object than it is to communicate with a human being. For me, playing trombone comes naturally. I can communicate very well and articulate what I'm saying with it. But when I'm talking to people, I have a hard time communicating. I get misunderstood, and my actions get misinterpreted. I get ridiculed, made fun of, and bullied due to my lack of social understanding and awareness.

When I'm playing my trombone, I can't talk, and I'm not communicating to a person directly. I am communicating to them indirectly by providing a musical sound that they can enjoy. Without having to worry if I'm doing something wrong or unacceptable, I'm able to relax and find much more enjoyment. Even if I was to go bowling in a group or putt-putt golfing, I wouldn't be able to enjoy myself because there is a lot of social interaction expected. So therefore, it's so easy to see why an individual with an autistic disorder develops special interests. Special interests are easy to communicate with, making them virtually stress free. The person doesn't have to say anything to them. They don't have to worry about the interest making fun of them or judging them, and they can keep and maintain the relationship at ease for a lifetime.

### *How do we handle the special interest in an autistic individual?*

I hear a lot of talk from professionals who are frustrated with the special interest. They are frustrated with the special interest because it is hard for them to deal with. It's hard to take away something that is loved by someone so much that it's almost a part of who they are. However, the special interest can cause trouble and be hurtful to the person with autism or Asperger's because they can talk about a subject too much to the point that they overwhelm people. They can lose friendships as a result. As they get older, the special interest or interests can change. Sometimes these can involve other people. For example, it is quite common for an adult with Asperger's syndrome to develop a special interest in making friends or even in dating and understanding or relating to women. This is when the special interest can be complicated to deal with.

The neurotypical person who wouldn't know much about autism or a special interest would see all of this attention from someone with autism as borderline obsessive. Dr. Tony Attwood provides an excellent quote in his book The Complete Guide to Asperger's Syndrome. He says "adult males with Asperger's can develop an interest in a woman they like and can fixate on them or adore them. While some women will view this adoration as obsessive, it is really just an adoration or appreciation for someone." Therefore, it's important that we handle the special interest because it affects other people, but it's also a part of who the person on the autism spectrum really is. So we're in a catch-22 position. We shouldn't change who someone is. But we can't let it affect their interactions with others.

This has been the most frustrating part of my adult life. In terms of dating, I so often hear people say, "Just be who you are. Girls will like you for who you are." But then in all reality it's the characteristics of Asperger's syndrome, such as the creepiness or weirdness in social interaction, that scares girls away and makes them want nothing to do with me. Unfortunately, those creepy and weird characteristics are a part of who I am. So I'm left really with no choice but to change who I am in order to be liked by others.

It is unfortunate that nearly all professionals whom I have encountered don't know how to handle the special interest and the only thing they can recommend is to take it away. However, taking away the special interest is harmful to the person on the spectrum. A special interest can possibly be modified or toned down with the proper treatment, but it is hard to completely take it away and make it nonexistent. I can totally understand how you could become frustrated with the individual with the interest, so I have thought about this for some time, and I really think that I have come up with a few effective ways to handle the person's special interest.

First of all, it's extremely crucial that we remember the special interest is not just an interest. The special interest could actually be the person's best friend. So whenever you think about trying to eliminate an interest in an autistic person, please try to remember that you're not really taking away an interest but a friend the person loves. You're also dealing with more than just a want. You've got more of a need on your hands. The special interest is like a need for survival in the person with autism. It could be the only thing that they have to look forward to in life. Taking it away can lead to severe isolation and depression. It's like a leg for a normal person. Life is going to be pretty difficult if you don't have both legs to walk with. If you take a leg away, what happens? You limp around and maybe get by in life, but with the leg you are able to hop, skip, and run just like everyone else.

What I am getting at here is the special interest in an autistic individual is his or her best friend. So when you're trying to eliminate the special interest in someone with autism or Asperger's, it's going to be painful for the person. Compare it to losing your wife or a close loved one. Obviously, this is going to cause a lot of discomfort that could be damaging to the individual. So I suggest that as long as the special interest is completely appropriate, we don't try to eliminate it completely. If it's so intense that it's interfering with the person's lifestyle or the lifestyles of anyone around the person, then I propose trying to control the intensity level of a special interest. Taking it away from them completely could be tragic.

### *What if it's an inappropriate interest?*

So what do we do if an interest is inappropriate and disturbing to society? I'm not sure there is a good way to handle a situation like this that we know of yet. I had the opportunity to hear about a wonderful young teenager. He is autistic and has developed a special interest in girls' feet. Yes, a foot fetish. However, because it's a special interest and not just an interest, the intensity level of the interest is overbearing and inappropriate. More often than not you'll find that a special interest is really just a neurotypical person's interest or fetish multiplied in intensity, making it a special interest. This child will walk up to high school NT girls and tell them that they have beautiful feet. This may come off as a little creepy to the average high school girl. It is situations like this that have been most frustrating in my life.

To the autistic individual, it is hard to understand the concept of "creepy." Neurotypicals have this filtering system that recognizes when things are a little off or creepy. It's just a feeling that a neurotypical is able to get from their subconscious level. As someone with autism, I don't get this feeling from anyone and am unable to tell or understand when I am putting out this signal to others.

Creepy is frustrating because society has made it out to sound like such a horrible word. When someone says I'm creepy, I automatically think I'm a horrible person because I've hurt them in some way. In my mind I think very logically about social situations. For example, one of the things that I always do wrong is send a dozen roses to a girl to tell her I like her. This comes off as creepy to neurotypical women. Neurotypicals have translated creepy to mean "bad, scary, hurtful, weird." When a guy is creepy around a neurotypical woman, the woman will automatically put up a shield and want to run as far away from the person who is being creepy as she can. The way I see it isn't creepy at all, though. I see giving a girl a dozen roses as showing her that I think she's an interesting person that I'd like to get to know. When I break this down logically, I don't see anything coming from this that could be hurtful or weird. How is giving a woman a dozen roses and saying "I like you," hurting her? It's not.

One of the things, however, that the neurotypical world has done is come up with something called "implied meaning." Somewhere along the lines neurotypicals have said that it's bad for a guy to bring a girl a dozen roses on a first date. It means he is creepy. Girls have told me that it can appear creepy to them because it implies that you are trying too hard to impress them and it puts a lot of pressure on the girl. Implied meaning is something that I never understand. Again, the difference here is that the autistic individual doesn't see how he is harming the neurotypical individual by his actions. It's almost like the neurotypical individual is trying to tell me what I mean or want just because I sent them a dozen roses on a first date or even before a first date. The neurotypical has come up with her own rule, a rule that I have not read anywhere. It's just an implied meaning situation that society has invented on its own and that most people with autism will never fully understand.

It's the same situation with the guy who has the special interest in girls' feet. There's no rule written anywhere that says you shouldn't tell a girl she has pretty feet. There is also no harm whatsoever in telling a girl she has pretty feet. It doesn't hurt her. It's the hundreds of thoughts that this neurotypical girl will have on her own that seem hurtful to her. It's all about implied meaning.

As I've mentioned, the special interest is like the individual's best friend. So as weird as it might sound, the feet of these girls are this young man's best friend. Now, it would be extremely hurtful and tragic to the individual if you were to eliminate his interest in their feet.

However, there are a couple of options to help diminish how intense it is and how it's affecting those girls who have the beautiful feet.

A special interest can never be eliminated completely from the autistic individual, but it can be controlled. The best way to accomplish this is through Applied Behavioral Analysis, known in the autism community as ABA therapy. The simplest definition of this is that it's a system of rewards/punishment or take away. When the person complies with a request, they are given a reward. The reward can be anything from a compliment to an object or something they want. The take away is used when the person is unable to comply with a request. So for this situation about the feet, we might say, "If the student can go a day without complimenting a girl on her feet, then we will give him a reward at the end of the day." However, if he can't make it through the day without complimenting her on her feet, then something such as a video game could be taken away at home that night. The problem with ABA therapy is that most who don't fully understand autism expect it to just automatically work and perform miracles, and that's not what it does. Just like anything else, it is an ongoing process.

Another way to approach this would be to try to modify the interest. Notice I said modify, not replace or take away. By modifying it, the person is still able to find enjoyment in the interest but maybe in a different way. Maybe the behavioral consultant could get him to rethink the thought before he says it to the girl.

The consultant should try to get him to not act on his thought so fast. This will allow him time to think and maybe change the thought into something that is more appropriate. If when he has the thought, Holly has beautiful feet. I'm going to tell her that, we could get him to think and switch it to something like, Holly looks really nice today, or Holly is beautiful today, or even, Holly has pretty eyes today, this might come off as a little more appropriate and prevent any tension at school between him and girls. It's quite possible that he's interested in girls in general and not just their feet. It just happens that he's got an obsessive interest in the way their feet look. So see how we modified this interest? He's still complimenting a girl he thinks is beautiful, but he's giving her a much more appropriate compliment that she might not take offense to. In fact, she might even feel flattered. We didn't take an interest away; we modified it.

Please understand that this is not something that is going to be easy to do with an autistic person. This will take hard work on their part but probably more from the person who is trying to modify the behavior. I cannot stress to you enough how important it is for the person working with the autistic individual (whether it be a professional, friend, adult, parent, or other family member) to recognize when the person is making progress and let the person know that you've noticed that he's making progress and doing better. We people on the spectrum really do need encouragement. If we are encouraged, then we are more likely to want to adapt to the modification in behavior because we will learn that with the modification comes a reward.

There is one other way we can handle this situation. Now, I recognize that this way might be difficult to execute. It will be easier on the person with the inappropriate special interest. However, this involves some cooperation and understanding from NT females.

If we could just find a couple of mature girls to recognize what the situation is and be accepting of it, then we could train the individual with the interest to go to those girls who understand and are aware of his situation. Unfortunately, with his age, this option would be hard, as the other girls at the high school level probably aren't going to be mature enough to handle a situation of this nature. If the individual could even have an older female in her twenties who understood, then we could modify the behavior so that he would know that when he has that thought about a girl, he has to go to the certain girl to tell her, and that would prevent him from offending girls he doesn't know all that well and who don't understand him at all. If we can just get him to think about the action that comes after the thought before he acts on it, we would be successful. It is important that he understand that it's okay if he has the thought that women have beautiful feet but not okay to tell them that. Then we would have modified the behavior but still allowed him to have his special interest, which is his best friend, without offending anyone.

## *Importance of Being Able to Escape into Imagination*

The ability to escape into imagination is a useful tool for someone who's dealing with autism or Asperger's syndrome. I found it to be a way to connect with someone. Even though these actors and actresses have no idea who I am, I still feel that I can put on a movie or watch a rerun of Saved by the Bell and connect with these people more than anyone in the world.

It's good for individuals on the spectrum to be able to find this type of connection with someone, even if it is in a make-believe world. Without being able to do this there would be a lot more depression and maybe even suicidal thoughts. Let's face it. Having no one at all to communicate with is lonely. Having someone, whether it be an animal or a make-believe character, to connect with could do wonders for people on the spectrum. I highly recommend getting a puppy for anyone who has a form of autism. That will help ease the loneliness, as the puppy will also be someone who will not judge you. (As long as you feed him, that is.)

## *Danger of Escaping into Imagination*

While I do believe that being able to escape into imagination is often extremely beneficial to an individual on the spectrum, I also want to caution of the chance of it becoming a dangerous situation. There's a chance of the person escaping into imagination too often. If this were to happen, the person could seclude themselves from the real world. Even though the real world is often a very hurtful place for us on the spectrum to live in, it is necessary for us to return from that state of imagination and get out into the real world and try to do our best at fitting in.

Since we are not yet to the point to where NTs will accept us, it's important that people on the spectrum still seek counseling to gain social skills and acquire knowledge about coping with autism. If the person stays in the imaginative state for too long, they will become comfortable with what life has to offer them. They might quit trying to learn social skills and norms and just seclude themselves. There have been times in my life in which I've just withdrawn from society completely because I didn't want to get hurt anymore. I would seclude myself in my house. As it got worse, sometimes I would even seclude myself in my bedroom. Sometimes I wouldn't even want to eat dinner at the family dinner table with everyone else, as I just wanted to be alone.

I know and understand how painful the real world can be for us on the spectrum at times, but it's very important that we get out in the real world and try to learn how to live in it. This is something that I'm working on even to this day. Getting out into the real world is hard for me. Recently, I went to a club that I hadn't been to in about two months. I felt extremely out of place and awkward. I attempted to have a few social interactions, to which most were duds and ignored me and some just looked at me with the "Why are you saying hi to me?" look. I've become very familiar with the "Why are you saying hi to me?" look. It's hard to hold your head high when rejection is all around you. You're being rejected for something that you have no control over. But it is so important to continue to put yourself out there and try. The harder you try, the more rejection you're going to face, but you have to try. If you don't try, you're going to shut down and lose the ability to feel any emotions at all and basically become a computer. Try to find something positive out of each social interaction you have with someone. No matter how challenging this must be, there is always something positive.

### *How can we tell if escaping into imagination is becoming too extreme?*

There are a couple of things to watch for here. The main thing is watching to see how the person acts at home. If the individual is still socializing with family members, it's okay. However, if it gets to the point where the individual doesn't even want to be around his or her family anymore, we've got a problem, the problem being that escaping into imagination or that make-believe world has become too comfortable. There's no pain in there. The individual has no motivation to come back into the real world now because they've managed to find a pain-free environment.

Tony Attwood says it best in The Complete Guide to Asperger's Syndrome. When an individual on the spectrum is by themselves, there is no impairment. The impairment doesn't happen until there is another individual with them. So with the people in their own make-believe world, with no other real human beings around, it becomes safe; life becomes easy, as there is no communication to worry about. I couldn't agree more with Tony.

Another way you could catch that this is becoming a problem is if you're able to listen to the individual talk when they're around you. If you feel that they're constantly talking about it like it's becoming their special interest, then it's time to step in and try to change it.

### *What is the best way to correct the interest?*

There is no clear-cut, simple way of correcting the make-believe interest and changing it into an interest of something that's in the real world. Cognitive behavioral therapy is probably the best solution to this problem. It's about reshaping the mind and thoughts in it. Remember earlier I talked of the little boy who had an obsession with female feet. Correcting a special interest that is make-believe works the same as correcting a special interest that is inappropriate. If you believe that the individual's interest of escaping into imagination is becoming harmful to them, then, by all means, please take action.

Correcting this situation could be more painful for the individual on the spectrum. Because a make-believe world has become a place of comfort and security, taking that security blanket away will not be easy to do. Please allow time. Giving someone who is on the spectrum time to adjust or time to change something or time to do anything is the best gift that you could ever give them. Often, if the individual is given enough time, they will comply with the request. They are just slower at it. It takes them longer to process changes.

### *Giving an Ample Amount of Time for an Individual on the Spectrum to Comply*

If you are support staff and working to correct a behavior in an individual, you need to be patient. People often expected me to adapt to change or fix something in an instant, without giving me a chance to practice or internalize the thought. This became extremely frustrating for me. I often see people who are so impatient with each other, but time is something that the individual on the spectrum needs. They need to be able to process your request and then think about it for just a little longer than the average individual who is NT.

I bet if someone were to do a study on people who were autistic, they would find nearly all, if not all, were able to comply with a request to change a behavior if they were given an ample amount of time.

### *Physical and Emotional Abuse*

For an individual on the autism spectrum, there can be many things that can present a danger for them. Depending on the severity of the autism, the dangers could range from not being socially aware and making social mistakes or going as far as doing something that's dangerous and could cause them to get hurt or worse. These individuals on the spectrum are simply just not aware of the many dangerous things there are in this world. I know for me this has been very much the case through my entire life. I would be easily taken advantage of. Therefore, it's crucial that we are aware of this information and can hopefully come up with a way of preventing someone with high-functioning autism or Asperger's syndrome from being put into harmful situations.

### *How can we help teach people on the spectrum of the dangerous things they might encounter in life?*

There are a few great programs out there to help with educating people on the spectrum about abuse. One of the more helpful ones that I've encountered as an adult on the spectrum is a program called "Bringing the Birds and Bees Down to Earth: Sexuality and Sexuality Education for Persons with Autism." This program is done by Lisa Mitchell, LCSW. Lisa has a very interesting presentation, and she teaches at a level that people on the spectrum can understand and relate to. She's also very good at teaching at a level that support staff and professionals in a field can relate to. I would highly recommend that this program be a must-see for not only people on the autism spectrum but also support staff and other professionals who are working within the autism field.

This particular presentation that I've seen is put out by "Autism Speaks." It's time to listen. You can find more information about "Autism Speaks" and this particular presentation by visiting www.AutismSpeaks.org. There are a few other programs for people who have an autism spectrum disorder or who are working with someone or related to someone on the spectrum. The Autism Society of America is one that is very helpful: www.autism-society.org.

We just have to continue to be aware that individuals on the autism spectrum do not think in the same way that NTs do. NTs are always cautious and aware of the dangerous things that are out there in the world. In fact, sometimes I wonder if girls don't come with this internal instinct that sends an alarm off to them when something is a little different or out of place. While this is a great thing for a woman to have, it's important to remember that just because something appears to be a little different, it doesn't automatically mean something's wrong. There might be an inside factor that is not visible in the person. Therefore, because of the internal instinct that NTs seem to have, they are quickly turned off by the autistic world. This is quite simply just a misinterpretation.

As I have so often been told by other people on the autism spectrum, they feel that no one understands them or they are constantly misunderstood. This is something that we all have to come together and work on by providing adequate education both to the NTs and the autistics. It's all about compromise. The autistic individual must try to learn the norms of society and become more aware of appropriate and inappropriate actions while the NT individual must become more in tune with autism and how it affects the individual. Let's all work together and try to understand each other.

I can't stress enough how important it is that we train autistic individuals and people who have Asperger's syndrome to report something when they have a problem with someone. No one else will be able to tell because Asperger's is such an invisible disability. If one does not tell or seek out help, it could be harmful to not only his self-esteem, but he could end up being physically harmful. There were several situations in which guys would make verbal threats to me and tell me I was stupid and I should do whatever they told me to. I was able to fight this off for a long time before I would give in to doing what a guy told me to; when I did, it was because I was convinced that I was stupid and didn't know anything and this guy knew it all. I would end up thinking that anyone but me was smart and that they had all the answers and I should listen to and do everything they told me to. This was a huge mistake, and because I wasn't even aware of having Asperger's at this point, I didn't think anything was wrong. I just thought that was how people treated some people and I just had to accept it, deal with it, and move on. In fact, I was scared of reporting it to anyone because I wasn't sure if I would get threatened or hurt by the person I was telling on.

People with autism or Asperger's syndrome should become aware of whom they can trust and whom they can't. It's extremely helpful to let your place of employment know that the person has autism or Asperger's and get them involved. This will allow them to be on the lookout for any bullying. They might even seek out a mature coworker to explain the situation to and take the Aspie or autistic individual under their wing. This will help protect them.

Please note that an autistic individual will work much better and faster if he or she is in a safe environment where there is little or no threat of being hurt. For me, my work has often suffered when I felt like I was in dangerous situations and I was stuck in them because I was working. One will become really anxious and be less focused on the job and make more mistakes. Having a safety net or security blanket, so to speak, allows the individual to relax and focus more on his or her tasks. People with Asperger's are just as hard workers as anyone else. They just have to be put in an environment that is safe, with little or no distractions so they can focus on their task.

It's important to be aware that there will often be at least one or two people in a crowd who will be able to tell that the autistic individual is incapable of standing up for themselves or saying no to someone. They will take advantage of this to the best of their ability. This has happened to me time and time again, and because of the level of desperateness to have a friendship or even relationship with a girl, I've kept putting myself in these situations. I've sometimes put myself into harm's way as well.

There is no good way to prevent being put into a situation where we are going to be taken advantage of. We must simply prepare ourselves and practice saying no to someone to avoid being used and hurt. We can do this by bullying education. We can teach people on the spectrum—and, yes, even kids who aren't on the spectrum—to detect a bully and how to stay away from them. We can teach them to be with someone at all times who knows that they are vulnerable and will try to protect them. Then, of course, we have to teach them to know how to report any type of bullying or abuse that is going on.

Being on the receiving end of so much bullying in my life, I can't express to you the amount of pain that goes through the individual who is being bullied. It's like you're stuck inside of a horrible dream. No matter what you attempt to do, you can never escape it. If you tell someone, the bully will find out, but if you don't tell someone, he or she will keep bullying you and could cause severe mental trauma. I hated going to school so often due to the fact that I knew the class bully was going to be coming after me, trying to do something to me in some way that could hurt me. I tried to avoid him most of the time. This was not always possible, though.

### *Importance of the Individual Being Aware of What's Going On*

I've now set out on a mission to make sure that the same things don't happen to other children on the autism spectrum. I would hope that we would be able to recognize the signs of this happening in our schools and take steps to prevent them from occurring. Unfortunately, the person with an autism diagnosis might be gullible and unable to even tell when this is happening. I mean, sure, they can tell when someone's hitting them and it physically hurts, but oftentimes they have a very high tolerance for pain. The sad thing is that sometimes even if a person with autism can recognize that some form of abuse is going on, they don't often have the necessary skills of knowing how to report it. This leaves the person in a completely vulnerable and dangerous position.

Obviously, as we know, it's extremely difficult for a person with an autism disorder to make friends. Therefore, this next thing is a difficult task, but it's crucial for the person with Asperger's or autism to have someone to look out for them, someone who's educated about the autism spectrum and understands that these individuals might not always be aware of making the right decision when it comes to being taken advantage of or being abused. It's more than likely that they will allow themselves to be taken advantage of, even if they do recognize that it's going on, or abused. If we could just get one peer to understand our people, then we'd be taking a huge step toward success. It's extremely important that children in middle schools and high schools get education on autism. All students should receive some type of training and education. I would even go as far as saying that this is something we could start doing with them as early as fourth grade. It is also important that our teachers are trained and able to recognize signs of autism in their students at early ages. We must become more aware of this so that we can prevent abuse from happening. To me, this is one of the most important things that we could do.

---

Marching band would provide many experiences for me. It's extremely beneficial for someone who's on the autism spectrum to become involved with extracurricular activities at the middle school and high school levels. Maybe it's something that's a special interest to them. This is also a good way of attempting to make friends. For us on the spectrum that have to work so hard at making friends, making them through a special interest can seem easy. Making friends through the special interest is a lot less stressful for the autistic individual.

Think about this. When an autistic individual is setting out for the sole purpose of trying to make friends and form a friendship, they can become so focused on it that it is overwhelming to them. The person on the spectrum has to work so hard to think through every social situation to the point that it can emotionally drain them. By making friends through a special interest, the autistic individual becomes more focused on the interest as opposed to making friends. While there's no guarantee that a friendship is just going to randomly appear in one's lap as a gift, it's highly more likely that the individual on the spectrum will be able to talk to people in a more comfortable way, which could allow the NT individual to become interested in them.

I can recall the situations where, for whatever reasons, I was more focused on doing something—whether it be playing basketball or playing trombone—than I was on making and developing friendships. It was these days when I had some successful social interactions with individuals—never to the point to where amazing friendships would blossom out of it, but at least I was able to socialize.

---

If I had a dime for every time in my life I've heard a woman say, "Well, he treats me so bad, but I can't leave him." Sounds like an oxymoron. This is a very true statement, though. What happens is that these women are tricked into falling in love with these men, and once they're in love, it's hard to leave, no matter how badly she wants to. This would be the same situation to an extent. For example, I could often tell that someone was using me for money or using me to provide something for them, but because I so desperately wanted friendships, I stayed and didn't run. This is the biggest mistake and the most costly mistake I have ever made in my life. You see, staying there might make you feel good for a short period of time because that person is giving you some attention. But at the end of the day, when you part ways, you go home and realize that that person doesn't care about you one little bit. They just wanted your money or something of value to them that you had. This in itself is really damaging to one's self-esteem.

There have been several occasions even in my adult life in which I've had women tell me they'd have coffee with me or go to a movie with me if I took them shopping or paid some of their bills for them. It hasn't been uncommon for me to be asked to pay a woman's rent at her apartment complex or to pay her phone bill in order to have dinner with her or coffee. While even to this day I know that this is wrong and it ends up hurting more in the end, I'll still pay someone's bills in order to have them spend just a couple of hours with me because I know that due to having Asperger's syndrome this is something that is required of me. I'm completely convinced that I have to pay anyone my age to hang out with me or spend time with me.

### *The Friendship/Acquaintance Ratio*

At this particular point in time in my junior year, I had no idea about the friendship/acquaintance ratio. I didn't know what it was or that it even existed. It's actually something I came up with about three or four years ago that I've used as a way of explaining my social interactions with people. I often tried extremely hard to develop peer relationships. It seemed like the harder I would try to develop a relationship or friendship with a person, the more that person would hate me or think I was creepy or psycho.

The friendship/acquaintance ratio is a relationship between an autistic individual and a neurotypical, or NT individual. The autistic individual might have anything from autism to high-functioning Asperger's syndrome. What happens is that the person with autism or Asperger's is trying so hard to develop a friendship with the NT. To the individual on the spectrum, as soon as an NT individual so much as says hi to them and/or smiles at them, the NT has become the person's best friend, while the NT individual was just saying hi to be friendly and might not even be interested in learning the person on the spectrum's name.

You see, neurotypical individuals have established a social network that is full of many different people. It's full of many different types of friends. They have guys that are friends and girls that are friends. Some of them will even have a boyfriend or girlfriend. To the neurotypical individual, meeting the person who's on the spectrum won't mean anything at all to them. Because they know how to develop friendships appropriately, they know that you do not just make a friend from saying hi to them or by even smiling at them. The person with the autism diagnosis doesn't understand this, and even if he or she did, they still would have a hard time with it because it just makes them feel so good that they didn't get ignored or even worse.

So what happens is that the NT person becomes the person on the spectrum's best friend instantly, while to the NT individual the person on the spectrum just becomes an acquaintance (someone they might or might not have an interest in seeing again). Due to the excitement in the person on the spectrum, they will become overly anxious and want to develop a friendship with the NT individual more quickly than the NT is comfortable with. This will cause the NT to accuse or assume that the individual on the spectrum is being disrespectful and purposely missing these cues or common knowledge about building a friendship that NTs come preprogrammed with. The person on the spectrum might end up calling the NT too much or too often or texting and e-mailing them too much. This can become overbearing to the NT individual, and they will retreat and try to get rid of the individual on the spectrum.

I know this is something that has happened to me time and time again. When you end up getting rejected or made fun of, you can't understand because you just don't realize or comprehend what you've done wrong. For me, even when someone would explain it to me, it wouldn't make much sense, and I just couldn't understand why they were reacting that way to me. An example would be with texting. I don't understand how it could be possible to text someone too much. There is nothing harmful about a text message, unless you are saying mean things in it. But if I'm texting a girl and I send her three hundred nice messages per day, I don't see how this can bother her or upset her. I just can't understand it. I feel as if girls punish me because I'm nice to them. I can't see how something "nice," no matter how intense it is, can be hurtful or harmful to girls. It makes no sense to me.

### *Importance of Looking Past Negative Effects and Finding the Positive*

While it's easy for a person on the spectrum to sit around moping about the negative effects that Asperger's syndrome or autism has on them, it's important that the individual realizes there are several positive traits to having Asperger's or autism. There have been a great many individuals with autism who have gone on to live very inspiring lives, some acquiring PhD's, some running businesses, some providing counseling services, and some just by being creative and using what they have as a gift. It is extremely beneficial that the friends, family, and professionals living and working with the individual on the spectrum recognize these qualities that are positive and unique about the individual and feed that back to them. There can be nothing more helpful to the self-esteem than to have someone tell you something positive about yourself. This will give them a little more self-confidence and hopefully motivate them to work a little harder at developing these great qualities and using them as gifts.

There are a great number of things that an individual on the spectrum's special interest and positive/unique qualities can lead to for them and others, one of which could be helping them find a job. By using our special interest, we can gain employment. If you can find a career field that has something to do with your special interest, you will be an expert at your job. No one else will be able to perform it better than you. So this is another reason it's crucial to not discourage someone from having a special interest, even if it seems a little too intense. It will be more intense than a NTs normal interest level. This intensity is what will allow them to become an expert at something in which they are good at and can use to help not only them succeed in the world but to educate others.

### *Social Unawareness of People on the Spectrum*

I was one who just didn't comprehend basic social interactions and didn't know how to interpret them. For example, when I was younger, whenever I wanted to go on a date with a girl, I'd just walk up to her and say the words, "Hey. I think you're really beautiful and incredible, and I'd like to get to know you. Would you mind going on a date with me?" I don't think I received one yes when I tried to ask girls out like that. But to me, that made perfect sense. If you want to go on a date with a girl, then you should ask her to go on a date. It wasn't until much later on that I learned that dating was more of a game than it was about two people actually having emotions and feelings for each other. Well, it's not just a game; there are emotions and feelings involved, but it seems like you must play a game of being hard to get and toying with a woman's mind in order to get her attracted to you.

I would get made fun of by other guys so often due to the way that I would try to ask a girl to hang out with me. I didn't understand the meaning behind playing hard to get with them. Today, it seems like you almost have to imply that you aren't interested in them but you are interested in them at the same time. This philosophy makes no logical sense to me, and it frustrates me like none other.

People on the spectrum often take things to be very logical. For example, in my situation, when I wanted to ask a girl to go on a date, it was logical to me to simply ask her to go on date, and that's what I did. Unfortunately, I should have had a more illogical approach. I'm still working on learning how all of this works, but people on the spectrum will often take anything you say very literally. So it's important when you know someone who's on the spectrum that you are very careful with things you say and make certain that the individual understands what you're saying.

---

This is often something I overanalyze and don't enjoy doing due to the amount of stress it causes me. It's not that shaking hands at all is a bad thing, and in fact, shaking hands in itself doesn't bother me. It's everything that has to happen before you can actually shake the person's hand.

For NT individuals who aren't on the spectrum, this is something that they can do with ease and without even thinking about it. It's like they have been programmed as to exactly how to do it. They don't have to think through the steps that someone who has Asperger's syndrome or autism might indeed have to think about before they can extend their hand to shake someone else's. There are at least five crucial steps to this process that someone on the spectrum has to think about or analyze before they shake.

> How do I know what hand the other person wants to use for the handshake?
>
> When exactly do I extend my hand out to shake his or her hand?
>
> How do I know how hard to squeeze the hand of the person I am shaking hands with?
>
> When do I let go of the other person's hand?
>
> Where am I supposed to be looking when shaking the other person's hand?

Not only do I have to think about these things, but I have to think about them in great detail and consider all possibilities that could occur. This isn't something that I just think about and do. It's something I have to think about, analyze, and then do. For NTs, this whole process can take two to three seconds. For me, it can take ten to twenty seconds before I have analyzed the situation and am ready to shake someone's hand. This creates a little awkwardness for the NT individual, as they aren't quite sure how to react to it or what to do while they're waiting on me to extend my hand.

## *Socializing Can Be Exhausting*

For people who have autism and Asperger's syndrome, socializing is not only stressful and confusing, but it can very well be exhausting. It's exhausting because the individual has to think about so many things that are going on within a social situation that their brain will just become worn out.

For people on the spectrum, any social situation can be very demanding and exhausting. There are just so many things for us to think about that the neurotypical doesn't even have to think about for a brief second. It's like someone being an engineer. They are an expert in their career field and don't have to think too much about something that has to do with their job. But if you were to bring an accountant in to do the engineer's job, the accountant would have to spend a lot more time thinking about what to do and more than likely wouldn't be able to be very successful at accomplishing the tasks.

Socializing works a lot like this. Neurotypicals come preprogrammed in the socializing profession. They aren't necessarily born with these skills, but they are able to acquire them with very little effort in their childhood. Meanwhile, we have people on the spectrum who for one reason or another were unable to acquire these social skills during childhood. It's kind of like neurotypicals took a class in school on socializing that wasn't offered to the people on the spectrum.

Imagine if you were put into a job or profession you knew very little about and were expected to perform at an outstanding level with little or no problems at all. You would probably be scared to death, as feeding your family and your basic survival would depend upon how well you performed. It's no different here. People who have autism or Asperger's syndrome are put into a job or a profession with no training and no knowledge of how to perform the duties and skills necessary to succeed at that job. The profession is socializing, and while I do know that this is not an actual job, so to speak, the profession itself seems very challenging and overwhelming to the individual. It's like the accountant being thrown into the engineer's job without any training and without ever even having a college course in engineering. What's going to happen in this situation? Most likely, unless the accountant is a genius and somehow has superior skills that are very rare, he or she would fail miserably.

We wouldn't typically think that socializing is a job because it's not something that we receive a paycheck for. I mean, there's no pay involved in walking up to someone and initiating a conversation with them. We don't get rewarded with pay if we say hi to someone. The neurotypical individuals out there probably don't even perceive socializing to be much work at all.

But let's look at this for a minute. Socializing is a tool that is used in a variety of ways, one of which is to go to an interview for a job. If a person has good enough social skills and great work history, as well as references, they will more than likely have a chance at getting the job. After obtaining the job, the individual must then use those basic social skills that he or she has acquired over the years to perform the job. While there are some jobs that don't require socializing to be successful, the majority of jobs have some sort of socializing involved. I mean, a product can't be produced or sold if no one is doing any communicating or talking. Therefore, it's necessary to have good social skills to excel.

Not only are these social skills necessary for performing the job description, but they are necessary for surviving in the work environment. Employers who often aren't educated in the area of autism will not realize that an autistic individual might have trouble fitting in or getting along with the rest of society. They will more than likely come across situations at work that they are unaware as to how to handle. This can cause tremendous discomfort. This could either lead to the person on the spectrum getting fired or quitting on their own due to the amount of stress that the social situations have presented.

This will cause the person to receive a horrible reference and create a substantial amount of difficulty in acquiring another job. The ability to excel at socializing is a key to unlocking a successful career and obtaining a good job.

The social skills gap between the NT world and the autistic world causes numerous concerns in survival for the person who's on the spectrum. Unfortunately, we live in a world where money is necessary for survival. We on the spectrum are eventually forced to come out of our make-believe world and enter the real world, where it's necessary to gain employment so that we can earn money to help provide for not only ourselves but also our family. There are many people on the spectrum who are able to get married and start a family. However, in order to do that, one must have a full understanding of themselves and be okay with who they are and their diagnosis.

Therefore, when we are forced into uncomfortable situations in places of employment in which we are unable to fit in or always be appropriate, we are unable to keep a job. This puts us out of work and back on the streets. This is why getting the people who are on the autism spectrum the adequate social skills training is extremely beneficial to the person on the spectrum surviving and obtaining a career that is worthwhile.

It would be beneficial if we could somehow educate employers on autism and Asperger's syndrome. This country's constitution says that all people in this country are to be treated equally and given a fair chance at employment opportunities. We are not to be discriminated against based on religion, race, color, or anything else. This would also include that we aren't to be discriminated against based on having a disability.

You can quickly see the significance of social skills and employment. Without social skills, there is no chance of succeeding in most jobs. Therefore, social skills should be taught at a high school and university level. It would be beneficial for everyone to take a couple of social skills classes at the university level. Even for the best neurotypical socializer, a class could give them a chance to understand and appreciate that socializing doesn't come as naturally for everyone as it does for them. They are just as important to an individual's survival as studying their major in college. Without the basic social skills, knowing everything in the world about your major could possibly not be enough. You have to be able to understand how to communicate what you know.

I have often wondered where other individuals have learned all of the social norms and rules that are supposed to be used in our culture. Where did I miss out on this in school? Somewhere at some place, at some time, a teacher had to teach me about social skills somewhere, right?

This isn't the case. Unfortunately, social skills are taught in what I call the hidden curriculum. There is not a single class in middle or high school in which these kids are taught how to say something, or when it's appropriate to say something, or how to say it. There's no class that teaches them how to read body language or nonverbal communication. It's all done on instinct.

They are able to just do it as if there's nothing to it at all. I mean, it just flows for them. Yet it's such a struggle for me to know how to say something sometimes or even just to look someone directly in the face or eyes. It takes a tremendous amount of courage and effort on my part to even sustain a conversation. I've gotten to the point where I know how to say hi to people. However, at times I feel as if I'm hurting someone or disturbing them by saying hi to them. This is a result of trying to get to know people throughout my entire life and being rejected over and over again. Yes, other people's responses to you can and do affect your self-esteem. As frustrating as it is, your self-esteem can be completely destroyed because people think you're creepy as a result of a social disorder. This is something people on the autism spectrum deal with on a daily basis throughout their entire life. Some people on the spectrum would freely say things without worry, as they may not even be aware to the fact that they could be saying something completely off the wall that is going to cause people to have negative or weird thoughts about them, while some people on the spectrum have to go about their daily life being completely focused on trying not to say something off the wall that is going to cause people to have negative thoughts about them. The goal for everyone is for other people to have positive thoughts about them.

I would simply conclude that neurological people are more equipped to obtain a career in a field of their choice. Unfortunately, at this time, only 20 percent of people with Asperger's syndrome are employed, with 12 percent of them in part-time employment. This means that only 8 percent of people who have Asperger's syndrome are successful at obtaining careers or full-time jobs.

This has nothing to do with the individual's ability to work. It has nothing to do with that at all. In fact, many people with Asperger's syndrome would be some of the company's best workers. The problem, however, is within the profession of socializing, which is a crucial tool in obtaining and finding a job. Let's put it this way. You can have a bachelor's degree, a master's degree, or even a PhD, but if you are missing that one small piece of the puzzle, then you will not have your life completed, and you'll miss just one important piece that could be the key for making it all fit together.

Those of us on the spectrum often refer to life and autism as a puzzle. In general, I'd say that everyone refers to putting together his or her life as some kind of a puzzle. Some people are missing more pieces than others. Eventually, everyone finds all of the missing pieces and completes the puzzle. Unfortunately, for people with autism, that one missing piece will often be the only piece that's not there. I've spent many years trying to find this piece of the puzzle. There were times when I didn't even know or understand that I was looking for a missing puzzle piece but just felt different. But knowing my diagnosis now, I know that I was different because I was missing that one final piece in finding success.

## *Lying Associated with Asperger's and Autism*

It is often true that when an individual is on the spectrum, he or she will have trouble with lying. This is something that has been common in most Asperger's diagnoses. Not only will the individual have trouble due to believing the lies that the neurotypical individual tells them, but once they believe the lie that the neurotypical tells, they will eventually adopt it into memory and their belief system. Once it's liked inside of someone on the spectrum's brain, he or she might not be capable of determining if the lie is true or not.

I'm particularly referring to the lies that a neurotypical individual will tell someone on the spectrum such as, "You're not cool unless you drink. Even worse, you're not cool unless you drink and drive like the rest of us." or "You're not going to be good enough for me if you don't pay me money to hang out with you."

There are so many fibs/lies that a neurotypical individual will try to tell someone on the spectrum. Because of the social unawareness of the individual on the spectrum, they will have an extremely difficult time with this concept. I've personally bought into the fact that it's necessary for me to pay people hundreds of dollars just to hang out with me. I was so socially naïve and desperate that I was willing to do anything in order to have a social interaction with someone. Even if it was only paying $500 to hang out with someone for two minutes, I would have done it, and I'd still have a difficult time saying no and walking away from the situation. Because I knew that if I didn't pay them to spend time with me, there was not a chance that they were going to become my friends.

This is a major trap that our people on the spectrum could fall into. It's very important that others who are involved in the child or young adult's life try to look out for situations like this, in which the individual might be getting taken advantage of or believing the lies that the world is telling them.

### *The Relationship between Creating a Make-believe World and Lying*

When individuals on the spectrum spend their entire life trying to learn how to fit in and be just like everyone else, it's easy for them to try to change the way they approach getting to know people in hopes that the change made will be the solution to all of their problems. This was the case for me. I would spend numerous attempts at getting to know someone only to fail at it and have this big rejection looming over my head.

For a long time, I would try the same things over and over again, thinking, Maybe next time it will be different. I was holding out that last bit of hope for the longest time. Eventually, as time went on, that hope became smaller. Eventually, any hope that I had at having a friend or even a girlfriend was completely gone and I'd all but given up.

People who are on the spectrum will often retreat to a safe place in which they feel that no one can hurt them. After being rejected so much, they'll end up using their imagination to retreat to this little make-believe world that they've created all in their own head. They will feel much safer and less vulnerable there. As I mentioned earlier, there are many advantages to this but also some disadvantages of this happening and some things that we need to be aware of.

Imagine that you were someone who didn't fit in and you wanted to know how to. What would you do? I know myself. I've actually done Google searches to learn how to make friends or even get a girlfriend. Unfortunately, these advertisements that will often come up on Internet sites saying, "How to get a girlfriend," are often scams, and they really aren't intended to help you. Sadly enough, they're really just in it to take your money.

Sometimes people on the spectrum will spend their entire life wondering why they don't fit in or why no one even wants to talk to them. Eventually, one gets desperate and decides to try to do something about it. You begin trying to change some things about yourself. You change what you do, how you do it, when you do it, to what extent you do it, and you change so much more.

I was frustrated to the point to where I would try to read lines of what to say to people off of the Internet. I tried to pick up on some conversational skills from a few Web sites and change my vocabulary. In doing this, I'd try a new thing or two and quickly evaluate and realize that they didn't work either. So then I'd go back to the Internet and find another technique I could use and try again. I was doing these things over and over while still having no success in social relationships with peers. This became so frustrating and tiring.

After spending days, weeks, months, and even years trying to change and mold yourself into something you're not that will be accepted by society, eventually you can become confused and lose track of who you really are. This happens because you've tried to mimic so many people and learn from them that you've changed who you were. You no longer remember who you are, what you originally stood for, and what your purpose is in life because you've spent such a significant amount of time trying to fit in and become someone you're not just so people will give you the time of day and, if anything, maybe so they won't abuse you verbally, emotionally, or physically. After spending so much time trying to be someone else, I forgot who I was and what I stood for.

When this day happened, I started to forget what the truth was. I couldn't remember who I was, what I liked, or why I liked it. Everything that was once a part of my life was no longer with me because I'd decided to let it go or change it into something else so I could get someone else to like me. Needless to say, trying to change who I was and become someone whom, at that time, I thought was better than me was a setback to developing myself and my own self-esteem. I needed to be spending my time trying to become more accepting of myself instead of trying to change who I was to please someone else.

One day later in my life, when I was terribly depressed and miserable and kept trying new things to figure out exactly how to be cool or liked by other students my age, I just lost it and started bawling in front of a bunch of people. Someone pulled me aside and made the following comment to me, "You don't know who you are, do you?" Wow. This comment couldn't have been more accurate. I had no idea who I was. I had no clue as to who I was because for a year or two I'd been trying all of these different techniques to make friends. I had tried so many different approaches and styles that I'd completely forgotten who Travis was and how Travis would approach a situation. I became a book. Whenever I had a social situation come up, I no longer said, "Okay, Travis. What should I do in this situation?" Instead, I said, "Okay. Now what would this book tell me to do in this situation?" I spent so much time trying to recall what the book would tell me to do in this situation that usually, by the time I thought of what I was supposed to do, the situation was gone.

### *Seeking Therapy to Provide Answers*

Therapy is a really wonderful idea for someone who is going through depression or anything at all. However, as I would find out, if the therapist just wasn't aware or trained in autism or Asperger's, there was no way that they were going to be able to tell me that I had any form of autism.

I went to visit several therapists. When I walked in and asked them what was wrong with me, I was asked several questions. They wanted to know what exactly was bothering me, so I told them that I thought other people hated me and I couldn't make friends. I told them I was sure girls hated me and I'd never get a girlfriend. I wanted to know why. I was asking the counselor why no one liked me and why it was so hard for me to make friends.

Immediately these counselors would start drawing conclusions. They would ask me things like, "Are your parents split up? Are your parents dead? Are you adopted? Were you abused as a kid?" At first, I immediately knew the answer to all of those questions. No, my parents weren't split up; they were still together and have been for twenty-seven years. No, my parents weren't dead. That was an obvious statement. I wasn't adopted, and I was never abused as a child.

I told a few counselors this, and they kept saying, "Well, there has to be something, something that's bothering you and holding you back." I swore to them that I'd never been abused nor had any of these problems in my life. They kept suggesting that I probably did when I was younger. I went to a handful of counselors, and they all kept saying the same things.

Eventually, after visiting anywhere from fifteen to twenty different counselors within a couple of months, I started to question myself. I began wondering if maybe some of those things had really happened to me. They suggested that I couldn't remember it because I wasn't wanting to or I was just trying to deny it. They had me stumped.

Somewhere along the way, counselors convinced me that the problems I was having in social interactions with my peers were because of my parents. They kept saying that it had something to do with my parents. After hearing that so many times, I began to wonder, and I eventually started to believe it.

I became kind of bitter, and my home life started to suffer. Now not only was I struggling in the social world, but I started to question my parents about things. I just wondered why I was different and wondered if the counselors were right and if something severe did happen to me during my childhood. I kept questioning my parents about what happened as a kid and why they didn't seem to have a lot of social interactions with other people their age.

As time would go on, there would be a few counselors who continued to harp on the fact that my problems had to be related to my home life. It's highly important that when one is seeking therapy, you recognize that not all psychologists are trained about autism or Asperger's syndrome. So therefore, when you don't realize yourself that you have some sort of autism- or Asperger's-related problem, you'll be easily persuaded into believing that your problem is whatever that particular counselor tells you they are.

Even once a person has already been diagnosed with Asperger's syndrome, it might not be a good idea to just walk in to any counselor and say, "Hey, I have Asperger's syndrome. Please help me." You would think that this would be okay to do, as these people have been put through at least four to six years of undergraduate school and graduate school. Most people you're going to seek therapy and counseling from will have at the least a master's degree in clinical counseling.

I strongly recommend that you search really hard and find someone who's already obtained a doctorate in clinical counseling. Even then, there are still a few psychologists with doctorates who might not know what Asperger's syndrome is. Most, however, will be familiar to some extent with autism.

I have visited with several clinical counselors who didn't have much background as to what Asperger's syndrome was and couldn't really help me out much. All that they could do was refer me to someone else who might. If at all possible, I would recommend asking ahead of time before you make an appointment with a counselor to see what their background is on Asperger's syndrome or autism in general.

After being passed back and forth between several counselors for about a two-week span, I finally started to believe what they were telling me. Somehow, I gathered from everything they were saying that I had been adopted and my real parents were dead. Somehow, I created that out of what they were telling me.

It was possible for me to create this because I thought that these individuals were well respected and would know everything and I should believe and trust them. Between them telling me that they thought that something had happened in my childhood and me having the characteristic and ability to create my own imaginary/make-believe world, I started to really believe this scenario. I thought that I had been adopted and my real parents were actually my adopted ones.

This is not the case, as now that I've became more stabilized, I've been able to do some reasoning for myself. At the time, though, I totally had myself convinced that I was adopted and my parents had died in a car crash somewhere along the line. I began telling this to other peers, thinking that maybe I would make more sense to them.

Eventually, I kept thinking more and more about it and becoming more and more miserable toying with the idea of deciding if I was adopted or not. It was like I was being brainwashed by an outside source telling me that I was adopted and my parents were dead but at the same time fighting with what I knew from the inside about my parents being real and alive and very nonabusive. It was a rough time period. I questioned my memory of the events of my childhood at one time, thinking that maybe I was just too young to remember my parents ever abusing me in any way and, indeed, maybe they actually had.

I couldn't tell. I just couldn't get a grip on things, and I couldn't figure them out myself. I was lost and confused more than ever and would cry as I went to sleep every night. I was wondering who I really was and why I was here.

---

For someone who has Asperger's syndrome or autism, sleep problems are a normal thing to have. It's not because you're not tired or the fact that you have a problem with sleeping itself, but it's due to the experiences you've encountered during the day.

Once the day is over and you've had a chance to wind down and do some thinking, you begin to replay social situations in your head. You think about something that you were made fun of or ridiculed for and try to analyze it to figure out what exactly was done wrong. Once you analyze it and come up with some sort of idea of what you have done wrong (which might be correct or incorrect), you begin to think about different situations inside your head and imagine situations in which you could have done it the right way. This is so intense that it can interfere with your ability to just fall off to sleep. If you're an adult and having trouble with this, I would recommend talking to your psychologist or family physician.

Unfortunately, kids who have autism or Asperger's syndrome aren't going to be able to understand or know that this could be a reason why they aren't sleeping. They could toss and turn all night and never have any clue as to what kept them awake. If you're a parent of someone on the autism spectrum, it's important you check in with them from time to time. Just ask them how they're sleeping. If they report to you that they are having problems falling asleep, then you could guess it's possibly due to the overanalysis of social events that have occurred throughout the day. This is not something that you will be able to just take away or make it go away for them. There are medicines that could help, and talking to a qualified psychologist would be recommended and preferred in my opinion.

## *Lack of a Social Life Leads to Depression*

For those of us who are on the autism spectrum, this is all too familiar a topic. This is a topic that varies for individuals on the spectrum. You see, some individuals on the spectrum have no or little desire to develop a great social life. They are completely content with being alone and don't want anything to do with anyone and would rather no one bother them.

Then there are those of us who want to develop peer relationships and make great friendships with people. Both groups are alike in the fact that we have no idea how to go about socializing or developing peer friendships. The difference is in the fact that one group wants to be successful in the social arena while the other group doesn't.

I've recently had the pleasure of meeting quite a few younger people on the spectrum. I've seen my fair share of people who want to connect with others so badly but don't have the tools to do so. Then I've also seen some individuals who don't have any desire to be included in society at all. In fact, some will do everything within their power to avoid society. Both groups need support, and we shouldn't forget about either group.

Even in the group of us who don't have any desire for social relationships, there is still some need for social and peer acceptance. Unfortunately, what has happened is that these individuals have made numerous attempts to connect with society in the past and have been embarrassed, made fun of, bullied, or ridiculed, and they've lost the desire for forming peer relationships. They've put up a shell to society, so to speak. This isn't at all because they have no need for social interaction, but it's because withdrawing from society and becoming a loner is a much safer and pain-free solution.

For the group of us who want to fit into society, life can still become quite miserable. After several attempts to build friendships that lead to rejection, the individual on the spectrum will lose any self-respect that he or she has ever had for themselves. Their confidence and self-esteem will drop like you've never seen. Unfortunately, self-esteem is one of those things that's easy to lose but twice, if not three times, as hard to build back up.

### *Self-esteem Becoming a Road Block to Social Success*

Once an individual on the spectrum's self-esteem has been ruined, we have to clear yet another hurdle. Before we can continue teaching our people social skills, we must cure their self-esteem problem. There's just no way around this. The saying, "You can't expect others to like you until you like yourself," sounds so cliché, but it's the complete truth.

Throughout the last few years, I've read many articles and books on self-esteem. I don't think there's any one book out there that I've read that really unlocks the secret answer to the question, "How do I build my self-esteem?" Unfortunately, positive self-esteem develops through positive experiences. This is kind of a hard situation to understand because, as I said, I don't think we can teach individuals on the spectrum appropriate social skills until they like themselves for who they are. So the self-esteem is a roadblock to teaching social skills. You can also say that the lack of social skills is the roadblock to someone developing their self-esteem.

You might need to consider doing some role-playing with the individual on the spectrum in which positive social skills can be learned but, more importantly, positive comments can be made back to the individual on the spectrum both by the clinical counselor or behavioral consultant and the other people who are acting in the role-playing. To me, there's nothing more rewarding than hearing someone tell me that I did something right in a social situation.

I spend so much time and expend so much energy in trying to learn and comprehend social situations that getting positive feedback makes me feel like it was worth my time and that I'm learning. Doing something right and getting positive feedback for doing it properly goes a long way toward building up my self-esteem.

We must overcome our low self-esteem before we can expect to make friends. If you're struggling with this as an adult with AS, it's important to find the right kind of therapist for you. There are actually many things you can do that will build your self-esteem without even having to see a therapist just for this one thing.

One of those ways is to put yourself out in the world and do things you enjoy. Partake in things that you like doing and things that you are good at. For me, there's nothing more boosting to my self-esteem than to pull out a trombone and whip through a couple of passages. In fact, I've found in the past that on an occasion in which I'm feeling brave and wanting to go out and try to fit in on the social arena, picking up my trombone and playing a few notes does wonders. Not only does it build up my self-esteem a little because I'm doing something that I'm good at, but it also calms my nerves. Therefore, I will feel a little bit less anxious in social situations.

I'm not saying this will work for everyone, but try partaking in something to do with your special interest or something that you really enjoy doing before you hit the social arena. This will relax your mind and allow you to think more clearly out in public. It's crucial that we are as relaxed as we can be when we meet new people and begin socializing. Being overly anxious can cause us to make more mistakes than we normally would.

Playing trombone builds the self-esteem enough to be able to have more confidence and at least attempt to be in social situations. Everyone likes to feel like they are good at something, and when we feel this way, we are more excited about life. It makes it easier to put yourself out there.

### *Beware: Social Unawareness Leads to Being Misled by Peers*

What I am going to talk about next is something that I find very troubling. It's something that happens to people on the spectrum all too often. It's definitely something that we need to educate our people about and prepare them for, as they will definitely encounter this at some point in their teenage or early adult years. This is something that I cannot believe is happening.

What I am talking about is being misled about social situations by peers with bad intentions. As I was reading The Complete Guide to Asperger's Syndrome by Tony Attwood, I came across a section of the book in which he addressed this same issue. As I was reading, I couldn't believe what I was reading. The exact same things have happened to me in my life over and over again. Dr. Attwood has really hit a lot of things in his writing about Asperger's, and this is one of the most important ones.

It's unfortunate that it's a fact that we have to beware of predators in society who are going to recognize the situation of people on the spectrum and use it against them in so many ways. Not only is it enough for the person to take advantage of us on the spectrum, but they also feel such a need to mislead us and cause us to do things that are even more socially inappropriate.

For someone on the spectrum who already has a hard time fitting in, doesn't understand how to develop friendships, and knows absolutely nothing about talking to people of the opposite gender, it's easy to go to other people whom you see being successful in friendships and dating interactions with people. Unfortunately, this is something I've done quite often, and I can honestly say right now that I wish I would have never sought help from a guy in this matter—at least not from a guy in my peer group.

People with Asperger's really need to be educated on the nonverbal cues and facial expressions of body language for dating. Dating is very much a nonverbal thing. There are so many social cues that people are expected to pick up on. There are several places on the Internet that will offer to help you learn how to date, but be wary of scams where people just want to take advantage of people who don't know any better.

### *Reaching Out for Help Is Hard But Must Be Done*

For anyone on the autism spectrum, reaching out and getting help will most likely be the most difficult task we encounter. Once we've been able to work up the courage to ask for help, we are then provided with an unbelievable amount of resources. I can't begin to tell you just how much support is out there for us. The hard part, as I said, is building enough confidence to put yourself out there and go get it. Unfortunately, the help is not something that can just come to you without you asking for it. No, fellow Aspies, it's not just going to appear in your make-believe world. We'll actually have to take a trip outside of our make-believe world and come to find the help that's in the real world. When you are able and capable of taking just this one giant step, you will have accomplished more than the majority of your counterparts. There are many people out there in society who probably have some sort of Asperger's syndrome or autism but are too afraid to step up and admit it to get the help they need.

I know for me, when I first got my diagnosis in October of 2007, I didn't want any part of it. I hated the diagnosis even though I didn't understand exactly what it was. I knew I didn't want it to be a part of my life, and I would spend six months or so trying to push it away and pretend it didn't exist.

Once I was finally able to convince myself to accept the diagnosis and move on with my life with Asperger's being a part of me, I was able to begin reaching out for help. I was also able to embrace it and begin studying it as much as I could. I decided that I wanted to learn more about who I was and what I was all about. It was obvious that I was wired differently than the average person in society. I just had to find out why and how.

## *Unable to Make Safe Judgments Due to Need for Friendship*

Someone with Asperger's syndrome might be unable to make decisions that are in the best interest of their own safety. We can get put into dangerous situations and be either unaware of them or willing to put up with them in order to gain peer acceptance.

I know that this was the case for me on that day when I was tied to a tree and forced to submit to a royal beating. I didn't care how much physical pain it caused me. I had already experienced more emotional pain than I could ever experience physically. While

I didn't exactly want to get hit, punched, and kicked, I was willing to allow it because I wanted to be a part of the group.

This is something that we have to watch out for in someone with autism or Asperger's syndrome. Sometimes that need for friendship and connection can be so great that we can be willing to put ourselves into harm's way to achieve acceptance and friendship. We are just unable to realize that there could be a dangerous situation involved. There are even times in which I remember recognizing that the situation might be dangerous and involve me getting hurt, but again, because of the great need for making friends, I thought that it was just something I had to endure in order to make a friend.

### *The Need for a Peer to Look Out for Us*

Due to the fact that people with autism or Asperger's syndrome can be so socially unaware and naïve, it's important that we try to find people on the spectrum, at least one peer, who can understand them and their diagnosis and help look out for them and hopefully stand up for them as well as keep them from being taken advantage of or, even worse, allowing themselves to be put into dangerous situations just to gain the approval of others.

When I first started attending the local support group, I had a chance to talk about myself a bit, and I was explaining some serious issues that I was facing in my life that had to deal with Asperger's syndrome. One of the issues that has always been a huge struggle for me was talking to girls. One of the parents in the group quickly suggested the book Asperger's and Girls.

Most of us are familiar with the likes of Dr. Tony Attwood and Dr. Temple Grandin, but I'd like to introduce you to a woman by the name of Lisa Iland. While I don't know Lisa and have never even had a chance to talk with her, I can tell you that she is a highly intelligent woman. I read through the chapter in this book that she wrote for girls about how to fit in socially, and she touches on a lot of great points. If you are a woman with Asperger's or if you're a parent of a little girl with Asperger's, this book is a must-have.

Lisa has an older brother with an Asperger's diagnosis, and she had grown up with it being a huge part of his life. Lisa was only a couple of years younger than her brother, and they both attended high school together. It was during this time of attending high school with him that she saw how much her brother needed help with social skills.

At an incredible young age of just sixteen years old, Lisa began writing a book about the unspoken rules that comprise the teen social code. She then took her brother under her wing and began teaching and working with him. When he was out with friends, she would pay extra attention to him and help guide him.

As you can tell, having someone like Lisa around to help look out for you and prevent you from being taken advantage or put into dangerous situations can be extremely helpful. If only everyone had a sibling who was as much of a go-getter as Lisa. People without siblings need to look for mature people within their peer group to seek out friendship with. It should be someone who seems honest and isn't misleading, someone that won't try to use you to get something that they want. Professionals offer great guidance and help, but they are only available for your use an hour or two a week, in which very little is accomplished. It's important to have someone your age you can go to for advice in social situations. Without having someone to look out for us, it's more likely that we will get hurt not only mentally and emotionally, but we could be put into social situations in which we are naïve and will be hurt or physically abused.

### *Sometimes People's Actions Aren't Intentional*

I have come to the conclusion that while some people are just mean, arrogant, and rude and will blow you off and purposely ignore you and make fun of you, there are others who might really want to be your friend and connect with you, but just as you don't know how to connect with them, they don't know how to connect with you.

This is because both of you have totally different mind-sets about socializing. Again, the neurotypical individual has multiple channels of communication within his brain that he or she can switch to at any time, almost instantly. Meanwhile, the person on the autism spectrum often only has the one basic channel. Therefore, even if the NT wanted to really be friends with the person on the spectrum, they would have to work really hard at finding the channel on which the individual was stuck and really bring out that channel in their interactions together.

I often refer to this as if I am a defective television set. Most television sets come programmed with the capability for you to flip the switch and go through several different channels before finding the one that you want, while the defective television might not allow you to change the channel. Neurotypicals come with multiple channels and are normal television sets. Individuals on the autism spectrum come with one channel and one channel only; we can be defective television sets.

If the individual with Asperger's is extremely shy, it will be very hard for the NT to connect with them in any way. The individual with Asperger's is more than likely going to have many impairments that will delay or affect the way in which he or she processes a social interaction.

Time delay is a major disturbance to individuals with Asperger's or autism. Time delay is the amount of time that it takes for one to have the initial thought and then act on it. For example, I put my hand on a hot, burning stove. My sensory or central nervous system is telling me that it's hot and burning my hand, and without hesitating, the brain tells the hand to retreat.

When an autistic individual puts his or her hand on a burning stove, it can take a few more seconds before the brain is able to process the thought, *This is hot. Move my hand*, which can cause one's hand to become burnt.

The correlation to Asperger's syndrome is that it takes those with Asperger's longer to react in social situations. We will need a longer response time, especially when it comes to figuring out what someone's body language or tone of voice means. A lot of times people with Asperger's syndrome will do much better socially in online conversations where there's nothing nonverbal going on and they have more response time. In most cases, a person with Asperger's can figure out body language and facial expressions, but it will take them much longer to do so.

### *Social Networking Sites*

Social networking sites are very useful for someone who is on the autism spectrum but also very dangerous. Imagine being someone who already struggles in social situations. Then, all of a sudden, you have this tool called the Internet, where all you have to do is type and you'll be able to talk to people.

This would make your life more simple and complicated at the same time. It could make your life simpler because an individual on the spectrum is able to sit at home in front of a computer with no other social disturbances around and communicate with others. As Dr. Attwood states in The Complete Guide to Asperger's Syndrome, "When an individual on the spectrum is alone or by himself, there is no social impairment. There has to be at least one other person there with the individual on the spectrum to cause a social impairment."

The downside to social networking Web sites is that they can make an individual on the spectrum's life extremely difficult and challenging. There are so many avenues to social networking sites. There are also so many Web sites out there, for example, Facebook, MySpace, and Twitter, just to name a few.

Using such Web sites can be complicated for a neurotypical individual. Imagine how much more tremendously confusing that they can become to someone who has Asperger's. While I do use social networking sites, I've had to teach myself the proper way of using them so that I can avoid coming across as weird, creepy, or psycho.

There could be a strong relationship between using social networking sites like Facebook or MySpace and escaping into imagination or creating the make-believe world for people on the autism spectrum.

Imagine that you are in your early twenties and sites such as Facebook and MySpace are being launched. You have also been diagnosed with Asperger's syndrome. You've finally figured out that the thought you've had for many years—Something is horribly wrong with me—is completely true.

So your suspicions that you don't fit in socially are finally confirmed. Once again, you feel rejected and like you just want a break. You're depressed because you can't make friends and can't get anyone to even notice you. So what do you do? You explore the world of social networking sites.

Social networking sites allow you to meet people online before meeting in person. They also allow you to do this from the safety of your own home. Unfortunately, when someone has autism or Asperger's syndrome and has been turned down by people nearly his/her entire life, the fact that you could possibly talk to someone on a networking site is exciting. Once you start making connections via Facebook or MySpace and talking to people, it can become quite addicting. These people are only here for you to talk to when you're on Facebook. Well, what happens when both of you can't be on Facebook at the same time? Then there is no friendship. I have many Facebook friends whom I've never met, and I consider them to be sort of like my imaginary friends.

Being in the social networking world might be good for those of us on the spectrum for some time, as it allows for us to experience a little bit of social success. With not having to be in person with someone, there is no social impairment and we are able to be more relaxed, with less anxiety. This could decrease the number of social mistakes that we make.

For someone with Asperger's, it might become a way to feel better about yourself. When one is seeing and experiencing positive social interactions via the social-networking world, it would become rather easy for them to just become addicted to socializing via the Internet. It is extremely crucial to limit the amount of time that one spends socializing on social networking sites. It all goes back to the problem that spending too much time in the make-believe world will cause us to withdraw from the real world and pretty much seclude ourselves into this creative imaginary world that we've made up.

Social networking sites are extremely useful and helpful for someone who is on the spectrum. I am one who does use them every day. I do, however, try to limit the amount of time that I spend on them daily, as I'm afraid that spending too much time on them will cause me to become addicted to the make-believe world and its surroundings and seclude myself from the whole world.

So social networking sites are useful for those of us on the spectrum, but they need to be used in moderation and mixed with going out into the real world to try to make real friends with real people. Social networking sites can be a nice getaway and provide one with a huge confidence boost, but again, it's important that we don't overuse these networking sites and lose track of our real life in the real world.

## *Getting Too Excited*

For me, whenever something good happens in my life socially, there is tendency to grab on to it and want to wrap my arms around it and keep it in my life. This is something that I have to continue to work on every day. When something good happens, it's okay to get excited about it and feel great about it. However, if you are too obsessively excited about it, there can be some problems—especially if it's another human being. Sometimes excitement scares people off.

This is the case sometimes for individuals who aren't on the spectrum. You see, neurotypical individuals are so used to getting attention from other individuals that sometimes they become annoyed or bothered with too much attention. NTs already have this awesome network of people set up that includes friends, coworkers, relatives, and other businesspeople. They have so many people in the sea to pick and choose from when they need someone or want someone to talk to that all they need to do is pick up their phone and dial someone's number. There's always someone that wants to talk to them or hang out with them.

For those of us on the spectrum, we hardly ever have anyone pay attention to us. We spend so much of our lives being ignored that when someone finally does decide to try to get to know us, we tend to jump on it and want to take it in all at once. While I'm not saying that this is a bad thing at all, I can completely understand and relate as to why people on the spectrum would do this. It is an observation of mine that if we're trying to establish a relationship of any kind with a neurotypical individual—whether it be a friendship with guys, a friendship with girls, or a dating relationship with a guy or girl—when the person does show us a little bit of attention, we like it, and we jump on it too fast and get too overly excited about it and will most likely scare the neurotypical person away. This is simply because to them this seems creepy. I have often been told by girls in particular that I'm creepy. I have no idea why I am creepy because I certainly don't intend to be, but I've learned that it's probably because I come on too strong because of how excited I am and they are used to guys who play the game of being hard to get.

There are ways to help with the intensity of things, but it's very difficult to change the way we interact with people. This is another complicated issue for me, as I feel like I have to change who I am. I constantly hear people say to just be yourself and people will like you. But yet I've found people are uncomfortable if I come on too strong. This is a very confusing issue and one that I'm still trying to figure out for myself. Cognitive behavioral therapy is the best way to help change these unwanted behaviors, but even with therapy I believe people with Asperger's will always struggle with the intensity of social interaction.

You see, it is said that Asperger's syndrome is an invisible disability. This means that it's a disability that doesn't show up on the outside. No one's going to be able to recognize the fact that I have Asperger's syndrome without actually talking to me or taking more than a few minutes to get to know me.

I was having a conversation with a group of people once, and I asked them to tell me the first five traits or characteristics that came to mind when they looked at me. I heard all kinds of things from funny to intelligent, ambitious, and motivated, but the two words that I didn't hear were autism or Asperger's syndrome. This didn't surprise me at all because I'm so used to this. Since getting my diagnosis, I've felt comfortable enough with disclosing it to a few people who have been patient with me and allowed me a chance to try to get to know them. When I disclosed my diagnosis to them, not only did they not have the slightest clue as to what it was, but they had no idea I had it and couldn't believe it.

Now, when I speak at events, I usually open with asking for five or ten volunteers to tell me the first quality or characteristic that comes to their mind when they first look at me. I open with this to prove a point. The point is that Asperger's in itself is invisibly visible, meaning it's very invisible when you're first getting to know someone, but it becomes extremely visible after the getting-to-know-you process begins.

Today, it is my goal to work on helping both the autistic world and the neurotypical world compromise on these issues and come together as one. I would like to see Asperger's continue to be an invisible disability because I believe that disability is one word that it is not. However, what I would like to see is that Asperger's becomes a more visible characteristic in the individual.

# About the Author

Travis Breeding was diagnosed with Asperger's syndrome at the age of twenty-two. Currently Travis is pursuing a bachelor of communications from Indiana Purdue Fort Wayne.

Travis has just recently begun to embrace his diagnosis and is starting to see it as more of a gift than anything else. He is working hard to organize and establish a foundation called "Educating the World about Autism with Our Special Interests."

Travis is actively pursuing speaking engagements across the Midwest as well as the rest of the country. He has a story to tell and believes that it's crucial everyone hear it and not just people who are on the spectrum. Travis's goals are to create camps that combine special interests along with autism education for individuals both on and off the spectrum to attend to learn more about each other.

If you're curious in learning more about Travis, please contact him at: travis@travisbreeding.com or by visiting his Web site at www.travisbreeding.com